# On the House

# On the House

## A Washington Memoir

———————◆———————

# JOHN BOEHNER

### Former Speaker of the
### House of Representatives

St. Martin's Press
New York

First published in the United States by
St. Martin's Press, an imprint of St. Martin's Publishing Group

ON THE HOUSE. Copyright © 2021 by John Boehner. All rights reserved.
Printed in the United States of America. For information, address
St. Martin's Publishing Group, 120 Broadway, New York, NY 10271.

www.stmartins.com

Design by Susan Walsh

Library of Congress Cataloging-in-Publication Data

Names: Boehner, John, 1949– author.
Title: On the house : a Washington memoir / John Boehner.
Description: First edition. | New York : St. Martin's Press, 2021. | Includes index. |
    Summary: "A memoir by former speaker of the house John Boehner"—
    Provided by publisher.
Identifiers: LCCN 2020045308 | ISBN 9781250238443 (hardcover) |
    ISBN 9781250277183 (ebook)
Subjects: LCSH: Boehner, John, 1949– | United States. Congress. House—
    Speakers—Biography. | United States. Congress. House—Biography. |
    United States. Congress. House—History—20th century. | Legislators—
    United States—Biography. | United States—Politics and government—1989– |
    Ohio—Biography.
Classification: LCC E840.8.B595 A3 2021 | DDC 328.73/092 [B]—dc23
LC record available at https://lccn.loc.gov/2020045308

Our books may be purchased in bulk for promotional, educational,
or business use. Please contact your local bookseller or the Macmillan Corporate
and Premium Sales Department at 1-800-221-7945, extension 5442, or by
email at MacmillanSpecialMarkets@macmillan.com.

First Edition: 2021

10  9  8  7  6  5  4  3  2  1

*To my grandsons, Alistair and Zak, two people who may
one day care about this*

# CONTENTS

# INTRODUCTION

When you've been around politics as long as I have, you see a lot of strange things. You may even think you've seen everything. But every now and then something happens that still has the power to knock your socks off, to show you that democracy can be full of surprises. Something like watching Donald J. Trump take the oath of office to become president of the United States of America.

I'd known Mr. Trump for decades. We'd played golf, chatted on the phone, seen each other at various events. But never once in my mind, not for a single second, did I ever think, "There goes the future president of the United States." I never would have even guessed he'd sweep away a crowded field of Republicans—all of whom I knew, and some of whom I even liked—to become my party's nominee.

On that improbable election night in 2016, when he took the stage to the music from the Harrison Ford movie *Air Force One* and declared victory, he taught me something about underestimating people. I was far from the only one who learned a lesson that night——and it wasn't the first time "the Donald" had offered me one.

The first time I met him was on one of his own golf courses: the Trump National in Westchester, New York. This was a high-end kind of place, with a big fountain outside the clubhouse, a grand staircase inside, and a hundred-foot water-fall on the course. Whatever you may think about Donald Trump as a politician, he sure knows how to put together a golf facility.

I was House minority leader then and on a fundraising run, scheduled to play golf with two high-profile insurance executives. We needed a fourth, and out of nowhere, we were informed that Donald Trump himself would be playing with us. I didn't know Donald Trump at all, except from television. But his name was on the door of the club, and if he wanted to come out with us, none of us were going to say no. I had no idea what to think. The big loud guy I had seen on TV did not strike me as an ideal companion for 18 holes of golf. When we got to the course to hit some warm-up balls, there he was: the man himself, with the shock of bright yellow hair, tanned face, dressed in a typical golfing outfit, ready to hit the links.

He was very friendly, but in an in-your-face, this-is-how-they-talk-in-New-York kind of a way that I was not used to at all. Direct, loud, intense. Pretty much the same guy who got elected to the White House. I can tell you that with Trump, what you saw was what you got—for better or worse.

"Boehner!" Trump said when we were ready to start. "You and I are gonna take these two turkeys on and whip 'em." That was okay with me.

As we were getting ready to start, Trump went over to John Criscuolo, a young staffer of mine who came out with us and whom we called "BJ," and asked for the insurance executives' names. "I think they're Joe and Jeff," BJ told him. So Trump said hello to Joe and hello to Jeff and we set off. (Their actual names, by the way, have been changed to protect the innocent.)

Then we went around sharing our handicaps. One of the guys was a 12, one was a 14. I was a 10.

"What's your handicap?" I asked Trump.

"Five," he said, matter-of-factly.

*There's no way this guy is a five handicap*, I thought to myself. *I'm going to have to carry him around on my back all day.*

But Trump ended up birdying three of the first five holes— that's going one under par three times, or one under the standard number of strokes a hole usually needs, for those rusty at golf terms. It absolutely blew me away. *Holy shit*, I thought, *this guy can play golf.* He and I won that day, beating Joe and Jeff soundly. Over 18 holes, we talked about this and that. Nothing particularly memorable, but had I known back then I was walking around with the 45th president, I might have paid better attention.

As we were coming off the course Trump was in a great mood, as winners generally tend to be. We shook hands— "Good match, Joe," "Well done, Jeff." Finally, one of the guys stopped us. He had kind of a weird look on his face, and I could see something awkward was coming. "Guys," he said, "our names are Mike and David." We had been calling these guys the wrong names over and over, all day long, and they were either too polite or too shy to correct us the whole time.

All I could do was laugh. Sure, it was a little embarrassing. But was it my fault these guys just let us walk around for 18 holes looking like assholes because we were spouting the wrong names? They could have said something earlier, but they didn't.

But Donald—well, Trump did not laugh. This sort of

glower fell across his face. The kind of look I could tell that you didn't want to see too often if you happened to work for him. He marched over to BJ and got right in his face to the point that BJ might have had to take a step or two back. Then Trump shouted, "What are you, some kind of idiot?" He pointed to the rest of our impromptu foursome. "These guys' names are Mike and David!" Then he gave the young man a piece of advice that he—and I—have never forgotten. And I hesitate to put an expletive in the mouth of a former president of the United States, but here it goes anyway. "You want to know how to remember somebody's name?" Trump asked. "You fucking LISTEN!" Poor BJ—he looked like he wanted to melt into the ground and pull the turf over his head.

We laughed about that at the time, and since—BJ still works with me—but there was something dark about it too. I'd never seen anybody treat a staffer like that—not in politics, not ever. This was more than New York bluster. This was real anger, over something very, very small. We had no idea then what that anger would do to our country.

And Trump didn't even take his own advice once he became president. He didn't listen to most people—let alone me. Our conversations became less frequent over the years—maybe he just got busy, maybe he didn't like my advice. But as for me, I've learned that if you want to be successful at anything, it helps for you to pay attention. As Speaker of the House, you don't hold on to the job long unless you do—noticing how a president tells you something so you can see he doesn't really mean it, or a member promises their vote on a tough bill but has a funny look in his eyes when he does, or when a group of rebels always seems to be staring at their feet when you walk by.

Over my years of listening, I've put together my own set of rules—handy sayings and phrases—that have helped to keep me sane no matter what got thrown at me. Some of these I made up myself, others I heard somewhere and committed to memory. At some point somebody decided to call them "Boehnerisms," and people started keeping unofficial running lists. You can skip to the end for the official list, but here and there throughout this book, I'm going to share some of my favorite Boehnerisms and how they've helped me see the humor, or even the lessons, in some of the weird spots I've found myself in. And there have been plenty of weird spots, for sure, but you can learn something from them. One of these Boehnerisms is my own definition of wisdom: wisdom means you've made a lot of mistakes in life and you've learned from *some* of them.

That's what I've tried to do, at least. So hopefully some of these stories will entertain you, educate you, and maybe even inspire you to take on a leadership role in your own life. Because, God knows, we need good leaders now.

I don't think it's a secret to anybody that our country faces unique challenges today. You might even say we're about halfway through a double-decker shit sandwich, served up to us by an outrage-driven media and a self-interested political class. An unprecedented global pandemic thrown into the mix certainly came as no help. Then there was a close election in 2020 in which red America got redder, blue America got bluer, and President Trump was replaced by Joe Biden, who took office along with a deeply divided House and a 50-50 Senate. America was split smack down the middle. Trump's refusal to accept the result of the election not only cost Republicans the Senate but led to mob violence. It was painful to watch.

Americans are well aware that our government isn't working the way that it ought to. In part, it's because of a cable news world in which controversy sells and outrage and rebellion are rewarded. In part, it's because of people who come to Washington intent on promoting themselves instead of working together. They claim to be true believers and purists, like the right-wing "Freedom Caucus" or the left-wing "Squad," but they really are just political terrorists, peddling chaos and crisis so that everyone keeps paying attention to them. And they can embolden *actual* terrorists, like the ones who stormed the Capitol and "occupied" my old office on January 6, 2021. That was a low point for our country, and it made me want to cry.

I've seen so many "purists" abandon their principles when it suits their political needs. After all, the Freedom Caucus, which was supposedly the great conservative bulwark against government spending, barely said a peep as a Republican administration outspent Barack Obama. Some of the self-proclaimed fiscal hawks with the shrillest screeches even joined that administration and presided over significant spending increases and growth of the national debt, which they didn't seem to care about anymore. You can hold your nose tight enough to stomach anything, I guess.

Part of the problem, if we are going to be really honest about it, is that we the people put up with all this malarkey. We prefer the easy outrage over focusing our attention on tough questions that don't have five-second solutions. We reward amateurs who know and care nothing about governing instead of having faith in seasoned officials with experience and patience, who are trying to make some changes to a democracy where change is meant to be hard. The left's promises of a Green New Deal or abolishing the police? They are pipe dreams, I'm sorry to tell you. They're recipes for division and anger. And they're perfect for cable news. But there are more realistic approaches that will help us solve our environmental challenges, or at least move the country in the right direction. One problem is that nobody has enough patience to be realistic. You can't do a quick TV segment on something requiring rational thought by people who actually know something on a subject——that would make for boring television, and no producer in their right mind would set it up.

But the last thing I want this book to sound like is some old guy railing at "these kids today." There are a lot of shitty things that come from getting older. Sometimes my back goes out and I can't play golf. I don't know what TikTok is, and I probably will never bother to find out unless someone makes me. I see more years of my life in the rearview mirror than are ahead. But age also brings wisdom and lessons and hopefully good humor, and that's what I want to share here.

I want this book to be filled with hope. Because I do think we can solve these problems. I believe in this country and in our system. There wasn't a day that went by when I was in Congress that I didn't feel damn lucky—the son of a bartender who made good, or at least tried to. And I'm going to guess the vast majority of the men and women I served with, Republican and Democrat, feel the same way about themselves. They aren't *all* trying to rip you off. They aren't *all* charlatans and liars. In fact, most of them aren't. They believe, as I do, that this is a great country and a great democracy. And the same goes for the vast, vast majority of the people that they serve, the American people who really do just want the best for their families and their neighbors. The Americans I've met from all kinds of places over my decades of traveling around the country certainly believe that.

All we need to get back on the right track is maybe just a little tough love. This book is my effort to pass along what I've learned over the years in the hope of helping us do that.

A lot has changed about Washington and the world since I left office. But one thing hasn't changed: yours truly. I walked out of the Capitol the same jackass I was when I walked in 25 years earlier. After serving at the top levels of government—second in line to the presidency, having met kings and queens and every president from Richard Nixon to Joe Biden—I have my regrets. Who doesn't? But I'm proud, at least, that I stayed true to who I've always been.

That's how I'm going to tell my story. I didn't want to write another boring drag through Washington's "halls of power." And I thought the best way to keep that from happening was to do what I've been doing for decades: just be me. That was how I stayed sane all those years in politics (and unfortunately, not everyone makes it out that way). So I'm going to tell it like it is, or like it was, in plain English. And I'll try to use expletives sparingly—but no promises. If you're looking for Shakespeare, or my 15-point plan to save the world, this isn't the book for you. But if you're looking to hear from a regular guy who went from working in a bar to holding a pretty big job, and got to see some incredible things and learn some things that just might help others get through their lives, then have a seat. Get comfortable. Pour yourself a glass of something nice. You're going to enjoy this.

*John A. Boehner*
Marco Island, Florida

# On the House

# The Art of (Real) Power

Nancy Pelosi has a killer instinct—something I never had (well, not much of one anyway). In fact, I think she may be the most powerful Speaker of the House in my lifetime, maybe the most powerful ever.

There are many reasons I say this, and some I'll get to in a moment, but one that really stuck with me involves one of her former Democratic colleagues in Congress—a legendary fixture on the Hill, the late, great John Dingell. John was the so-called Dean of the House, the longest-serving member, having been first sworn in under President Eisenhower in 1955. He was a World War II veteran and remained a favorite of both sides of the aisle due to his charm, sharp tongue, and eccentricity—including his punchy embrace of Twitter in his eighties.

He was also chairman of the House Energy and Commerce Committee. To those of you with normal lives who live blissfully outside of Washington, this may not seem like much. But sitting on a big and powerful committee like this one—known as "E&C" for short—is a major deal on Capitol Hill. And becoming chairman? Well, that's what people in Congress live for. You get to hold hearings, and issue subpoenas, and investigate pretty much whatever the hell you want if you come up with a reasonable pretext. And Dingell was ferocious in that job—tough, nasty, powerful. People dubbed him "Big John" and "The Truck."

Personally, I liked the guy a lot. We met in 1991, my first year in Washington, at—of all places—an NRA press conference. For some reason we quickly struck up a conversation, which turned into a friendly relationship for the next 25 years. He was a great guy to spend a few minutes with sitting on the House floor, to ask his advice or just hear him wax on about the institution of the House, for which he had a great love. When he came to office in 1955, it was in a special election to replace his own father, who had died in office after serving since 1933. The place was in his blood. He'd grown up with it. His depth of knowledge was amazing.

For this reason, lobbyists, CEOs, presidents, fellow members of Congress, and everyone else who happened to cross his path were scared as hell of John Dingell. Everyone except Nancy Pelosi.

Sometime after Pelosi became Speaker, her fellow Californian, Henry Waxman, made what many of the smart set in DC saw as a surprise move to unseat Dingell as chairman of that committee. There were a couple of things that may have motivated Henry. Maybe it was an ideological thing. Dingell was a Michigan moderate who didn't follow the progressive line on issues like climate change and auto emissions standards. Waxman, on the other hand, was a staunch liberal, a "Watergate Baby"—a member of the large class of Democratic representatives who came to office in 1975 in the wake of President Nixon's resignation and voters' general dissatisfaction with Republicans. And as the second-highest ranking Democrat on the committee, Waxman had been "waiting his turn" to take over the chairmanship for years and years. Maybe he just got tired of waiting.

Anyway, when Waxman announced he was leading what at first seemed like this nutty suicide mission against Big John, Pelosi stayed officially neutral. But anyone with two peas between their ears knew that Henry wouldn't have dared to challenge Dingell without Nancy's approval. He certainly would not have won, which he did, without her tacit support. She didn't have to say much, and she didn't show her hand in public. Nancy is one of those people who doesn't leave a lot of fingerprints. But she was all over this. I could just smell it.

Waxman's 15-vote victory made all of our necks snap upright. Pelosi had gutted Big John Dingell like a halibut she found floating around San Francisco Bay, then calmly sat back and had a cup of coffee afterward. His entrails were left on display for everyone in the House of Representatives to see—and to remember. I don't think Nancy relished mounting Dingell on her wall—she certainly didn't brag about it—but that's not the point. The point is she did it, and I have no doubt she slept just fine that night.

After that gutting, there wasn't much of a role for John Dingell. It's hard to leave a perch that powerful and still feel relevant. Nobody was afraid of him anymore. He retired from Congress in 2015 and died a few years later. When his funeral mass was held at Holy Trinity Church in Washington, Pelosi was Speaker again. She attended, but did not give a eulogy. I spoke, as did a number of John's former colleagues, but the highest-ranking Democrat to address the mourners was the majority leader, Steny Hoyer.

I didn't often agree with Nancy's politics—well, I pretty much never agreed with her—but I respected her. Her family had political power in Maryland, but she moved across the country and came up in California politics on her own strength. In many ways, she and I chose similar paths once we got to the House. She set out from her first term, just like I did, to join the leadership. And she got there, just like I did, in part by throwing herself into fundraising for her colleagues. She was a formidable political operator who knew how to count votes and dollars, an essential skill for building coalitions in a nuthouse like Congress. She knew how to tell the difference between bullshitters who promised their support and people who would stick by you until the last dog died. When she became Speaker the first time, she held her entire conference in line, passed Obamacare, and wielded power with sometimes ruthless enthusiasm.

I like Nancy. Don't get me wrong. But while we may have taken similar paths to the Speakership, I'm still not sure I could have done what she did to poor John Dingell. And it wasn't just Dingell—there is a pretty sizable pile of victims on the Democratic side of Congress that Nancy Pelosi turned virtually into non-persons. Pelosi understands power, and she is not afraid to use it. That gets me thinking a little bit about what this concept of "power" really means, especially in Washington.

—◆—

Ever since I came to our nation's capital, I've heard people babbling about power. You always hear the same phrases: the "corridors of power," the "power players," the "most powerful" this or "least powerful" that. They can go on and on.

I'm not about power, and I never have been. I couldn't care less about it. Well, I guess that's not wholly true. Maybe more precisely, I couldn't care less about conveying an image of power. "Being powerful is like being a lady," Margaret Thatcher famously put it. "If you tell people you are, you aren't." People running around calling themselves powerful look about as ridiculous as those telling everyone they are a genius. That's why President Trump didn't do himself any favors with his declaration that Article II of the Constitution gave him the power to do "whatever I want" as president. All that does is leave you vulnerable to attack from people who want to prove you wrong.

As Speaker of the House, second in line to the presidency, I was considered a pretty powerful figure in town. Most of the time I found this an annoyance. I couldn't always do what I wanted, like go play a round of golf or go out to dinner with some friends, without making some U.S. Capitol Police officers tag along with me. The black SUVs, the security detail—I guess some people would call those "trappings" of power, but to me they were just embarrassing. Sometimes it was nice to speed through stoplights if I was late to a meeting or pull up to an airplane right on the tarmac rather than having to go through security lines and wait for my seat to be called. But sitting in some entourage, followed around by people with sunglasses and guns all day long—that's not my style at all. I often felt like I had to justify the extravagance. It's hard to just veg out at home and watch TV when people are keeping you under 24-hour surveillance. The taxpayers are really paying some guys to stand outside my house while I watch television? Give me a break. I wish I'd thought of the term "executive time" when I was Speaker, but Trump was way smarter than me on that one.

Maybe one of the reasons I've been reluctant to embrace the "power" label is that I saw how quickly and casually power can be abused. Not just by world leaders like Nixon or Clinton or whoever, but by ordinary people like me and you. Something happens to a lot of good people when they start feeling powerful. As for the bad people, well, power just makes them all the more dangerous.

I saw it time and time again in Washington. Some people could barely hold power in their hands for a hot second before they became jackasses, using it either for their own gain or somebody else's loss—or both. The way the House leaders abused their power to take advantage of the already dirty earmark process—in which members basically were bribed with special pet projects in their districts to vote in favor of legislation—was one of the worst examples, but there were plenty of others. Some members would wait years to settle scores with people over some minor grievance, like voting against a bill of theirs. Maybe it's a little ironic that one of the biggest abuses of power I ever witnessed ended up propelling me to a more powerful position of my own.

I'd been a member of Congress less than nine months when, in September 1991, I stumbled across a little item in *USA Today*. They reported that a federal agency, the General Accounting Office (GAO), had done an annual audit of the House of Representatives' bank—yes, we had our own bank. It wasn't even a bank, really. It certainly wasn't regulated in the way that every normal bank in America is regulated. It was just a little operation run out of the House sergeant at arms office (dating back to 1789) where members' paychecks were deposited, and from which members could then write checks. But the GAO found that members had bounced thousands of checks without penalty. Nobody seemed to have paid much attention to that story. But I did.

I hadn't liked the idea of the House bank from the moment I heard of it. When I first showed up, they tried to get me to set up an account for my paycheck. "No thanks," I told them. I liked my bank back in Ohio. I'd been dealing with them for years and saw no reason to switch. "You can't do that," I was told. "The only way you can get paid is to have an account with the House bank." Well, that got me nervous. I didn't like hearing that there's only one way, through one entity, to get something done. These guys had created a nice little monopoly for themselves. My nose started twitching. It didn't smell right.

It turned out I wasn't the only one who felt that way. Charles Taylor, another freshman Republican, from North Carolina, had had a similar experience. Charles owned banks back home, and he understandably wanted his check wired back to his own institution. But like me, he was told you couldn't get paid unless you took part in this little venture. So Taylor and I talked to a few other freshmen we knew, and then we started asking around more generally. Here's what we found: nobody who had been in Congress for any length of time seemed to want to talk about the House bank. Some members would start looking at their shoes whenever you mentioned it to them.

We figured out what was happening. The House bank was a sweet little perk for all these guys. They were letting people overdraw their accounts with regularity. At home if I had zero dollars in my bank account, I was out of luck unless my bank gave me a loan and charged me interest. Here in Congress, if I had zero dollars in my account, I could just write checks and someone else would pay for it. I guess you'd have to pay the House bank back at some point, but nobody seemed to be too bothered by that. And guess who paid for this great perk? The American taxpayer. The rest of you were footing the bill for members who couldn't balance their own checkbooks. Why this came as a surprise to me, I couldn't say. But it did. And I wanted all these guys to admit it.

One day, Scott Klug from Wisconsin and I, along with Rick Santorum from Pennsylvania, introduced a privileged resolution on the House floor—a special measure brought up outside of the normal calendar of House business—that demanded an explanation of what was going on with the bank. The Democrats controlled Congress at the time, but I like to think we would have done the same thing if it were the Republicans. I'll be honest—the fact that the Democrats were the ones up to their necks was a nice cherry on top. When their leadership figured out what was actually going on, they converged on us. Speaker Tom Foley came down to the well of the House, as did Majority Leader Dick Gephardt. But then it turned out the Republicans weren't innocent in all of this. Our Republican leader, Bob Michel, joined the group as well. They really seemed to be against our resolution being introduced. In general, their explanation sounded like, "We didn't do anything wrong, and we won't do it again."

We were going against the most powerful people in Congress. So we needed to turn to people with immense power of their own: the press corps. The press gets such shit from members of Congress—often deservedly so—but they were the ones who first brought this scandal to light. We guessed that the American people would not like the idea of their representatives passing bad checks with taxpayer money. As we expected, once the story got out, it not only grew legs but also started running all over town and into pretty much every member's office on Capitol Hill. By Monday, the story of a few freshman congressmen exposing the cover-up of the House bank was everywhere, and people were pissed off. Americans were pissed as hell at Congress. Our colleagues were pissed off at us. By Tuesday, the House had voted to close the bank and ship the whole matter over to the Ethics Committee.

We had gone against the most powerful people in the House, but now the power had passed to us. Here's how I knew it: I got a call from Speaker Foley's office. For months the Speaker hadn't returned my calls asking for a chance to introduce myself as a new member. Now it seemed that the Speaker had finally found time to meet with me—but apparently not much. I was told that Foley would soon be leaving his office to walk over to the House floor, and if I wanted to talk with the Speaker, I should hustle over to the Capitol and walk with him. I decided to decline. I didn't feel like a walk just then.

The Ethics Committee took up the matter, and I was skeptical from the beginning of their investigation. It seemed to me that this was just a way of keeping everything "in house." On April 1, 1992, they published a list of the top 22 check-bouncers, and probably hoped that would be the end of it. But we fought for full disclosure, and finally, some two weeks later, the list of all members who had bounced checks at the House bank was released. Hardly anybody was spared. Speaker Foley was on the list, as was number-two Democrat Gephardt. Nineteen different committee chairmen had overdrafts on their accounts. Democratic representative Gerry Sikorski of Minnesota was one of the worst check-bouncers, having written nearly seven hundred bad checks from his account. He tried to pawn off the blame on his wife—a real classy move. Plenty of House Republicans were on the list too, including two rising stars: Newt Gingrich of Georgia and Vin Weber of Minnesota. Weber chose not to run for reelection, but Newt stuck it out. The hapless Buz Lukens, who had held my seat in Ohio's 8th District before resigning over an improper relationship with a minor, was sent back to jail—this time for bribery—as a result of the House bank investigation.

Charlie Rose—a long-serving congressman from North Carolina, not the former journalist—used to say that the House was "run like the last plantation in America," meaning that the members who ran the place, especially the leadership and the committee chairs, were lords and masters of their own self-contained domain, and nobody, least of all the American taxpayers, could tell them how to do things any differently on *their* turf. And he was absolutely right. The House bank scandal was the first shock to that system. After that, people began to take more notice of how deep the rot went in the institutions of the House. On March 26, 1992, as the bank scandal was unwinding, veteran *Washington Post* columnist Jack Anderson described the "image of a Congress that fiddles while Rome burns."

"Congress runs up the national debt and gets free overdraft protection at the House Bank," Anderson observed. "Congress eats a salmon lunch for under $10 while America is brown-bagging it." He pretty much hit the nail square on the head.

Here's another reason I knew I had power: after the bank issue blew wide open, my phone never stopped ringing. People were coming out of the woodwork to tip off my office about other little perks and freebies that were hidden away in the House of Representatives system. Some were burrowed in so deep that there was no way any investigation would have uncovered them. A lot of these tips were anonymous. Some were cranks, but some of them turned out to be legitimate.

Those cheap gourmet lunches Jack Anderson wrote about? Those were specialties of the House restaurant, which soon became another target of our reform efforts. At that time the restaurant was run by the House itself, as opposed to an outside catering firm on a contract. That meant they could get away with a lot more. Only members and guests they sponsored could eat there, and while it was used by outside groups a fair amount, the sponsoring members were ultimately responsible for making sure outsiders' tabs got paid. We got a tip that the stack of unpaid bills at the House restaurant had reached the neighborhood of $60,000. Before long we had the receipts to prove it. That was all unpaid-for food, prepared at taxpayer expense for members and their pals. We gave all of our colleagues formal notice that if these tabs weren't paid off in 30 days, the rest of the information would be disclosed. Well, they got the message. Within 30 days, every dime was repaid.

Then there were all the problems with the House post office—formally known as the Congressional Post Office. Members would buy stamps and charge them to their office account, and then use them as currency in an underground congressional black market. Stamps were being traded for cash. Under federal law, you can't sell your stamps back to the government, but some members were getting away with it. One way the stamps were "laundered," so the rumors went, was through late-night poker games where they would play in stamps. Thousands of dollars' worth of USPS stamps were apparently changing hands. And you couldn't just buy stamps at the House post office—apparently you could buy cocaine too. You couldn't make this stuff up. No wonder people were sick of Congress. This place was being run like the side streets of Mexico City.

Several investigations were opened into the House post office, including by the Capitol Police, the House Administration Committee, and the Postal Service itself. Eventually the

House postmaster was charged and pled guilty, which in turn threw light on the involvement of two members—Joe Kolter of Pennsylvania and Dan Rostenkowski of Illinois—and one staffer. All three of them were charged, but only Rostenkowski, or "Rosty" as I knew him, got sent to jail.

That was a tough one. Rosty was a good friend, a good member, and a good man—but he was also one of the last of the old-school big-city politicians. Rosty exemplified the "Chicago Way," and he played by different rules than the rest of us. Now, here I was having to go on television as the "point man" for the House reformers arguing that Rosty deserved to go to jail. Sometimes they'd book me and Democratic representative Charlie Rangel of New York—another old-school big-city political veteran—and have him defend Rosty. It was hard coming down on my friend from Illinois, but it's what we had to do. Both Rangel and Rosty grew up in a political system with a set of rules that went back to the 1950s. Obviously the rules had changed quite a bit over the decades, but these guys hadn't. They weren't bad people, they just operated under different rules than what society was going to accept forty years later. So Rosty paid the price. And a little more than a decade later, so did Rangel, when he was censured for violating House ethics rules.

It wasn't personal with Rosty or the guys who bounced checks at the House bank or anybody else who got caught up in the reform efforts of the 1990s. Right was right, wrong was wrong—and something had to be done about all the mess. And those of us who found ourselves out in front of it, the freshmen of the so-called Gang of Seven, quickly became despised by our colleagues, Republican and Democrat alike. To the leadership, we were toxic. Some members would come up to me in the hallways and say, "Boehner, what are you screwing up today?" Often they used less polite language than that. Others wouldn't even look at me at all as they shuffled past. But they were afraid of us. I had been a member of Congress for about ten minutes, and I was a guy that mattered. I don't say that as a boast. It was just true. When a member of Congress saw me or one of my boys walking their way, they looked like they wanted to either strangle us on sight or jump under their desk.

But I was kind of used to my colleagues hating me. So I kept right on going. I had been elected to office to do something, and now I had the power to get people on my side. That was what led me, as a freshman member in 1992, to sue the House of Representatives in federal district court. I had retained outside counsel, and the general counsel to the clerk of the House was representing the legislative body. I was joined in the suit by about two dozen other current members, and needless to say we were not popular among our colleagues.

They were pissed enough about losing out on free money and free meals. And just a few months before, I had been part of the effort to ratify the 27th Amendment to the U.S. Constitution, which made it harder for members of Congress to increase their own salaries. Now they were trying to do just that through the backdoor method of a "cost-of-living adjustment," called a COLA for short. This seemed like a sneaky way to violate the very amendment that the Congress and the American people had just supported—despite the grumbled objections of some senior representatives. Congress had made a show of agreeing with the new constitutional amendment, but now they were trying to raise their own salaries on the sly. So I took my own legislative body to court.

As strange as it may sound, this story started all the way back in 1789. The Bill of Rights, as most Americans know—

and every American *should* know—is made up of the first ten amendments to the Constitution, and they clearly lay out the fundamental rights and freedoms of every citizen. Originally though, there were twelve amendments proposed for the first round of additions to our founding document, and two didn't make the cut.

One of these, written by James Madison himself, read simply, "No law, varying the compensation for the services of the Senators and Representatives, shall take effect, until an election of Representatives shall have intervened." This just means that if members of Congress vote to give themselves a raise, that raise couldn't take effect until after the next congressional election. That way it's left up to the American people to determine whether or not to vote them back into office to enjoy it.

In a June 1789 speech in Congress, Madison observed that "there is a seeming impropriety in leaving any set of men without control to put their hand into the public coffers, to take out money to put in their pockets." That made sense then, and it made sense more than two hundred years later. But at the time, Madison's colleagues were less than enthusiastic. Only six states—Maryland, North Carolina, South Carolina, Delaware, Virginia, and Vermont—initially ratified the amendment.

It stayed mostly forgotten for nearly two centuries, but since there was no time limit given for ratification, it still had the potential to become part of the Constitution if a total of 38 states ratified it. Ohio was the only state to do so in the whole nineteenth century—in 1873. Wyoming got around to it in 1978. But things really took off in 1982, when a University of Texas student named Gregory Watson got a C on a government class paper that argued for the amendment's ratification. Watson took on the cause and started a nation-

wide campaign to raise awareness about this commonsense amendment and build up grassroots support. As a result, more and more state legislatures ratified the amendment through the 1980s.

By the time I took office in 1991, the amendment had been ratified by 35 states (though technically it was 36—Kentucky originally ratified it in 1792 but apparently everyone, including the Kentucky legislature, forgot about it until the mid-1990s). Three more were needed.

The grassroots work was amazing, but in Washington, the idea still needed to gain traction. I knew that this provision belonged in the Constitution. It was the right thing to do for Congress itself to get involved, to show its support for fiscal responsibility. It was time to play some politics.

The older members of Congress weren't happy about this—they didn't want any obstacles to raising their own pay when they felt like it—but I figured that the newer members, my fellow freshmen, would feel differently. A bunch of us had a different, more modern perspective on how the House should be run, and we had the momentum to change things—plus, it wasn't a bad way to make our mark as reformers early on. The Capitol Hill newspaper *Roll Call* asked me about it at the time, and I told them, "We believe if you're going to have real reform, you must push from the bottom up. Once you're here three or four terms, you have a vested interest in the way things are run."

Counting on my classmates paid off. In August 1991, when I sponsored a resolution in support of the 27th Amendment, every one of my fellow Republican freshmen signed on. So did a substantial number of Democrats in the Class of 1990. Even our class Independent—Rep. Bernie Sanders of Vermont—jumped on board, honoring his home state's ratification of the original amendment back in 1791.

Still, the resolution only got 59 cosponsors, less than 14 percent of the total House membership. There was serious resistance to the idea. Meanwhile, I was helping out the grassroots efforts. I worked with state legislators, I wrote letters, and in May 1992 the deal was done: Alabama and Missouri ratified on May 5, and Michigan clinched it on May 7.

You could practically hear the harrumphing from the House leadership. Democratic Speaker Tom Foley of the state of Washington groused about challenging the ratification in court. Rep. Don Edwards, a Democrat from California who chaired the Judiciary Subcommittee on the Constitution—and who had made a name for himself promoting civil rights legislation—complained to the *New York Times*: "If James Madison had been interested in this provision, he would have put it in the Constitution. He was sitting there the whole time."

But a week later, the archivist of the United States, in charge of officially adding new amendments to the Constitution, announced that the ratification process had been carried out properly and he would approve it. That, plus the overwhelming support for the amendment from the American people, took the wind out of Foley's sails. He admitted at a press conference, "As a practical matter, it will be considered a part of the Constitution." A few days later, on May 20, the House and Senate both passed resolutions to recognize the new amendment.

Congress had agreed to limit its ability to pay itself more money, an effort spearheaded by the House Republican freshmen. But the fight wasn't over yet. In 1992, once the excitement over adding the newest constitutional amendment had died down, Congress tried to raise its pay again with its so-called cost-of-living adjustment under the Ethics Reform Act of 1989, passed before my fellow freshmen and I had arrived. That was

when we decided to take Congress to court, arguing that they violated the amendment they had just approved.

*Boehner v. Anderson* was decided on December 16, 1992, by Judge Stanley Sporkin of the U.S. District Court in DC. It did *not* go my way. Judge Sporkin declared that "the Court finds that any pay raises stemming from the Ethics Reform Act of 1989 unquestionably meet the requirements of the 27th Amendment." It might be worth noting that federal judges get the same pay as members of Congress, and typically there's a provision that allows the Congress to give federal judges the same raise that members of Congress give themselves. Anyway, the opinion ripped me to shreds.

I didn't win that one, but the 27th Amendment is still in the Constitution. Not many members of Congress can say they've been part of the time-honored amendment process laid down by the Founders. That is something that no one can take away. It was a humbling experience, and an educational one for a freshman member still learning how the DC game was played. I knew we were doing the right thing for the right reason . . . but that didn't mean we couldn't flex some political muscle to get it done.

Having that kind of power was a scary and also a heady feeling. We confronted folks who were using power for misguided ends, while we were using it for what I thought were good ends. But I could feel that tug—that tug that comes to anyone with any authority. People were listening to me now. There's always some voice that can pop into your head. That says something like, *Maybe I can use this power to destroy anyone I don't like. Maybe I can use it to get something I want for myself. Maybe I can use it as blackmail.* You could see how people went down this road. But I tried to be sparing with power and not make examples of people, no matter how pathetic they appeared—such as when a sitting member of Congress ended up on his knees in my office, begging forgiveness.

This was Mark Meadows, a founder of the so-called Freedom Caucus, whom I had first met when he was running for Congress in 2012, just one of hundreds I'd campaigned for over the years. I was doing a swing through North Carolina supporting Mitt Romney's campaign for president. This was back in the days when Mitt was the next great conservative hope, before the rabble-rousers decided he wasn't a big enough lunatic for their liking.

After speaking at a Romney rally in Asheville, I made time to stop by one of Meadows's campaign events as well. He was grateful to have my support, but that was just part of my job. Meadows went on to win his race, and that's when he became my problem.

When Meadows showed up in Washington, DC, one of the very first things he did to thank me for campaigning for him was to vote against my reelection as Speaker. His vote wasn't much of a surprise, since none of those Freedom Caucus folks ever seemed to know how to keep their mouths shut. I knew there was a small group getting together to vote against me, because they had decided I was some left-wing accommodationist or something. Meadows's name was on that list. You may find it hard to believe, but I didn't bear him any ill will. At least he had the courtesy to knife me from the front. And I still won. He was far from the first person to work in Congress for a day and a half (in his case literally) and then decide they were an expert on how to run the place.

Not long after the vote—a vote that like many of the Freedom Caucus's efforts ended in abject failure—I was told that Meadows wanted to meet with me one-on-one. That was no problem. I had made it clear to my staff that I would meet with any member, anytime. So we set up the meeting, but I didn't have a clue what he wanted. Meadows came into my office in the U.S. Capitol and sat down on the couch across from me. We couldn't have talked for more than a second or two. Before I knew it, he had dropped off the couch and was on his knees. Right there on my rug. *That* was a first. His hands came together in front of him as if he were about to pray.

"Mr. Speaker, please forgive me," he said, or words to that effect. I was so startled I can't remember exactly what the hell he was saying. For a moment, I wondered what his elite and uncompromising band of Freedom Caucus warriors would have made of their star organizer on the verge of tears, but that wasn't my problem.

I hadn't expected any sort of apology, and I really hadn't expected to see a man huddled on the rug at my feet. So I did the only thing that came to mind. I took a long, slow drag of my Camel cigarette. Let the tension hang there a little, you know? I looked at my pack of Camels on the desk next to me, then I looked down at him, and asked (as if I didn't know): "For what?"

Yeah, I said, I'd forgive him. But I knew he was carrying a backpack full of knives—and sooner or later, he'd try to cut me again with them. Which, of course, he did.

The funny thing is that Mark Meadows was not the only guy I campaigned for who ended up trying to shiv me once they came to Washington. Take another member of Congress, this one from Florida, by the name of Daniel Webster. As I think about it, having a name like that, linked to a historic figure, is almost a natural in running for office. But believe me, the same name is the only similarity the two men ever had. Of course, Webster showing up to be a pain in my ass was kind of my fault in the first place. Years before, when it was known that he was considering a run for Congress, I was down in Florida for a fundraiser. Webster was there too, and while we didn't get to meet, other people had pointed him out and said good things about this former Speaker of the Florida House and then state senator. So when my ride was leaving, and I saw Webster walking off by himself, I put the window down in the back of the Suburban and shouted: "Webster, for God's sake, run!" We had a few follow-up phone calls where I helped convince him to make a bid for the U.S. House, which he did in 2010. By 2015 he was running against me for Speaker and then later against Paul Ryan too. You never can tell with people.

Then there are times when you find, despite a title or seniority or ranking in the hierarchy, that the person across from you has more power than you do—they just wield it in a way you may not expect. There was another one-on-one meeting with another kooky member that went very differently.

When Michele Bachmann took her seat in Congress in 2007, she had already made a name for herself as a lunatic. While a member of the Minnesota Senate, she cautioned that showing kids the Disney movie *The Lion King* was "normalization" of homosexuality, because a gay man, Elton John, did the songs. In 2009, she suggested that it was "an interesting coincidence" that swine flu had broken out under one Democrat in the 1970s, Jimmy Carter, and then cropped up again under another Democrat, Barack Obama. That wasn't factually true, but that never stopped someone when they were on a roll.

When she first came to town, Bachmann was largely a bomb thrower, complaining about a lot of nonsense to get attention. I don't know how many people paid attention to her. I barely did. She was a kook, no doubt about it, but not the only one. There had always been a few of them around.

In 2010, the situation changed. Suddenly the kooks were

joined by a whole bunch of new friends, who had helped Republicans retake the House majority. The Kings, Gohmerts, and Bachmanns who "prepared the way" (in their view) were only too happy to welcome the new arrivals. And they weren't above taking advantage of the situation for themselves. I generally had a good read on my folks in the Republican Conference. But in this case I didn't see her coming.

Bachmann came to meet with me in the busy period in late 2010 after the election as we were getting ready to take over the majority. That would mean a reshuffling of committee seats, and she wanted a seat on the Ways and Means Committee, the most powerful committee in the House. She had a few years of seniority at this point, but there were still a number of members in line ahead of her for a post like this. People who had waited patiently for their turn and who also, by the way, weren't wild-eyed crazies.

There was no way she was going to get on Ways and Means, the most prestigious committee in Congress, and jump ahead of everyone else in line. Not while I was Speaker. The idea that she could have even asked seemed strange. In earlier days, a member of Congress in her position wouldn't even have dared ask for something like this. Sam Rayburn would have laughed her out of the city. I told her no—diplomatically, of course. But as she kept on talking, it dawned on me. This wasn't a request of the Speaker of the House. This was a demand. Her particular circle of crazy had gotten a lot bigger in the years since she first came to Congress. She was kind of a folk hero of the freak show set. And she had no problem letting me know it.

Her response to me was calm and matter-of-fact. "Well, then I'll just have to go talk to Sean Hannity and everybody at Fox," she said, "and Rush Limbaugh, Mark Levin, and everybody else on the radio, and tell them that this is how John

Boehner is treating the people who made it possible for the Republicans to take back the House."

I wasn't the one with the power, she was saying. I just thought I was. She had the power now. She was right, of course. She was a conservative media darling and, by then, the conservative media was already eyeing me skeptically. More on that—a lot more—later. In Washington-speak, I was in an untenable position. More frankly, she had me where it hurt.

It wasn't even a decision I could make on my own. The Speaker doesn't have hand-of-God power to place whoever he wants on whatever committee he wants. At least not these days. That power belongs to a little-known but very important group called the Steering Committee. The Steering Committee has about 35 members, including the party leadership and members drawn from all the regions of the country. If there's a real "power behind the throne" in the House, it's the Steering Committee. They are the ones who decide which of their fellow members get to sit on which committees. I had a lot of influence, of course, and I guess if I pulled out all the stops I might have gotten my way. But I wasn't about to do that for her anyway.

I knew there was no way the Steering Committee would approve putting Bachmann on Ways and Means. The votes just weren't there. If I even pushed the issue, they wouldn't have let me leave the meeting without fastening me into a straitjacket. But then, Bachmann wouldn't go on TV and the radio to explain the nuances of House Steering Committee procedure. She'd just rip my head off every night, over and over again. That was a headache I frankly didn't want or need.

But then a solution presented itself. The House Intelligence Committee is a "permanent select committee," which means the party leaders *can* personally appoint the members. They get approved as a slate by the whole House Republican Conference, but they don't have to go through the Steering Committee. And "Intel," as the committee is known, deals with serious issues and gives their members solid chops to talk about national security, which puts them in demand for media appearances whenever some global flashpoint gets hot. It also was a good perch for anyone wanting to build up their foreign policy chops for a run for president, which she was already considering—Lord help us all. I suggested that committee to Bachmann as an alternative, and mercifully, she liked it.

The man preparing to take up the gavel as chairman of the Intelligence Committee was Rep. Mike Rogers from Michigan, an army veteran who had also served in the FBI. In Chicago. In the organized crime and corruption division. He was a straight shooter, a true professional, and not somebody who could be pushed around. You can imagine how he reacted when I went to him and told him, "Next year, your committee is going to have a new member," explaining who it was. I thought he was going to rip my head off, but the choice was between Rogers ripping my head off once and Bachmann ripping it off every night on television for God knew how long. So I took my lumps from Rogers, and Bachmann took her seat on the committee.

The funny thing is, Michele Bachmann turned out to be a very focused, hardworking member—even though she spent a few months later in 2011 on a short-lived campaign for president. She showed up to the committee, did her homework, and ended up winning over her fellow members with her dedication. Mike Rogers was impressed—and I have to admit, so was I. The whole situation ended up working out well for everyone. As one of those old Boehnerisms goes, "Get the right people on the bus, and help them find the right seat."

The Bachmann and Meadows maneuvers—theirs and mine—demonstrated the varying ways people can wield power, successfully and not. What I never wanted to do was wield it the way some of the leaders before me had. I saw the way earlier Republican House leaders like Tom DeLay and Dennis Hastert and their handpicked committee chairmen ran the show. They thought they ruled the roost, and that they were entitled to feast on taxpayer-provided pork-barrel spending. To protect their spoils, they imposed an autocratic, top-down system on the rest of us that didn't sit right with me from the beginning. One day in my first term, I saw just how far some members would go when they felt their share of the spoils was threatened.

Rep. Don Young of Alaska is a tough old son of a bitch. When I say tough, I mean tough. The kind of tough that only comes from living in the Last Frontier for nearly as long as it's been a state in the Union. The kind of tough that earns you the right to cover the walls of your Washington office with the heads and pelts of wild animals you bagged in the woods and mountains.

And when I say old, I mean old. Representative Young first came to Congress from Alaska in 1973. He became the Dean of the House—the longest-serving member in the chamber—in December 2017. In March of 2019, he passed another milestone and became the longest-serving Republican in the history of the House of Representatives, breaking the record held by former Speaker Joseph Gurney Cannon, who retired in 1923.

If you're going to survive in Washington or in Alaska for that long, you've got to be a real hard-ass.

At some point during my freshman term, we were on the floor of the House, and I was making one of a whole lot of speeches I made over my career calling out other members for making earmarks. As I told the people in Ohio's 8th District during my first campaign, if they wanted somebody to go to Washington just to steer money their way, they should find somebody else to send. When they sent me anyway, I thought I would do my best to make life hell for the other members—Democrats and Republicans—who just couldn't seem to live without this pork-barrel spending. Don Young was one of those members with a special talent for bringing home the bacon—so to speak—to Alaska. He had a whole state to look out for, so I could understand his point of view. Members fought for those crumbs tooth and nail—or in Young's case, with a 10-inch knife.

He didn't like what I had to say about earmarks. It certainly wasn't complimentary. As I finished my speech and walked up from the well of the floor—where the main podiums stand in front of the Speaker's rostrum—I saw Don marching toward me. I didn't know him well, but I could see that he didn't exactly have a smile on his face. Before I knew what was happening, he had shoved me up against the wall of the House chamber, pulled a 10-inch knife from his pocket (he was known for carrying one or more knives everywhere he went), flipped the blade open, and held it up to my throat.

"Don't you ever do that again," he growled.

I didn't have time to think about any of this in the heat of that particular moment, but there are certain defining moments in Congress, as in life, that force you to decide what kind of person you're going to be. Are you going to be your own man or are you going to be part of the flock of cackling chickens following behind whoever is in charge, tossing out the feed? Don Young was no cackling chicken. And I sure as hell wasn't going to be, either. The way I figured, if God sent me to the House of Representatives to end up getting gutted like a dead caribou by a wild man from Alaska in the middle of the chamber, then hey, there were worse ways to go.

I looked Don right square in his eyes and said, "Fuck you."

He quickly took the knife away from my throat and we went our separate ways. The whole thing was over in a matter of seconds, and it was out of the range of the C-SPAN cameras. Still, the story has bounced around Washington ever since. The funny thing was that, despite this unusual getting-acquainted meeting, or maybe because of it, I don't know, Don and I actually ended up becoming good friends. I was the best man at his wedding, where I told the knife story for probably the thousandth time. As Don likes to say nowadays: "Each and every time you tell this story, Boehner, that knife gets a little bigger and gets a little bit closer." Well, I know what I saw! Sometimes I can still feel that thing against my throat.

The real moral of this story is that there was something very wrong with a system that made good, upstanding U.S. representatives fight like wild dogs over leftover scraps of taxpayer money. The rot went deep. That's why the first thing I did as Speaker was get rid of earmarks for good. But it wasn't even just about the money. The money itself wasn't the corrupting influence. It was the power.

As I ended up in leadership myself as Conference chairman and got to see more of "the system" up close, it only soured me more. Nobody made these people God, and they had no right to act like it. And this attitude filtered down from the leadership to the chairmen of the individual committees. Throughout my career I was struck by what a little power could do to people's heads. I saw perfectly decent, rational members get appointed chairman of a committee and then turn into autocrats. They'd turn into somebody you didn't even recognize. It all went to their heads. I could name names here, but I won't. The point is, you never knew how power was going to change people.

So I decided that, if I ever got the chance, I was going to do things differently. When I became a leader in the House, I sure as hell made sure that I didn't turn into one of those power-mad assholes that kept that system of abuses going in the first place. Only on rare occasions did I give my approval for actions "punishing" individual members—and even then, it wasn't about punishing that certain member but protecting the team as a whole.

For instance, the House Steering Committee, as I mentioned earlier, could put members on committees, but they could boot them off too. They wanted to use their power to weaken members who made it their "brand" to vote against leadership. There were always people like that—who thought the easy and cheap way to look like a "maverick" or "reformer" was to stand against whoever was in charge on almost anything. I say this with some irony, since I was one of those people who went against the leadership during the House bank scandal. But I did it for what I felt were the right reasons, though I guess some of these people who became nuisances to me felt the same way.

In some cases, the Steering Committee did carry out punishments. Tea Partier Tim Huelskamp from Kansas; so-called libertarian Justin Amash from Michigan; ex-Democrat Walter Jones of North Carolina; and Dave Schweikert from Arizona, who'd kept his seat by knocking off a fellow GOP member in an especially nasty primary—all of them ended up losing committee assignments. That wasn't my idea, however. In fact, I often thought it was a bad idea. I argued to the Steering Committee that it would just help them with their brand-building by making these guys into bigger martyrs, and give them a platform to fundraise with outside right-wing groups and take potshots at party leadership in the media. But the will of the Steering Committee and the rest of the leadership was clear, and I signed off on it. I could understand their logic too. These guys were actively hurting the team, so why should the team continue to help them? Let them whine about it. They could go soak their heads.

Still, there *were* other ways of dealing with difficult members that I found much more my style. Most members, for instance, like to travel. Anything to get outside of the Beltway. Members of Congress get to travel all over the world on fact-finding trips called "congressional delegations," or CODELs for short. They get their pictures taken with foreign leaders, and they look like big deals back home. People love to rip on these trips as taxpayer-funded junkets, but take it from the guy who got rid of a lot of lush perks for members of Congress—CODELs are usually worth it. If members of Congress are going to be in charge of funding and oversight for American projects around the world—military operations, aid work, business initiatives—it helps to see how these things work firsthand. It helps to know other foreign leaders and to see the United States from their point of view. It is also a good idea to see for yourself if things abroad are working out the way a president or a secretary of state says they are. Not to say you can't have some fun seeing the world with your colleagues too . . . but there will be time for CODEL stories later on.

The committee chairs and the leadership determined who got to go on CODELs, and there was often a long list of people interested. Sometimes, when I made the determination that a certain member was acting in a way that was hurting the team, or just being a total jackass, I had to make a tough decision.

On a few of those occasions I went to the committee chairs and made clear that it wouldn't be a problem for me if we basically lost their plane ticket. Sometimes I said it more directly than that. I wouldn't go to the press or make a big announcement about how I'd punished someone or trash-talk anybody. It was more subtle than that—I just made my decision clear to a few key people. And the knuckleheads never got to go on CODELs. Period.

Of course the biggest institutional power of the Speaker of the House is by far the ability to decide which bills make it to the floor and which don't. The actual scheduling of the floor calendar is handled by the majority leader, the person on the rung directly under me in the leadership ladder. That's what it says on paper. But trust me, nothing came to the floor for a vote unless I said it was coming to the floor.

Members of the Knucklehead Caucus figured that out real quick. The bills on the floor reflected the priorities of the whole team. If these folks didn't want to be on the team, why should the team support their bill? Some of them got the message, some didn't. It was fine by me either way.

The role of Speaker of the House has an important ceremonial aspect too. The greatest expression of this is the president's annual State of the Union address to Congress, where the powers of the Legislative and Executive Branches collide. It's a logistical nightmare to pull off—getting all the members of the House and Senate plus the cabinet and Supreme Court justices and everybody else into the same place. Once during the George W. Bush years I got to the House floor late (a rare occasion for me) and couldn't find a seat. I was still looking out into the chamber to see if I could spot one when Bush took the podium. I didn't want to have my back turned toward the president, so I just turned around and sat down right there in the aisle. One of the photographers got a photo of it, naturally, and it made it into the next day's paper.

Once I became Speaker, of course, I had a direct role in the State of the Union proceedings and couldn't afford any screwups like that. It was easily the hardest night of my year. There I would sit for an hour and a half, next to "Uncle Joe" Biden, staring straight at the back of President Obama's head. Those occasions were all about the president, not the vice president or me or anybody else, and I knew that if I did anything, made even one off-kilter facial expression or—God forbid—yawned, the camera would catch it and I'd get roasted.

And so I would stare at the back of the president's head. I could almost tell you how many hairs President Obama had back there. I did my best to make no expression whatsoever. Usually that worked out alright. But even that wasn't good enough for some people. One reporter once said I looked "bored." Inside, I was making every facial expression known to man. There were plenty of times Obama said things I didn't agree with, or took jabs at Republican priorities, but rolling my eyes or shaking my head would have been totally unprofessional.

At least, that's what *I* thought. Apparently the new tradition enacted by Speaker Pelosi is ripping up her copy of the president's speech. That's a good 180 degrees from how I'd do things, but everyone has their style, I guess.

The first year I sat for a State of the Union as Speaker was 2011. Biden and I had a meeting about a week before, and I made a suggestion.

"Joe," I said, "we've got to stop this jumping up and down and clapping, where one side of the aisle tries to outdo the other. We've got to bring this to a stop." It's become an annoying tradition at these speeches—the strictly partisan standing ovations.

"Maybe we should lead by example," I offered, "and the two of us shouldn't hop up and clap for everything the president says."

Biden seemed fine with that. So maybe, I thought, this year's address would actually have some semblance of order to it.

On the night itself, I was standing up at the podium and everyone was walking in—senators, ambassadors, and all the rest. Biden came up to take his place next to me, and I immediately started telling him about a fantastic golf game I'd had out in the Sandhills of Nebraska a few months before. I was walking him through my round of the decade—I shot 72—until one of my staff came rushing over to tell me our mic was live. It turned out the mic at the president's spot was switched on already and picked up every word of our conversations. All I could think was, *Thank God we were talking about golf.*

Just before the speech started, Biden turned to me and said, "You know, I'm going to have to stand up sometimes." Maybe the boss had got wind of our plan. I told him I understood, of course. But for the rest of the night, every time Obama delivered an "applause line," Biden would shoot me a quick, apologetic glance that seemed to say: "Is it okay if I stand up now?"

The last thing I wanted to do was get "Uncle Joe" in trouble with the president. He and I had a long-standing relationship. Biden was a classic old-school pol—maybe one of the last of the breed. We were pretty close, always friendly, and could count on each other to be honest all the time—something that's rare in Washington or anywhere else.

Whether it's the scene of grand rhetoric or a partisan rallying cry, the State of the Union is in many ways a strange American institution. On the one hand, it's mostly empty theater these days. Everybody pretty much knows what the president is going to say. The members of the president's party in Congress will get up and cheer, and the opposition party members will sit on their hands, stone-faced (or at least hopefully not shout anything). It's just a show for the TV cameras.

On the other hand, only a president can command that kind of attention. The greatest power at the president's disposal is not the world's most powerful military force or an arsenal of nuclear weapons capable of destroying the world several times over. It's the power of the soapbox. The president of the United States has the biggest soapbox in the world, which if used correctly can shape and form national and even international opinion. How a president uses that platform is critically important to their success.

Effective communication is key to projecting real power. Most of our modern presidents have understood that. President Obama was very good at it. Even though I disagreed with most of what he said, I can admit that he was a great communicator. So was Bill Clinton—he was a fantastic talker (just ask Newt about his ties—more on that later) and a master of the bully pulpit.

President George W. Bush was also able to use power effectively, but in different ways. Bush was certainly underrated as a communicator, and he had a phenomenal partner in Dick Cheney. They were a great team who understood how to use the power of their offices to advance their agenda, in a way that they believed would help the country.

President Trump had a hard time using the world's largest soapbox in a way that benefited the country, or even himself. As everyone knows by now, he often preferred to communicate by tweet, which on many occasions got in the way of his own goals. Early on, the economy performed admirably, and the administration logged some major policy wins, like tax cuts. Of course, the 2020 pandemic was something nobody anticipated. But all along the way, the president's continual tweeting threatened to undermine his own success.

The bully pulpit for the Speaker of the House is pretty small by comparison, but it is still an office outlined in detail in the Constitution. That makes it more than just a partisan position. How one chooses to balance those roles, however, depends on the Speaker him- or herself.

That was another difference between me and Speaker Pelosi. When I was minority leader and she was Speaker, I watched how she handled the office. We obviously came from different parties and were different sorts of people, but if I wanted a shot at leading my party to the majority, I figured I'd learn all I could. And sometimes I learned what *not* to do.

One thing I learned watching Speaker Pelosi was that saying a lot of words is not the same thing as communicating. In my view, she spoke on the floor too often, and her speeches could be long-winded. That helped me understand that if I was going to go on the floor, it had better be about something important. As Speaker, I thought it better to hold my fire most of the time. I wasn't going to add my voice on any old bill, even if I supported it. If there was a need for me to speak on something, I'd do it. But when I did, I would get up, say what I had to say, then shut up and sit down. I didn't think being Speaker gave me any special opportunity to go over time limits and crowd out other members.

Some colleagues—from both parties—seemed to think that the longer they talked, the more points they were making, but I never bought into that. Long-windedness, to me, is power wasted. I learned a great saying very early on in Congress from Texas representative Larry Combest in 1992. We sat on the Agriculture Committee together. Combest had been a former staffer for Senator John Tower, and one day in the House cloakroom he told me a favorite saying of Tower's: "You never get in trouble for something you don't say." I've never forgotten that to this day. It's helpful for most people to remember in both their professional and personal lives.

The tighter you try to cling to power, the easier the hold can sometimes be to break. I saw Speaker Pelosi's iron grip on power backfire, ultimately bringing the Republicans back into the majority. Between January 2009 and the November 2010 midterm elections, she worked hand-in-glove with President Obama to pass two major pieces of legislation: the Affordable Care Act (or "Obamacare") and the American Clean Energy and Security Act (or "Cap-and-Trade").

The House Democratic Party had to be fully behind these bills. Speaker Pelosi would tolerate no dissension in her ranks. I saw pro-life Democrat Bart Stupak of Michigan hold his nose and vote for Obamacare because he was promised changes that never came. He decided to step down in 2010. I saw pro-coal Democrat Rick Boucher, who represented a coal-producing district in southwestern Virginia, vote for Cap-and-Trade, one of the most anti-coal bills in recent memory. He lost in 2010 to a pro-coal Republican.

In a sad twist for the Democrats, it was their moderates who lost the worst in the 2010 elections. Moderate Democrat seats swinging to Republicans helped us take back the House. I never forgot that lesson, and I knew that I wasn't going to endanger our majority by forcing controversial legislation through at ramming speed.

I just couldn't work that way. I'd let everyone have their say, and when the majority of the Conference was committed to a course, we'd go ahead. And those who didn't get their way just had to deal with it (which to them often meant running and crying to the right-wing press).

Consensus rarely meant unanimity, but that was fine with me. I just wanted to keep the decision-making process open, and I did that all the way through. It was more open than any Congress I'd ever worked in, and most of the members felt that way too. Even if they didn't always agree with me, they appreciated the chance to hear what was going on and have their say.

Mitch McConnell, for instance, has a very different approach. And the Senate is a very different beast. These points were made very clear to me by the man himself.

McConnell is one of the best politicians I've ever met. He's incredibly smart. You get the impression he's always playing a game of *Risk* inside the safe confines of his brain—and he's always winning. He's made a living out of being inscrutable. He holds his feelings, thoughts, and emotions in a lockbox closed so tightly that whenever one of them seeps out, bystanders are struck silent. To McConnell, information is power, and he holds it close. He keeps his cards so close to his vest, his members don't get to see them until he's ready. And even then, they only see the corner he shows them.

Mitch and I had a great working relationship. His staff got along with my staff. Rest assured the guy was a tough nut to crack. I like to get along with people, to have a few drinks and a few laughs, to not always make everything about work. Mitch McConnell has a professional façade you cannot shake. It's useless to try to loosen things up with a joke—maybe at the most you'll get the corners of his mouth to twitch into something that could be interpreted as a smile. But you never can be certain.

We have different styles for sure, and there's a reason I stuck to the House and he stuck to the Senate. Maybe his kind of leadership is more what the Senate needs than what would work in the House. But you can always learn something from those who lead differently than you—even if it's what *won't* work in your case.

In 2006, I was the House majority leader and McConnell was the Senate majority whip. That meant we were both the number-two man on our respective chambers' leadership teams, so we kept in touch frequently, as did our staffs. I didn't know him that well at the time, and despite coming from similar parts of the country—Cincinnati is right on the Kentucky border—we weren't gelling.

McConnell came over to my office in the Capitol to see me for one of our regular check-ins. I had friends in the Senate— several of my pals from the House like Saxby Chambliss, Richard Burr, and Lindsey Graham had moved over there by that time—and generally kept up with gossip from the other side of the Hill. I had a pretty good idea of what was happening over there, and I wanted to make sure Mitch knew it. I thought he might be impressed that I had the place wired.

After the meeting ended, I walked McConnell to the door. I held it open for him, and as Mitch walked out, he turned around in the doorway and gave me a little lesson in how he viewed our power dynamics, and how it was going to work between us. He looked me dead in the eye. "John," he said, with his usual expressionless face, "I'll never presume to know more about the House than you do. And trust me, you'll never know as much about the Senate as I do." And then he turned and was gone.

Now I knew how members of the Senate probably felt whenever they got sideways with their leader. Mitch McConnell had kicked me in the balls. I was stunned. I went back to my office and sat down to think about what I'd done, like I'd been dressed down by a parent or a teacher (and Mitch is not *that* much older than I am). He certainly got his message across. I never again made the mistake of acting like I "knew" the Senate. He was the powerful one in that chamber, and I was just a mere observer pretending that I wasn't.

Even if I wanted to, I could never operate like Pelosi did. The fact was, I *didn't* want to act that way, even though sometimes other people thought I should. A lack of transparency might work in the Senate, but it would never fly in the House, no matter how nasty things got. As Speaker, when I was dealing with members who were not only going against the team but also trashing the team to the press, I'd have staff and other members chastising me every day. "Boehner, you've got to be meaner," they'd say. I'd have to explain that I just don't have a mean bone in my body. I don't do mean. It's a waste of energy. I couldn't be mean to somebody if I tried—and I have no interest in trying! It's not who I am. Which probably means I ought to get around to telling you a little bit about where I came from.

# TWO

✧

## Cheaper by the Dozen

When you have 11 brothers and sisters, you can be forgiven if you can't remember all of their names every once in a while.

Late one night in Washington, after I'd been in Congress for a couple years, a lobbyist buddy named Bruce Gates asked me—after we'd had a few—if I could name all my brothers and sisters. In my defense I rattled off ten of them pretty easily. When I got to my youngest brother . . . I could picture his face like he was standing right in front of me, but for the life of me I just could *not* come up with his name. (Sorry, Mikey.) Needless to say, by the next day that story was all over Capitol Hill. I was child number two in the Boehner dozen. Pretty much every time I turned around, I had a new brother or sister. I'm supposed to remember them all on command? Give me a break. Anyway, years later, when Lesley Stahl came out to film all of us together for a *60 Minutes* feature, I made damn sure to not screw up again and wrote everybody's name down. In order. Just for the record: there was Bob, the oldest, then me. Then Steve, Nancy, Greg, Rick, Drew, Lynda, Pete, Jerry, Susan, and Michael. That's all of us. I think. All sharing the same little house in Reading, Ohio. My parents were plenty busy, obviously. And us kids were kept busy too.

Having 11 brothers and sisters isn't just a conversation topic. For those who are interested, it explains my whole life. There's a huge difference between being an only child or part of a family of four and being one of 14. First there's just the matter of valuing what you have. When I got a new jacket or a pair of pants all my own, I treated it like gold. Even fresh towels were a rare commodity in our house, with the whole platoon of us sharing a bathroom. I don't think I ever used a totally dry towel the entire time I lived there.

This probably explains why I had such little tolerance throughout my life for people wearing wrinkled suits, or loose ties, or scuffed shoes. Dress like you are grateful you have something of your own. My unusual upbringing also probably explains my reputation in some corners of having a Zen-like approach to chaos. When you live your formative years in a house where Greg and Nancy are fighting over watching the TV, Lynda is late for work, Jerry needs his lunch for school, Susan is complaining that someone is in the bathroom too long, Mom is feeding us all in shifts, and Dad just wants one minute of quiet, please, you can sure as hell withstand a maniac trying to blow up the Congress or a bunch of constituents yelling at you about some vote you made or members of Congress squabbling like kids over the office assignments.

I lived through a good-natured war zone all my life. I can handle anything. It also might explain my propensity for a cigarette or a glass or two of red wine. I love my whole family, but after dealing with all of that for so many years, wouldn't you need a drink too? And it also probably explains a lot about my work ethic. Which brings me to telling you about the most formative experience of my young life.

On Saturdays, at about quarter to five in the morning, starting when I was about eight years old, Dad would walk quietly upstairs and open the door to the room I shared with my brothers. At that point, there were only two bedrooms in the house, so the boys got one and the girls got the other. Mom and Dad slept on a pullout couch. Later, when I was in high school, we put a three-room addition on the house to give everyone a little breathing room—plus a room for my grandmother to live in after she developed dementia.

Silently, so he wouldn't wake up the little guys, Dad would come over to the bed—we all slept in a big bed together when we were really young—and gently shake his two oldest boys, my brother Bob and me, awake. We got out of bed, went into the single bathroom to get cleaned up, then got dressed, went downstairs and followed Dad out to the car. It was still dark outside, and usually pretty cold. Dad made sure to close the front door gently, since Mom was still asleep on the sofa bed in the living room. We were gone by five o'clock.

We drove through the darkness down the hill from our house in Reading through the Mill Creek Valley. The little farms and neighborhoods turned into factories and industrial yards as we got closer in to Cincinnati. It would just be getting light as we pulled into the Carthage neighborhood in the northern part of town. Dad parked the car in the normal spot, and we would walk over to the corner of 72nd and Vine Streets, to a bar called Andy's Café.

Some of the regulars were already lining up outside the door. They nodded at us as dad got out his keys to open up the bar. We didn't want to keep them waiting. If they wanted booze with their breakfast, that was their business. Our business was the bar. It was 5:30, and Andy's Café always opened on time.

When you're right in the middle of growing up, you're too busy to think about this kind of stuff, but as I got older and got to see a lot more of the world, I realized that Andy's—that little corner bar in north Cincinnati—was in many ways the center of my world as a kid. Sure, there was home and school and friends' houses and of course church—all places that were important to me in different ways. But Andy's was special. It didn't seem like it at the time, it just seemed normal to me. Some kids' dads worked in factories, some kids' dads were plumbers, some kids' dads were policemen or firemen, and my dad owned a bar.

But it was at Andy's that I learned a lot of the things that have really stuck with me the most over the years. It was where I learned about hard work, and the value of every dollar you got with your own sweat and elbow grease. It was where I learned about family, and how to keep one working together as a team. And, probably the most important lesson of all, I learned how important it was for every single person to be treated with respect. Everybody who came through the door of Andy's Café got treated the exact same way, no matter what they looked like, what they were wearing, or how much money they had to spend. It didn't matter if they were a local businessman, a bottling plant shift leader, a line worker, or even a lazy drunk. Well, the drunks were welcome as long as they behaved themselves, which most of them did.

The place was small, just a rectangular room with enough space for a bar counter with a bunch of stools, and some tables set up along the opposite side. Outside, the brick building was painted mostly tan, but the area around the front door and windows was a dark green, with some wood shingles that came up to about chest level. In those days, the area was mostly German, and from the beginning Andy's served cold lager beer in frozen mugs.

It was a basic shot-and-a-beer joint, and stayed that way from its opening all the way up until my family sold it not too long ago. They served food too—breakfast and lunch, but no dinner. Never dinner. Why? Because that's just the way it worked, that's why. You just didn't show up at Andy's for a steak dinner.

When my dad opened the place up at 5:30 in the morning, the guys getting ready to go to work at the factories or chemical plants nearby could come in for a shot and a beer and some breakfast. That may sound like an odd way to start the day, but it worked for these guys. Around the same time, the guys just getting off the night shift would come in for *their* shot, beer, and breakfast before going home to sleep.

Things slowed down a bit after the breakfast crowd left, but in the afternoon, people would come in for a shot, a beer, and some lunch. Some would be done with their shifts, and some were on break and fueling up before heading back to work. Finally, around five or six in the evening, people would come back in for another shot (or two) and a beer (or four) before they went home. A lot of customers would come visit Andy's three times a day—for breakfast, for lunch, and after work. You can see how they would become like family, and make for an endless cast of fun characters for a young kid to get to know.

The drink offerings were simple. You could get a shot of beer, a mug of beer, a glass of beer, a pitcher of beer, or, in the evenings, a gallon jug of beer we filled up from the tap for a dollar. As it turned out, buying beer by the gallon was the cheapest way to buy beer in town. It pays to buy in bulk.

Beer drinking was a family affair in those days, too. Husbands used to fill up extra gallon jugs to take home to their wives. They'd holler to my dad behind the bar: "I need to get more beer for Mama, she's doing the ironing tomorrow!" As a guy who does a lot of ironing, I'm not sure how beer helps—but I *am* sure that nobody was going to tell these Cincinnati German housewives they couldn't have their lager. Don't get the wrong idea though. These weren't super heavy "double IPAs" or whatever bartenders are pushing these days. They were crisp, cold, old-fashioned light lagers—just enough to take the edge off.

We had liquor too, but just the basics. You could get a shot of bourbon or vodka. The closest we got to any kind of "cocktail" was a vodka with club soda, or a bourbon with Coke or 7 Up. I saw exactly one martini served in the entire history of Andy's Café, and it was my fault. In 1976, when my dad was still running the place, I brought my boss—later partner—at Nucite Sales over for lunch. I was 26 and he was 73, but he still knew how to have a good time, and a boozy lunch was standard. He was used to a ritzier sort of place than Andy's though.

So the guy came in and ordered a martini, and everybody in the place sort of looked at each other. Then everybody looked at me. Sitting next to him, I cringed a little bit inside. But somebody found a way to pull together the ingredients and make him a martini. Seeing that drink sitting on the bar at Andy's was like coming across a fish in the middle of a desert.

If the drink options were simple, so was the food. This wasn't exactly a gourmet dining establishment, but they served up hearty portions of the kind of food you needed to keep you going during a long workday. Breakfast was eggs with sausage, ham, or bacon and a side of toast. The lunch options were soups and sandwiches, which included hamburgers.

There was a 30-gallon pressure cooker in the back that we used to make our own chili.

The types of people who came in were a cross-section of the community as it was in those days in that part of the country. The area north of Cincinnati, all up and down the Mill Creek Valley, was home to a number of manufacturing firms, some big, some small, but now mostly gone. Andy's would attract workers from "Ivorydale," the Procter & Gamble plant where Ivory soap was first made, and still is today. They'd also come from the William S. Merrell Company chemical plant— which later became Merrell Dow Pharmaceuticals and which played a big role in my life later on.

We'd get everybody from the factories—line workers, clerks, managers. We got the truck drivers who hauled their products up and down the Valley, looking to kick back after a long day on the road. Karl Mouch and his family ran a jewelry store right across the street and sent someone over to pick up lunch every day. The Mouches were family friends of ours, and their shop made the trophies for all the local youth sports teams.

Among this crowd there were always the regulars—the three dozen or so guys who would make several trips to Andy's every day. They were a real cast of characters. One of them was called Shaky. I never knew his real name. Sometimes, especially when he came in the mornings, the shaking was so bad we'd have to grab his beer glass to keep him from spilling it all over himself. My dad did *not* like to waste booze. But amazingly enough, after Shaky would have a shot, then chase it with a beer, then repeat that one or two more times, the shakes would calm down. The booze put him on an even keel. So he would hop off his bar stool, wave goodbye to everybody and head off to his job at the *Cincinnati Enquirer*.

That's the way Andy's Café had been run since the early 1930s, when my grandfather, Andrew Boehner, first opened it up. He grew up in Clifton, a neighborhood right in the middle of Cincinnati, the first member of our family to be born in the United States. Both of his parents had emigrated from Germany, and so had the woman he married. Even by the time I knew my grandmother, she still spoke broken English with a strong German accent.

As a young man, my grandfather went back to Europe as a soldier in the U.S. Army in the First World War. He faced off in the trenches against German troops who, for all he knew, might have been distant relatives. But he wasn't sentimental, and didn't worry one bit about ties to the "old country." Andrew was an American—his country called, and he answered.

Plus, there wasn't much room for sentimentality in the trenches of France. There, Andrew had a close-up view of the horrors that made World War I such an especially terrible conflict. His unit was attacked with poison gas. He survived, but when he came home to Cincinnati, his health wasn't as strong as it had been. The doctors told him he would live a little longer if he moved out of the center of the city and went somewhere in the country where the air would be cleaner. He was a practical man, so he followed doctors' orders and bought a small farm in Reading, Ohio, where my dad and his siblings were born.

In the 1920s, Andrew was working as a pipefitter at the National Distillers plant in Carthage, which made whiskies like Old Grand-Dad and Old Crow, but he didn't exactly enjoy it all that much. After going through Prohibition, he knew how miserable it was not being able to get a drink (well, legally at least). So at some point he got it into his head to start a bar in the neighborhood where he worked, to serve all the guys at his and all the other factories and plants in the area. He had learned something about the booze business, and he knew the market was there. In fact, Andy's Café may have started its days as a speakeasy, opening up just before Prohibition ended. That part of the story is a little murky, but either way the place has been going strong at 72nd and Vine for decades.

When the next war came along, my dad, Earl Boehner, did like his father had done and signed up to fight for his country. Dad served in the South Pacific driving DUKWs, amphibious vehicles the troops pronounced "Ducks." Their job was to haul men and supplies back and forth from island battlefields to ships waiting offshore. Besides being a "Duck driver," I don't know much about what my dad did during World War II, because like my grandfather and most of the guys in those generations, they didn't talk much about their service. It never came up—not once—and somehow we knew, even as kids, not to ask about it.

A bunch of those old "Ducks" survived the war and ended up being used as tourist vehicles. I guess people got a kick out of being able to go into and out of the water. There are still some of them chugging around Washington, and when I see them, I think about my dad—and how those things must have been a real bitch to drive.

When Dad and his brothers came back from the war, they went right to work helping out my grandfather at the bar, and gradually took over the day-to-day management of the place. They developed a pretty good system to divide and conquer the work: Dad tended bar and waited tables, Uncle Ken ran the kitchen, and Uncle Roy handled the finances.

Ken knew what he liked, and he stuck to that. One thing he *didn't* like was potatoes. I never got to the bottom of this, but in any event, Andy's never served French fries. Ever. Not even with burgers. There were no home fries at breakfast either. There was hardly a potato in the place. But he would personally boil, skin, and chop all the steer tongues to put in the "mock turtle soup." Adding fried fish to the menu on Fridays was his idea of a major innovation. He had his quirks, needless to say. But the kitchen was his domain, and that was that.

Roy was Ken's twin brother, and it was his job to manage the business side of things. He was always in and out, running back and forth to the bank. We usually let the regular customers pay their tabs for the week on Thursday or Friday. Roy would take their checks to the bank, deposit them, and come back with cash so Dad could make change at the register.

The weekends were also when we would wash down the bathrooms—always a fun job—as well as the windows on the inside and out. There wasn't a lot of "down time." Before we knew it, it was time to wash the lunch dishes, and then squeeze in a bite to eat ourselves. The good news was that Dad left a little early on Saturdays, so we all headed home around 2:00 in the afternoon. For the day's efforts, Dad would pay Bob and me each two dollars. Not two dollars an hour— just two dollars.

Still, two dollars was a lot of money for a kid in those days, and I knew for sure I'd earned every cent of it. From watching my dad and my uncles, I knew how important it was to put in our share of work in the family business. The work might have been its own reward, but that didn't mean I didn't like the cash too. When I got to be a little older, around 12, I decided to negotiate for a raise. I talked with my dad and said that now that I was bigger, and could help out more around the bar than I could when I was eight, I should get paid five dollars for a day's work. After some convincing, he agreed. And it was a pretty good early lesson in negotiation.

It wasn't long after the raise that I made the first big personal purchase of my life, and learned the importance of saving. Siler's Bike Shop was right next door to Andy's, and I used to admire the slim, shiny bikes in Siler's window while I was outside washing the windows of the bar. Mr. Siler would come over to get a cup of coffee almost every day, including Saturdays (always with cream and sugar), and we would talk bikes.

Not that we had any money for the kind of things in Mr. Siler's shop, of course. We had to make do with more budget-conscious options growing up. Bob and I would put together our *own* bikes from old junk parts we found lying around, picking up a frame here and some handlebars there. They probably weren't the safest things on two wheels, but they were fun. The idea of a store-bought bike of my own seemed ridiculous. I might as well have tried to buy a yacht. But once I started earning five dollars a week at Andy's, I also started to get ideas . . .

One day I noticed a secondhand Raleigh six-speed sitting in Siler's window. I mentioned it to Mr. Siler when he came in that day, and he could tell I was interested. We cut a deal—I could have the bike for $30. For the next six Saturdays, the five dollars was in my hand for only about the 60 seconds it took me to walk out of Andy's and over to Siler's, where I'd hand the bill to Mr. Siler. After six weeks, I got my first store-bought bike.

That bike opened up a whole bunch of other possibilities. Not only did I suddenly have a lot more freedom to ride around town with my friends, I could make this thing work *for* me. In a way it was the first big investment I ever made. For one thing, it meant I could ride over on Sundays to the Ridgewood golf course and caddy. I didn't know much about golf at that age, but how much did you need to know to carry some guy's bag? It was good money, and that was all I cared about. But clearly something stuck, because later on in life I came back to golf in a big way.

Caddying was just one of the many different odd jobs I found my way into as a kid. When I wasn't in school or playing sports or helping Dad out at Andy's, I was always on the lookout for a chance to make a quick buck. I would get a major windfall whenever it snowed. Bob and I would run out of the house with shovels and start knocking on neighbors' doors, working our way down the big hill we lived at the top of. In the afternoons, after school, I'd sell the *Cincinnati Post and Times-Star* for a nickel out in front of the factories to workers going home after their shifts. I figured out when shifts changed at different plants so I could run between them, sell to the most workers, and maximize my profits. I got pretty good at it and started putting money away.

I ended up spending a lot of time outside of the house—working, playing sports, or just running around—because there really wasn't that much room for me *inside* the house.

For us boys, it was easy enough to just answer the call of nature outside if our one bathroom was occupied, which it often was. At one point my parents started a renovation project to add an extra bedroom, but it took years to complete because they could only afford to pay the contractors here and there. By the time the third bedroom was finished and my parents were finally looking forward to leaving the sofa bed after so many years, my grandmother announced she was moving in. So she got the new room, the boys and girls kept one room each, and poor Mom and Dad were still stuck on the sofa bed.

Once there were too many of us to fit in one big bed, the boys' room got bunk beds. We were stacked three-high at one point. It was like an army barracks. As soon as they were set up, I made sure to claim a top bunk to myself, just to get a little bit of privacy. Unfortunately, I forgot that heat rises. Whenever it was warm enough, I would sleep outside. We had a "porch" that was really just a concrete pad with a chaise lounge on it, and I'd throw a sheet and pillow onto that and drag it out into the yard under a tree, so I wouldn't wake up with too much dew on me in the morning.

One night when I was in high school, I went to sleep out in the yard and woke up outside my best friend Jerry's house. I was in his yard, it was about three in the morning, it was dark, and I had no idea what I was doing there. Oh, and I was wearing nothing but a pair of jockey shorts. Once I came to my senses I got out of there as quick as I could, trying my damnedest not to wake up Jerry's family. I can't imagine the looks on their faces if they'd found me. They'd probably have been more confused than I was about the whole thing.

My motorcycle—I'd upgraded from the bike as I got older— was parked outside at the curb, in the same spot I normally left it whenever I went to visit Jerry. The keys were in the ignition, so I started it up and zipped home, praying that nobody would see me out riding through the streets in my jockey shorts.

To this day, I might have still thought the whole story was a dream if my mother had not been waiting for me on the porch when I got back. Mom had always been a night owl, and I guess she'd heard the motorcycle start up when I left. "What in the world are you doing?" she asked. I told her the truth: I had no idea. I'd just woken up outside Jerry's house. Mom took the keys to my motorcycle and went back in the house, and after that, I wasn't allowed to leave my keys in the ignition. But I never went sleepwalking—or sleep-cycling—any other time, before or since.

That was one of the stranger situations I found myself in growing up, but no matter how much mischief the 12 of us put them through, I never saw my parents mad. They were two of the most patient people I ever met, and were absolute saints to put up with all of us. We didn't have much money, but even that never seemed to give them stress. We just made do with what we had. Mom would darn our socks until the threads totally wore out. We'd even joke about it. Once my mom took me to buy new shoes (a rare occasion), and when she saw how much my feet had grown, she asked the sales-man, "Can you just give us two shoeboxes for free?" The two of them had a good laugh, but I didn't.

No matter how wild things got, with everyone running around every which way for school, sports, or whatever else, when 6:00 came around there was only one place everyone had to be: around the dinner table. I'm still not sure exactly *how* we all fit around that table, but we did. Mom would cook up enough to feed the whole army of us: some meat, some potatoes, and some vegetables, usually from extra-large cans. Sometimes there would be something special like fried chicken, or a big pot of chili. There was always bread, which we would dip in mom's to-die-for gravy.

Every now and then she'd make a giant German-style dumpling, taking bread (usually the less-fresh side), eggs, milk, salt, and pepper and mashing them all together into a soccer-ball-sized hunk. It would sit there in the middle of the table, like a doughy cannonball had been dropped right in the middle of our dining room. Then we would cut it up into slices, and cover them in more gravy. I haven't had it since I left home decades ago, but I can still taste it now. Just wonderful.

We never took a bite until we'd said grace, of course: *Bless us, O Lord, and these Thy gifts which we are about to receive from Thy bounty, through Christ our Lord. Amen.* There was another rule, too. The oldest kid (Bob, or after he left to join the army, me) could never have a second helping until the youngest (whoever that was at the time) had had their first. It was a fair system.

Somehow, even with so many of us in such a small space, we were able to keep things in pretty good order. Part of that, I admit, was because by the time I was a sophomore in high school, I had become a total neat freak.

Every night after dinner, Mom and Dad would head to the couch in the living room—the same one they would sleep on—while some of the kids worked on the dishes and others helped clean up. Dad would have the newspaper, and Mom would either be reading or watching the TV (once we got one). But always, inevitably, some squabble would break out between the younger kids that would soon blow up into World War III right there in our living room. Mom and Dad mostly ignored it, probably because this was the only time all day they could turn their brains off.

Somewhere in the middle of one of these, I snapped and started barking orders. I told one brother to get all the shoes off the floor. I told one sister to empty all the wastebaskets. I divvied up the work and made sure everyone stuck to their tasks. And in an hour, the whole place was ship-shape. Everything was organized . . . and then of course, an hour later it was back to a mess. So I'd have to go back to action again before long. Once I'd gained some control over the situation, there was no going back—I've been a neat freak for the rest of my life. That probably explains why I never leave the house to this day without ironing my clothes.

Pops's farm—"Pops" was our name for Grandpa Andy—was nearby, too. It was only about a five-minute walk. His yard alone was 3 acres, and the whole property was about 20. There was a barn and a chicken coop, and all sorts of places for a kid to get into mischief. I learned a lot out on that farm.

When I was about seven, I "adopted" one of his steers as a pet. I'd feed him every morning. He was my bovine buddy. Can you see where this is going? One day I went into the barn to feed him and he wasn't there. There was just a trail of blood leading out behind the barn. I walked out back and, sure enough, there he was, hanging from a big elm tree in the yard, freshly slaughtered, with all the blood draining out of him. That night, over a steak dinner, I learned a bit about the facts of life and death.

A few years later, I learned another lesson that made me feel as bad as that dead steer looked. Pops used to have picnics at his farm, where family members, friends, and neighbors all hung out under a giant elm tree. There was always a keg of beer in a barrel of ice. I must have been around 11 when I, figuring I was pretty much grown up, decided to fill up a mug of beer like everyone else from the keg. I'd tasted beer before, but this time I went back to the keg once, then twice. Meanwhile, all I was eating were raw green onions that had been pulled out of the ground that morning. We would wash them off, throw some salt on them, and just chomp down on the stalks, then wash them down with a swig of beer.

After about a dozen of these onions and three or four beers, I felt sicker than I ever got again in my entire life. The day after, I woke up with my first hangover—and one of my last, in fact. Because I learned early on how god-awful it felt to drink too much, I grew into a very strategic drinker as I got older. If your first experience with booze ended up with belching the unholy smell of beer and green onions, you'd learn to be a damn careful drinker too. Over the years, I found a preferred vice—a nice glass of wine. Or two. And then there was that other bad habit that people complain about, with good reason, to this day.

# THREE

## Smoke-Filled Rooms

When Paul Ryan replaced me as Speaker of the House, one of the first things he complained to me about—besides the nuthouse I'd left him to manage—was that the office he inherited in the U.S. Capitol reeked of cigarette smoke. Legend has it that he spent months cleaning out the smell from curtains and carpets and whatever. It did not agree with Mr. Health Nut who, as you'll recall, had a photo shoot done at the gym. I love Paul, but we are very, very different people.

To this day, people like to bring up my smoking and the fact that my new office in Washington contains a balcony that allows me to excuse myself from meetings to take a few puffs. Someone even wanted to title this book *The Smoke-Filled Room* until my daughter very rightly explained that I didn't want to encourage young kids to get hooked on the stuff. And that's the last thing I want to do, because I was just a kid myself when I got hooked on the stuff. I remember vividly the epiphany I had.

I was 19 years old, and I didn't like what I was looking at in the mirror. I weighed 273 pounds—I remember the number with that much precision—and had pants with a size 38 waist. The next size up was 40. That was a mental block for me. There was no way in the world I was ever going to let myself buy pants that size, so I knew I had to do something.

I figured I'd eat three meals a day and every time I got hungry between meals I'd smoke a cigarette. This was in 1968, and it was way before everyone under the sun was screaming at you about the dangers of smoking. Pregnant ladies were puffing cigarettes in those days. So was James Bond. You could smoke on airplanes and in restaurants and pretty much wherever you pleased. Large ashtrays were everywhere. So give me a little bit of a break, please.

Also, my idea worked. I lost 85 pounds, dropped a couple of waist sizes, and picked up a new bad habit in exchange for eating a bunch of crap all day long. At first I smoked Lucky Strikes with no filter, but whatever brand I started smoking they kept taking off the market. Now I just hope Camel stays in business—fingers crossed.

I'm not blind to the health risks, and I sure as hell don't encourage kids today to smoke. But I've told my doctors that I've made it this far in life by smoking, and the damage has been done. They don't stop trying to tell me what I should do, and I don't stop ignoring them. And it works out fine.

I did try to quit once. In 1985, my wife, Deb, and I both took a six-week class for that very purpose. It worked on my wife, and it worked for me for a while too. Until one day when I found a moment of weakness and smoked one cigarette. That was it. I started scrounging around in gutters for butts to light up. I did have at least one more moment of reflection on this when I joined the board of Reynolds American. It was a funny thing. I noticed that not a single other person on the board of one of the world's largest tobacco companies was a smoker.

Neither were the senior executives I knew. I never saw any of them touch the stuff.

One day during board meetings, I walked outside for a smoking break, and the head of R&D at the company came up to me. This was the guy who knew more about cigarettes and what goes into them than anyone else in that company, and probably as much as anyone in America. He didn't smoke either. "Hey, Boehner," he said, "you really ought to quit that." In more recent years, I found myself in a very different sector of the smoking community when I joined the board of Acreage Holdings, a cannabis company. But now, some people don't believe me when I tell them I've never smoked a joint. But I haven't. I'm not ruling it out though.

So I guess it's fair to say for most of my life I've been in smoke-filled rooms, which in the old days is what they used to call the back rooms of political intrigue in Washington. But before I ended up in the dark, smoky back rooms, my intrigues (such as they were) started out somewhere very different—a sunny poolside Fourth of July party in an all-American suburb.

I wasn't really a political person by nature. I didn't pay much attention to politics at all when I was growing up. But when I did, I usually took my cues from my parents, who were solid Democrats. We were a Democratic household, so I just went along with that and assumed I was a Democrat too.

Besides, I had so much other stuff to worry about that politics didn't even make the top ten. As I was getting ready to graduate high school, I was almost completely taken over by stress about what I was going to do next. I wanted to go to college, but I had no money. I did okay at school but wasn't *that* great, and I liked playing sports but wasn't *that* great at those either—which meant no scholarships for me. So I knew, whatever I did, I'd have to pay my way.

Between school and sports I was working every part-time job known to man. When I first graduated, I knew I couldn't try for college right away, but I still had to make money, so I kept working whatever job I could find. I took my first shot at college in the fall of 1968 at the University of Cincinnati, and that didn't go so well. Then I took a job in construction, and after a while I decided to join the navy to put that experience to use as a Seabee—but my screwed-up back put an end to that after just a couple months with a medical discharge. More on that later.

By September 1969 I was out of the navy and back into the odd jobs. I worked construction again, and roofing. Eventually I got myself into Xavier University, going part time because I needed to keep working all these other random jobs to pay my way. I picked up extra money refereeing high school sports too. It really wasn't that different from high school—I was either at school or at work. That was it. It wasn't easy, but I kept plugging along that way for a few years, still with no real goal in mind other than graduating college (eventually).

But things started looking up in the summer of 1972. People I knew around town who worked at Merrell Dow Pharmaceuticals had recruited me for their company softball team (I was a decent softball player in those days). To play on the team you actually had to work for the company, so they gave me a job as an overnight janitor, working from 11:00 PM to 7:00 AM. For anyone keeping score at home, between night work, day work, and college classes my time left for sleep was . . . well, not much.

One morning that summer, it was about 6:45 and I was cleaning off one of my last desks when this cute girl walked into the office. She was coming into work early that day. If she'd come in a few minutes later I'd have been gone and missed her completely. And I would never have met my wife.

Deb and I got married the next year. We had about $400 in cash between us. She had three rocking chairs, a TV set, and a few other furniture odds and ends. That was it. We may not have had a ton going for us, but we loved each other. Suddenly everything came into focus, and life had a lot more direction and meaning.

I finally got my degree from Xavier in 1977 and went to work full time at Nucite Sales, a small company that provided plastics and packaging to a whole lot of manufacturers all over southwest Ohio. I liked the sales work—getting to know people, finding out what they needed, putting the deals together. I'd finally found a job I could make into a career, and that's just what I did—I stayed with Nucite, helped it expand, took over as president after my boss died, and ran it until I went to Congress in 1991.

Deb and I moved into a new house on July 3, 1977, and the next day, my buddy Al Busemeyer, who lived nearby, invited us to the neighborhood Fourth of July celebration at the local pool. It was a great way to get to meet the neighbors, but I was in for more than I bargained for.

Somewhere in the conversation that afternoon, it came up that the seat representing my section on the board of the Lakota Hills Homeowners Association was vacant. Someone said, "How about the new guy?"

I'd been in the neighborhood for all of a day, and all of a sudden I was on the HOA board. Next thing I knew, I was Speaker of the House. A few things had to happen in the meantime though.

As the 1970s turned into the 1980s, I got a bit more serious about politics. Even though I was raised in a family of Democrats, I'd bucked the trend a few times. I voted for Nixon in 1972 and Ford in 1976. And now, because I was making a bit more money, the government was taking a bigger chunk of it. In those days, they took a lot. In 1978, I paid more in taxes than I made in gross income in 1976. In those days, once you made about $74,500, 70 cents of every dollar you made went to the federal government. I thought that was just outrageous.

Around the same time, there was somebody else emerging on the national scene who felt the same way: former California governor Ronald Reagan. He was talking about economics in a way that really made small-business folks like me sit up and pay attention. Things didn't have to be this way, he said, and sketched out a vision of new tax rates, supply-siding, combating inflation, and unleashing the power of the free market. So I finally looked around and said to myself, *I'm not a Democrat anymore, I'm a Republican. And I'm a Reagan Republican too.*

That turned out to be a little controversial in those days (as it is today, according to some). Everyone I knew that was involved in Republican politics was campaigning for George Bush in the 1980 Republican primary. Bush was supposed to be the "anointed one" that year, and he was, by the media. Reagan was portrayed as too old, too Hollywood, or too much of a right-wing extremist. Well, none of that bothered me one bit. I stuck with my guy. As far as I was concerned, the sun rose and set with Ronald Reagan.

While he was running for president, my own much smaller-time political career was ramping up as well. This was not something I had set out for, but things just seemed to keep moving. In the spring of 1980, I was asked to be president of the Homeowners Association. I was the youngest guy on the board, but I guess nobody else wanted to deal with the work.

As president, I was involved with coordinating with other local groups like the school board as our community grew and expanded. That led to meeting more and more people, and the next thing I knew, I was running for an open township trustee seat. I was only 31 years old, and the first day I went out to knock on doors, it hit me: Who am I to ask these people to vote for me? Who did I think I was? But I went ahead and did it anyway. Between me and a few friends, we knocked on almost every single door in West Chester, Ohio. We were welcomed in some places more than others.

One woman met me at the door with a snarling Doberman who looked like he was ready to rip my guts out on command. But because I stood my ground and delivered my pitch on the doorstep (with one eye on those sharp nasty fangs), she promised to vote for me. I guess this was some kind of sick "test" she pulled on people.

On the other hand, I still have friends to this day that I first met when they opened their door to hear my pitch back in 1981. That's meant more to me than winning the election itself—although that was pretty nice too.

I like to think that Ronald Reagan helped inspire me to run, in a way, even though party politics didn't do much good at the local level (which is much harder than governing at the federal level, by the way). I grew into a Reagan Republican, and I became more and more involved in the community. That's the philosophy I tried to stick with all the way—working toward a smaller, fairer, more responsible government. That's what Reagan stood for.

I don't think Ronald Reagan would recognize the Republican Party today. And he sure as hell couldn't get elected in it. As a matter of fact, Reagan would be the most left-wing candidate in the GOP these days—by a mile. Which is why

I laugh whenever all the politicians celebrate their fetish for Reagan. They don't have a first damn clue about who he was. Reagan didn't operate on the principle of "all or nothing." He knew that getting 80 percent of what you wanted counted as a victory. He believed in finding common ground, building coalitions and working across the aisle with the Democratic House Speaker, Tip O'Neill, to get things done instead of throwing bombs to score points with partisan media. We could learn a lot from that approach today, but unfortunately most of us probably won't. In fact, more often than not that approach got me into a hell of a lot of trouble once the crazies came to town.

---

Anybody who says there are "rules" to the political game is probably not very good at playing it. Rules can hem you in. I followed the law and my own code of ethics—especially remembering to do the right things for the right reasons—but beyond that, I tried to avoid hard and fast rules when it came to applying political pressure or working different angles.

Every situation was different, whether it was a constitutional amendment fight, the investigation of an internal institution like the House bank, or a tense negotiation with President Obama. They all demanded their own approaches, and all offered their own lessons. Mostly I learned from experience, letting the lessons of different successes and failures guide me along the way.

Sometimes, for instance, I ran up against so-called rules that just seemed made to be broken. That's what happened during my first campaign for Congress in 1990.

The Ohio 8th is a solid Republican district, so the real race was in the Republican primary. My top opponent was Tom

Kindness, who had represented the district in Congress a few years back. His name was tailor-made for politics, and mine, well, wasn't. It was a rule, I was told, that nobody's going to vote for you if they can't pronounce your name.

All through my life I'd heard my name pronounced any different way you could think of. In high school, of course, it was "Boner." I'd also heard "Beaner," "Bonner," and plenty of other variations. So we decided to lean into that in my first campaign, and cut a radio ad featuring an older couple named George and Helen.

"George," asked Helen in the ad, "who's this John Beaner guy?"

"No, Helen, that's John Boehner," George responded, pronouncing it correctly. "He's a small businessman from West Chester."

And it went on from there. The idea was to set people straight, but gently. We even put pronunciation guides in printed material, cluing people in that it was pronounced like B-A-Y-N-E-R. It took some people a little while, but they figured it out. And I figured out that the old rule that "they won't vote for you if they can't say your name" isn't always true. Who would have expected "Boner" to beat Kindness?

I wasn't sure what to expect when I got to Washington, but I do remember my first impression. *This is just like the Ohio legislature*, I thought, *but bigger*. I'd served in the Ohio House from 1985 to 1990 and met all sorts of people. I met some of the smartest guys I'd ever known, and some of the dumbest. I met some of the nicest people you'd ever want to meet, and some of the nastiest. When I got to Washington, I met many of the same sorts of characters. Any legislative assembly, anywhere you go in the world, is like that. All kinds of people thrown together to argue and hopefully get stuff done, all bringing their talents—and their strange baggage—to the table.

The strangest story I ever heard about a politician—which is saying something—concerned a public servant who once gave his daughter a ticket to a football game. It was one of the family's season tickets. This happened all the time. But when the woman arrived at the game, she found an unfamiliar woman sitting in the seat next to hers—also part of the family tickets. When she asked her neighbor where she got her ticket, she was told, "I got it from my dad." In response, the first woman said, "I got mine from *my* dad." And that was how these women discovered they were half-sisters, and that this gentleman had two separate families.

I know, I wouldn't have believed it, either—but my source is unimpeachable. Like I said, politics takes all kinds of people.

But some, apparently, are "more equal" than others. One person I didn't get to meet when I arrived in Washington was the Speaker of the House, Tom Foley. I couldn't even get near him. When I had first showed up in the Ohio legislature, Democrats had been in control for more than 20 years. I was the newest member of the minority party, which meant I was less than nothing on the pecking order. The Speaker of the Ohio House, Vern Riffe, was a Democrat from Scioto County, in the southern part of the state not too far from Cincinnati. He'd held the gavel with an iron fist since 1975 and would end up serving 20 years. I wasn't important to him at all, but he made time to meet with me when I first arrived, and I was able to get to know him.

U.S. House Speaker Foley, on the other hand, wanted nothing to do with me. Following what I had learned in the Ohio House, I called Speaker Foley's office not long after I got to Washington to set up a meeting to introduce myself.

The Speaker didn't have time for that, I was told. So I called again—and got the same answer. I must have called a dozen times in early 1991 when I first took my seat, and I got rejected every time. That taught me something, not just about Foley, but about what the pomp and circumstance of leadership can do to people. I made sure to file that away.

Two things I made sure to keep in mind from the very beginning were what I believe are the two responsibilities I had as an elected representative. First, I listened to my constituents. But second, and just as important, I had to consider my own background and experience. By combining those two together, I would come to a decision about the right thing to do (done for the right reasons, of course). The way I saw it, as long as I stuck to those principles and stayed right with the law and with God, pretty much everything else was fair game.

And things got pretty real pretty fast. My first major vote, beyond standard procedural stuff, was on the authorization for use of military force in Operation Desert Storm in 1991. I was a freshman in Congress. I had a lot to learn about the place. And here I was sending American troops into battle to potentially die for their country. It was a real baptism of fire. It made it clear to me, damn quick, that we weren't just talking to hear ourselves talk on the House floor or arguing about abstract things. This was serious.

As if the vote itself hadn't brought that home to me, something happened later that day that did for sure. I flew back to Ohio after the vote, and that evening Deb and I went to a restaurant for a quiet dinner, just the two of us, to catch up on things since I'd been gone. During the meal, a woman came up to me and introduced herself. She told me she had a relative in the military, who was ready to be deployed to the Gulf. She just had one question.

"Congressman," she said, "I'd like to know how you voted today."

I looked at Deb. I looked back to this woman. There was nothing I could do except to be straight with her.

"I voted to authorize the war," I told her. I braced myself, not sure what she would say or do. Anything could happen.

"God bless you," she said. "If you're comfortable with your decision, I can respect it." I still remember that conversation. It brought the reality of all the political crap people were slinging in Washington home to me. There were real people's lives at stake here.

A few days later, when the Gulf War actually began, I was interviewed about it in my living room by a reporter for the local Cincinnati TV news. His name was Bill Hemmer, and he went on to become a veteran TV newsman, first at CNN and then at Fox, his home for many years. But whenever I see him I think of the earnest young cub reporter in my living room.

Voting to send American troops to war kept my colleagues' whining over the House bank and restaurant in perspective. I took some early lumps for going after those "perks of the job." I guess that was a fair amount of shit for a new member to stir up. But it didn't bother me much. For one, I knew I was doing the right thing. Plus, I was making my own plans that looked further into the future.

As a new member, I had joined a group called the Conservative Opportunity Society. Some people looked at us as the "renegade" Republicans, but we preferred to think of ourselves as "activists." Newt Gingrich was a member, as were Tom DeLay, Dick Armey, Jon Kyl and Jim Bunning. We met every Wednesday morning and tried to find ways to make Republicans more effective despite being in the House minority. In the years that followed I would have a hell of a time contending with groups formed by so-called conservatives that also ostensibly were about making us carry out our policies more effectively. But there were some key differences: none of us were crazy—well, most of us weren't anyway—and we also knew our limits. We weren't for blowing up the entire government just because we could. And we even worked with and liked many members of the opposition party. Even though they were lording over us in a very annoying way.

At this point, Democrats had held an iron grip on the House for decades. Republicans had, over the years, gotten used to just accepting the crumbs that Democratic leadership left for us from their cake. They seemed to have accepted as fact the idea that they were always going to be in the minority. I would argue that in all those years, there had never been a serious attempt to regain a Republican majority in the House. That complacent attitude went straight to the top. Bob Michel, the Republican leader at the time, was very much of the Republican old school. At that time, that meant being a dutiful loser and taking whatever the Democrats dished out. I got along great with Bob, and had a lot of respect for him, but I knew if we were going to be effective as a congressional party, we would need someone new at the helm. Bob was like a school principal—nice, likable, able to deal with administrative issues. We needed someone with a sharper edge—like the assistant principal who was in charge of detention and seemed to enjoy it. And they needed to be meaner—like maybe a school lunch lady. I have a thing about lunch ladies, as you'll see later.

Enter Newt Gingrich. You may have heard of him. Where do I begin on Newt? He was smart, fast on his feet, and a sharp-elbowed campaigner. He was a historian by training, and had first been elected to Congress in 1978, so he'd been around a while and seen a lot. He also had that air of destiny about him, like he felt he was meant for great things. Someone got in his path toward greatness? Well, that was *their* problem. In late 1993, I started meeting every once in a while with Newt and a small group of members to discuss how we might make him the next leader. There aren't many secrets in Congress, and naturally Bob Michel was aware of Gingrich's ambitions. Newt also wasn't exactly known for playing it cool. As a result, there was tension between the two camps, for sure. But by having a good relationship with both men, I tried to keep things from getting too heated.

As it turned out though, there was no need for a leadership struggle. In early 1994, Bob Michel announced he was going to retire at the age of 71, which still made him something of a spring chicken among the old birds of the House. He wasn't a dummy. He knew he could either leave through the door or get tossed out of a window. We quickly rallied around Newt as his successor, but we knew that in order to make that happen, we had to do a better job of engaging *all* the Republican members in a way that had never been done before. People like being brought in—they like to feel like they have skin in the game. For all of Newt's other skills, that was one of his biggest tests.

The annual Republican members' retreat was coming up, when all of us would pack onto buses like kids going off to summer camp and head off to some hotel in the DC area for a weekend of presentations. Mostly we were "talked at" by leadership, pollsters, and so on. I decided, along with a couple of the other Conservative Opportunity Society guys, that instead of just being "talked *at*" we should talk *to* the members. It should be a conversation among the whole family, not just a bunch of kids sitting there while the adults in leadership lectured them. Nobody likes being lectured.

Well, it turned out to be maybe the best retreat we'd ever had. Suddenly, members were actually talking to one another, trying to understand one another, and working to get to a position where we knew who we were and what we were there to do. And we decided that we, after all these years, were finally going to bring back a Republican majority to the House. At that retreat, pushed on by this newfound energy, we began to hatch the plan.

President Bill Clinton's first term had not been going well. I couldn't figure out how he blundered so badly since his skillful campaign of 1992, where he managed to survive accusations of adultery, draft dodging, being a communist, drug running, and even mass murder. Some of those allegations were more credible than others, but I'll let you decide which is which. "Bubba" had run for president as this new kind of Democrat—a southern moderate—and yet the very first things he did were to pursue liberal social policies that many in the country just weren't ready for. A total takeover of our health-care system, for one, and allowing gays to serve openly in the military, for another, earned him a rebuke from national hero Colin Powell.

It was around this time that I first met a southern Democratic senator named Howell Heflin. Heflin was an old-school dealmaking pol. He was a former chief justice of the Alabama Supreme Court and a beloved figure in the state. There is no way he would be a Democrat if he ran for office today. He thought the Clinton crowd was a bunch of radical hippies who were taking over his party. Gays in the military as an issue—well, that wasn't his thing.

I will never forget our first meeting. I was at a DC restaurant, sitting with a group of other legislators and having a good time. Suddenly I felt a tap on my shoulder. I turned around to see a very round older man with slicked-back hair. It was Senator Heflin.

Seeing me holding a Camel in my hand, he said, with a thick Alabama drawl, "I'm glad to see you smoking a cigarette." He told me he had just gone to the White House that day, his first visit since the Clintons were elected. It was not a "kumbaya" moment.

"I lit up my cigarette like I always did," the senator told me, his eyes flickering with annoyance, "and these kids come running over to say, 'Oh, senator, senator, you can't smoke here.' And I looked back at them and I said, 'I can't smoke here? But would it be OK if I put a penis in my mouth?'"

Anyway, this was the cultural blowback Clinton was dealing with. His approval ratings were low and getting lower. The American people were souring on the Clinton charm. (Although I'm not sure how much "charm" there really was. I always thought he reminded me of Eddie Haskell, the kiss-up kid from the old TV show *Leave It to Beaver*.) But we couldn't just run against the president. We had to offer an alternative, something to get voters in congressional districts all across the country to take a serious look at Republican candidates. It was Newt who came up with the idea of the "Contract with America." Sometimes Newt would go into "eccentric professor" mode and come up with "pie in the sky" ideas without much follow-through, and at first we thought that might be what was happening here. But the more we looked at it, the more the idea gained momentum, and before we knew it we had focused on ten key issues and even written legislation that we promised to enact to advance this agenda. We raised the money to unveil this to the American people with a one-page ad in *Reader's Digest*, which at the time was one of the most widely read monthly publications in the country. In the run-up to the election, we held an event where everybody signed the contract publicly.

I don't know if the Contract with America got us the majority. Newt, of course, believed that it did. Personally, I think Bill Clinton got us the majority. But the contract certainly helped, and it gave all of us Republicans something to organize ourselves around. And in that regard, it soon became clear that we needed all the help we could get. We were about to get a crash course in the very distinct differences between politics and governing. That's a lesson a lot of people in Congress and the White House these days have never learned.

Election Night 1994 was a thrilling moment. All our hard work had paid off, and Republicans had taken back the House after all those years. But after we got all the celebratory shit out of the way, we realized we had no clue how to run the place. None. Nobody in the entire Republican Conference had ever served in the majority in the House. Not one. There was no institutional memory, and we had to figure it all out as we went along. We were given lists of offices to assign in the Capitol and had no idea who was currently in them. We didn't even know where some of them *were*. As the majority party, we were now responsible for the Capitol and coordinating with all the permanent, nonpolitical staff who made the building run—the engineers, electricians, carpenters, and so on. We had to schedule a special tour with the architect of the Capitol so that he could show some of us around and point out areas of the old building we didn't know existed.

Eventually, despite the fits and starts, we did take over, and 1995 began with Newt becoming the fiftieth Speaker of the U.S. House of Representatives. He was an instant superstar—on the cover of *Time* magazine, his news conferences carried live, recognized everywhere. That huge boost of oxygen would take a toll on even the most modest of men. And then there was Newt Gingrich.

As I say, Newt was one of the brightest people I've ever met, and I liked him. Still do. I credit him with a lot. But like any of us, he had his flaws. But sometimes the eccentric professor side of him came out. He had 100 ideas an hour, and maybe 90 of them made sense. Those last ten though . . . well, they could be trouble. Oh, how he loved to strategize. Unfortunately, we never had time to implement last week's strategic plan before he came up with a new one. Newt used to advertise his management philosophy on a sign mounted in his office, which read: "Listen, learn, help, and lead." Occasionally he'd even do some of these things. At one point, some of us on his leadership team turned the sign upside down so that the instructions were in reverse order, which reflected the reality. I guess he didn't think that was too funny, because when we came in for the next meeting the sign had been moved high up on the wall, out of reach.

Whichever way the sign was facing, Newt had to manage more than two hundred members all jockeying for position in the new majority. He didn't always have time or patience for that. If two members came to Newt with conflicting requests, his instincts would be to say "yes" to both of them just so he could get them out of his hair and move on to the next "big idea" he was interested in. While Newt was off on his vision quests, it was up to the rest of us in the leadership team to clean up the mess.

This was where I came in. When Newt became Speaker, I became the chairman of the House Republican Conference, the fourth-ranking position on the House leadership ladder. The body of all the Republicans in the House, taken together, is known as the Republican Conference. The Democrats call themselves a "caucus," because of course we can't do it the same. The job of the Conference chair is to keep the two hundred or so rank-and-file Republican members on the same page as the top three in the leadership—the majority whip, the majority leader, and the Speaker—and to make sure everyone sticks to the same unified message.

It might seem strange for a guy to spend his first couple years throwing bombs from the floor, often toward his *own* side of the aisle, only to end up as part of the leadership. Gingrich knew what he was doing by bringing one of the rabble-rousing Gang of Seven reformers into the leadership team. Besides, I'd had my eye on leadership from the beginning.

At the very end of 1990, after I'd been elected but before I got sworn in, I sat down with Barry Jackson and a few other friends—soon to be staffers—and had a simple conversation. They asked me, "What kind of member do you want to be?" We talked through the different types. For some members, it was all about the district, so they stayed focused on local issues. Some got really into their committee work, and became experts on the particular policy area they worked on. But then there was the leadership track, helping craft the agenda and keeping the team together to get things done. Well, I didn't have to think about it for very long. I was going to be a leadership guy, and that was that. And from there, it was pretty easy to figure out the end goal—if I didn't want to end up at the top of the leadership ladder, as Speaker, what was the point of climbing on in the first place?

So while I spent a fair amount of time causing trouble with the Gang of Seven, I also made a point to do everything I could for my fellow members to help them raise money. And, yeah, money talks. People liked that I was willing to show up for a golf outing or a dinner or a reception and give a little speech about how great a guy the candidate was. It's not like they had to twist my arm either. I was having a pretty good time.

When we took back the majority in 1994, I knew it was time to make a move. No, I hadn't been there very long, and yes, I'd ruffled some feathers, but I'd worked my ass off to help us take back the House, and I was damned sure going to help us run the show.

Naturally, I wasn't the only one with that idea. Before we even left to campaign for the final leg of the 1994 election, there had been discussions among the Republican members over how to proceed if we won the majority. Members were already angling for committee and leadership spots, and the top contender for the Conference chair job looked to be Rep. Bob Livingston. Livingston was a southern gentleman from Louisiana who'd been in Congress since 1977. Bob was, in many ways, the natural choice, and I'm sure he would have made a fine chairman. But I had other ideas.

After the election, with our majority official, I still hadn't declared myself in the leadership race. But I *had* been helping our transition team talk through committee assignments, which gave me an idea. I picked up the phone and called Bob Livingston.

"Bob," I asked him, "wouldn't you rather be chairman of Appropriations?" The Appropriations Committee held the purse strings for the entire government, since all federal funding bills had to originate in the House. Its chairman was one of the most powerful committee posts on the Hill, and even the subcommittee chairs—not usually the most glamorous titles—were unofficially called "cardinals."

Bob didn't waste any time in responding: "Yeah!"

"I'll tell you what," I offered. "You get out of this Conference race, and I'll do everything I can to help you." Sure enough, Bob called Gingrich to let him know he was no longer interested in the Conference spot. Of course, I had tipped off Gingrich and he went along with my plan. When the new Congress was sworn in in January, Bob Livingston took up his gavel as Appropriations Committee chairman. One down.

I was officially in the race by this time, and the only other formidable contender was Duncan Hunter, Sr., of California. My member friends, my staff, and I started working the phones hard, talking members' ears off and twisting their arms to try and get their support. We knew Hunter and his buddies were doing the same thing too. Until one day, they weren't. In the middle of this leadership race, Hunter had somehow just disappeared for a couple of days. He just dropped off the map.

Finally we figured out what had happened. He'd had a late-fall hunting trip scheduled for after the election but before Christmas. He'd been looking forward to it and wasn't going to let a leadership election spoil it for him. So he disappeared off into the woods over a long weekend, mostly cut off from the world (this was before our cell phones were genetically attached). That gave me all the time I needed. By the time Hunter resurfaced the following Monday, I'd already lined up enough votes to become the new Conference chair.

When the new majority took over in January 1995, the leadership team was Speaker Gingrich, Majority Leader Dick Armey, Majority Whip Tom DeLay (both Texans), and me. I knew that personalities were key to the leadership staff of any organization, but they can take on an outsized influence when politicians are involved.

Armey and I got along great. My staff got along great with his staff—which is key to making any leadership operation run smoothly. The staff have to be able to all work with one another. DeLay and his people, on the other hand, always seemed to be marching to their own beat. DeLay had a strong personality, and seemed to run his office like a dictatorship. His staff were either loyal or scared, or both, and they shut out everybody else. The staff problems got so bad that it seemed like his staff were carrying out vendettas against other leadership staffers. They were thorns in everyone's sides. And my personal relationship with DeLay wasn't much better either. I remember from some of the earliest meetings I attended as a new member, he looked at me funny. Maybe he saw a threat, hard to say.

As it turned out, it wasn't just me. On our first member retreat in the majority, Armey and I found ourselves with adjoining rooms. I ran into him in the hallway and asked if I could talk to him in private. He came into my room, shut the door, and shoved the rug up against the crack at the bottom. He was not playing around.

"What's up?" he asked.

"Help me understand Tom DeLay," I said. Dick had been around longer than I had, and I figured he might have some insight.

"You think I can help you understand him?" Dick came back. "He doesn't like me at all."

"Well, he doesn't like me either!" I responded, and neither of us left that day with any better understanding of how DeLay's mind worked. Or didn't, as the case may be.

He never got any easier to understand or work with during the rest of the time we served in leadership together. It was from DeLay's unique brand of political calculation that the idea came to campaign on a promise to impeach President Bill Clinton in the run-up to the 1998 midterms.

For those who don't remember what the Clinton case involved, here's a brief primer. Everybody with eyes and/or ears knew about Bill Clinton's reputation with women. When he got himself involved with a 22-year-old intern, Monica Lewinsky, and then appeared to lie about it and encourage others to lie, many people around town assumed he was done. I thought he'd die from embarrassment, or maybe at the hands of his wife. Whether what he did as president was a high crime and misdemeanor, requiring impeachment, was another story.

I've lived through three presidential impeachment inquiries—Nixon's, Clinton's, and Trump's. But there was only one—Bill Clinton's—where I was a participant as a member of the House leadership. I know what we all said at the time: Bill Clinton was impeached for lying under oath. In my view, Republicans impeached him for one reason and one reason only—because it was strenuously recommended to us by one Tom DeLay. Tom believed that impeaching Clinton would win us all these House seats, would be a big win politically, and he convinced enough of the membership and the GOP base that this was true. I was on board at the time. I won't hide from that. I won't pretend otherwise. But I regret it now. I regret that I didn't fight against it.

Impeachment of the president is meant to be a tool of last resort. Nancy Pelosi had it right—or at least she did at first when she contemplated impeaching Donald Trump: it has to be bipartisan. Not everyone in both parties has to be on board, but at least a good number do. A partisan impeachment simply does not have credibility to most Americans. That's exactly what we pursued against Clinton. Clinton probably did commit perjury. That's not a good thing. But lying about an affair to save yourself from embarrassment isn't the same as lying about an issue of national security.

DeLay however was absolutely convinced that that was the right thing to do, and so for the six weeks leading up to the election, all we talked about was the impeachment. Instead of gaining five seats like we expected, we lost five seats. Even though DeLay had been the one beating the impeachment horse hardest, the responsibility lay at the top.

Even putting aside impeachment, Newt had become a real problem for the Republican majority. His management issues hadn't improved.

Meanwhile, I was dealing with "management issues" of my own. By this time my two daughters, Lindsay and Tricia, had grown from two of the cutest little girls you ever hoped to see into—well, teenagers. They were still cute. And I still loved them to death. But two teenage girls, close in age, stuck at home with their outnumbered mother while I was spending half my time in Washington—it was a recipe for disaster. Deb was holding the fort, but I was always ready to help. There was no way those girls were going to get away with more just because their dad was away for work. There were plenty of times when I'd be sitting at my desk, on the phone on one line with some members trying to defuse a crisis in the House Republican ranks while on another line I'd have Deb telling me what trouble the girls were giving her and then Lindsay and Tricia themselves on a third line giving me their side of the story—and everybody trying to talk at once. It was around that time I gave the girls the nicknames "Bad" and "Worse"—and Lindsay was usually Worse (sorry, honey).

So you can forgive me for getting tired of Newt's "absent-minded professor" shtick after a while. And it wasn't wearing thin just for me. It sometimes got in the way of his getting along with his members. Because he was so busy thinking, he'd end up making snap decisions and then moving on. Or he'd be so wrapped up in thought walking through the halls of the

Capitol or the tunnels underneath or on the sidewalk up above that he wouldn't pay attention to his colleagues walking past. He wouldn't even acknowledge them, let alone stop and say "hi." Sometimes it felt like he was the star of some big college faculty and those of us in the rank and file were jockeying for time during his "office hours." Even when I was a pretty new arrival myself, I wasn't shy about giving him advice. "Newt," I'd remind him—respectfully of course—"when you pass one of your members in the hall, stop and say hello. These are the people who can vote for you or vote against you." He'd always promise to be better about it, and sometimes he was, but usually he'd go back to doing things his own way.

He had let his press attention get to his head—and the press love to feed on their own creations. And there was a sense that he was getting rolled by the Clinton White House, like every day. He was often disheveled, and back in the 1990s he wore some of the worst neckties I've ever seen. I remember telling him early on, "Newt, you gotta buy some new ties. Those are just awful." One time in early 1996, Newt hustled back from a meeting at the White House, and the first thing out of his mouth to all of us waiting anxiously for his report was, "Clinton really liked my tie." We all rolled our eyes. "And you probably believed him," I said. This was the same old Eddie Haskell–like "Clinton charm." He could steal your watch right in front of you and you'd be grateful when he told you the time. Clinton had been on the ropes when Republicans took power. But he was a survivor. He masterfully used Newt's weaknesses against him.

It was my job to break the news to Newt Gingrich that it was time for him to step down as Speaker. The day after the election, he called me.

"What do you think?" he asked.

"Newt, you're not gonna want to hear this," I told him, "but I think you've led the team as far as you can lead them."

It was clear that was not the answer he was expecting.

"As your friend," I told him, "I just don't think you'll have the votes come January to be elected Speaker."

He thanked me and got off the line. Then the next day, he called me again.

"Well, what do you think?" he asked.

"The same thing I thought yesterday!" What did I tell you about his listening skills?

That time he got the message, and by the next day he had announced his intention to resign. But Newt wasn't the only casualty of the 1998 midterm losses.

In late 1998, a member from Oklahoma, J. C. Watts, announced he was running to replace me as Conference chair. Watts was a charismatic former college football star who'd been elected in the class that helped us take back the House in 1994. I respected the challenge, but I expected to hold on. That was until I realized that Watts had some real muscle in his corner. Two senior members, Bud Shuster of Pennsylvania and Jerry Lewis of California, were supporting Watts's candidacy. Shuster and Lewis, it just so happened, were also two of the members who tried to dissuade me and the rest of the Gang of Seven from looking too deeply into the House bank scandal back in 1991.

Watts beat me fair and square. Interestingly, one of the members to vote for Watts in that leadership election was a new representative from Wisconsin who had just been elected but not yet taken his seat—a 28-year-old named Paul Ryan. He comes up later in this story.

By the time I made my second run at leadership, becoming House majority leader in 2006 and then minority leader in 2007 after the Democrats took over, I had learned a fair amount both from my years serving under Newt and in the intervening time since.

I knew, for instance, that it was better to have talented members with a rabble-rousing streak working *with* you rather than against you. Put another way, it was better to have them inside the tent pissing out, than outside the tent pissing in. And I knew that a great place to install these sorts of people, those who had true leadership potential, was in the position of Conference chair. I knew from personal experience that serving as Conference chair was a great way to understand how things really worked "behind the curtain" of leadership. There was a tendency, especially among the more firebrand rank-and-file members, to think that the leadership folks were always up to something, plotting behind closed doors. Bringing the skeptics in showed them that there really wasn't anything nefarious going on, that we were just trying to keep the team together.

In the later 2000s, much of the criticism from the Republican right flank came from the Republican Study Committee (RSC). There was no Freedom Caucus then—it later grew out of a more extreme wing of the RSC—but these guys were the self-styled "true conservative" members and were convinced that leadership was always trying to drag the party too far to the middle. The post of RSC chairman, while not an official leadership position, usually went to people who were trusted to speak for this faction.

Some of the guys elevated to that role showed real political promise, and I tried to spot that and help them along. One such talent was Jeb Hensarling from Texas, who went on to become Conference chair and then a very effective chairman of the House Financial Services Committee. Another was a very serious and passionate Indiana congressman named Mike Pence.

When he first came to Congress, Pence was a fire-eater, or was at least well on his way to becoming one. He came from the world of talk radio, where he hadn't been afraid to court controversy. As soon as he came to the House, he'd identified strongly with the RSC, serving as its chairman from 2005 to 2007. We'd clashed over policy before, like when Pence had come out against No Child Left Behind in 2001. We'd also clashed over leadership—Pence had run against me for minority leader in 2005. But still, I preferred to have him pissing inside the tent than outside it.

Pence was a good member, but he needed an outlet for his energy. I tried to guide him toward being more measured in his approach to governing, to show him that not every single action he may not have fully approved of needed its own scathing press release, and that sometimes you have to pick your battles. Over time, and certainly by the time he became Conference chair in 2009, he had developed into a calm, collected, unflappable professional—a skill set he used to great effect as vice president of the United States.

Maybe the most important aspect of House leadership is the Daily Management Meeting that takes place every morning around 9:00 or 9:30. Before that, the members in leadership all huddle with their senior staff. But when the members gather for their meeting, the real business gets done. The Speaker, the leader, the whip, and the Conference chair are the main attendees, with other members coming in and out. Members can bring a staffer or two along, and sometimes the meeting room—usually somewhere in the Speaker's suite—gets crowded.

I tried to run these meetings like a conversation. With

Newt, it was all over the place. When I was majority leader under Speaker Dennis Hastert for about a year, it was more of a lecture. Hastert had already decided what we were going to do and was issuing orders. That was just not my style. Hastert wasn't a particularly charismatic Speaker, but he did have the presence of a coach. He'd been a high school wrestling coach for years, and years later it was allegations of abuse of students stemming from that time that eventually sent him to prison. I was about to walk into a fundraiser at a lovely home in Pennsylvania when the news broke, and I was stunned. Then I ran into someone I'd known from the Hill who had worked for Hastert, and obviously he'd just heard too—he was as ashen-faced as I've ever seen a living person look.

Looking back on it, the time I spent in the leadership under Hastert was also the scene of another strange episode. Sometime in the spring of 2006, not long after I made majority leader, someone came to me and asked about Rep. Mark Foley of Florida and kids in the House page program, suggesting there was a problem. This was news to me. So I did what I thought was the right thing and went straight to Speaker Hastert. I told him what had been shared with me, and left it with him. He seemed interested at the time but obviously didn't do anything about it, because the story broke out of nowhere in late September that Foley had behaved inappropriately with young male pages. In fact, I was in a meeting with Hastert when he excused himself to take a call, came back, and told me it was about to break. I was livid. He'd had a chance to address it internally and clearly hadn't done so, and now the Democrats had a scandal to hang around our necks before the 2006 midterms (which ended up bringing the Democrats back into power). But before that we had to go through a whole ethics investigation. It was a mess.

That was just one incident, but in general I knew that when I became Speaker, I didn't want to run the House like the last Republican to hold the post. I wanted the back-and-forth, I wanted the honest feedback, and I wanted to know what people were thinking. It was a way for everyone to touch gloves so that everybody on the leadership team knew what everyone else was doing, and that no one was running into each other or doing things that would somehow set us up for internal conflict. Also it was a way to work together to avoid trouble.

As the Speaker, I would set the agenda, and I'd try to keep it to the main two or three things we needed to discuss. I tried to build consensus, making sure everybody felt comfortable as we decided on a course of action. There were very rare instances when I had to cut off discussion and say, "No, sorry, but we're doing it this way." That must have happened fewer than five times in the five years I was Speaker. Consensus was always the much better way to go. Sharing information honestly and openly was the best way to make sure nobody got blindsided.

But the responsibility of the leadership, and especially of the Speaker, isn't just to deal with other leaders. You have a responsibility to every single member of your conference. They were the ones who put you in the Speaker's chair in the first place (and you have to forgive the ones who didn't vote for you). You owe your time and attention to everyone from the most senior committee chairman down to the newest freshman.

Arguably, the more time a good leader spends with freshman members, the better. The early years can set the tone for someone's entire congressional career. They got themselves elected, sure, but somewhere along the line, they've got to learn how to become members of Congress. Especially when there's a big new class like there was in 1994 or 2010. Most of the "Tea Party" class in 2010 were just good solid Republicans, it's just that a lot of them hadn't served in office before. The leadership offices tried to provide as much help as we could—to help new members find the right staff, get on the right committees, and generally find their way around. Some of them figured it out, and some, well . . . you can't save them all.

Cultivating these individual members can eventually, if enough of them get on board, lead to the creation of a cohesive team out of two-hundred-some scrappy, lazy, smart, dumb, kind, nasty, opinionated, boring people all thrown together in Washington to represent millions of their fellow Americans.

I used to see being a "leader" as being more than whatever title you held—minority leader, or even Speaker. You're not just a figurehead. You're a principal. You're a dean of students. You're somewhere between a father and older-brother figure. There are all kinds of roles you need to be able to play in order to keep your team together. There were times when I had to bring certain members into my office—younger ones, usually—and let them know I'd got wind of them doing something they shouldn't.

"Come on, boys," I'd have to tell them, "you're just cruisin' for a bruisin'."

Keeping everyone under control not only protects the members themselves, but it protects the institution. A member of Congress behaving badly makes the whole House look bad, and can derail whatever legislative priorities you're trying to get done to actually do something for the people who elected you. Nobody has time for bullshit like that.

Speaking of bullshit, I learned early on that there is a high tolerance for that on the Hill, particularly in meetings. Some days it just seemed like you were slow-motion drowning in a never-ending stream of meetings. And there are a lot of people who show up for a lot of meetings, where they have lots of conversations, and then nothing happens. Nobody wants to step up and make a plan.

I figured out pretty quickly that in the absence of any other plan, your plan becomes the plan. After that, I made sure to never walk into a meeting without a plan. If we're going to spend all this time talking about some problem or other, we'd better be prepared to pick—or at least suggest—an option to fix it. Otherwise, what's the point? And so there were plenty of times when my plan became *the* plan, because there weren't any other ones. This comes in handy when you're dealing in negotiations at the highest levels—something I kept having to remember over the years as I figured out how things really worked in the smoke-filled rooms of Washington and beyond.

# FOUR

# Gerry, Jerry, and Me

Morningside golf club, southern California, mid-1990s. I'm standing on a beautiful green—can't recall which one, but it doesn't really matter. It's a beautiful course no matter where you look. There are plenty of palms and other majestic trees all over the place, and majestic mountains surrounding you, with more blue mountains beyond. It's just gorgeous.

But at that moment I don't give a shit about any of that. Sorry, Jack (Nicklaus—the course designer and my pal). Right now I'm doubled over, laughing my head off like a fool while a former president of the United States is stomping up and down, throwing the dirtiest word in the English language around in every direction. His face is crimson. He's mad as hell, angrier than I'd ever seen him. But even in that unguarded moment, he's one of the finest men I ever had the privilege to know.

Another scene: southwestern Ohio, mid-1960s. The grass is just as green and perfectly cut as the grass at Morningside, but it's a different kind of grass, and this time there are big white lines drawn across it every ten yards. Oh, and there are a couple thousand people on either side of me screaming their heads off—some because they love me, some because they hate me. It's not even me they love or hate, it's just the colors and the logo on the damn uniform I have on. And lined up across from me are some of the biggest, ugliest bastards I've ever seen waiting to stomp my head into the ground just for fun.

Up there on the scoreboard next to my team's name there's a big fat goose egg, and as for the other guys . . . well, let's just say they're already well into the dozens. But over on the sidelines, there's a guy wearing my team jacket, arms folded across his chest, staring right at me with hard eyes. He expects the absolute best from me no matter how beat up I feel or how bad things look. I know if I screw this up he's going to rip me a new one later. But even then, even though he scares the living hell out of me, he's one of the finest men I've ever had the privilege to know.

If you'll permit me, I want to take a brief break from the weird and wild tales of Washington to tell you about a couple of genuine American heroes. Maybe it's no coincidence that they both hailed from the middle of America or that they played the same sport. It surely is a coincidence that their names were both Jerry—although one spelled it with a "G." Both of them were great leaders of men—well, one led women and children too. One had a few more followers than the other. They both found their way to glory in very different ways, even if they had to put up with a lot of crap along the way. And I was lucky enough to learn from both.

There are a number of people who helped raise me up in my life. Deb still does, to this day—and so do Lindsay and Tricia. Of course there were my parents, and brothers and sisters, and friends I've had for decades. But two guys in particular loom large in my life as inspirations, and examples for leadership that I carried with me all the way to the Speaker's office. Frankly I think we'd all be better off as a country if we focused more on people like Gerry Faust and Jerry Ford, two legends in their respective fields, but more than that, two decent men who had a lasting impact on me and a lot of other people. I've had to deal with a lot of crazy shit—more than I ever thought I'd signed up for. When it got really bad, I'd pray, and then, probably with a little nudge from the man upstairs, I'd remember the example of these two guys. Knowing them, and learning from them, gave me a grounding that helped me get through a lot of different messes.

---

This story begins in a darkened classroom, where the only light came from a flickering screen at the front of the room. There was a short film about a brand-new local high school, Archbishop Moeller, that had only opened a few years earlier and was looking to recruit kids to join its newest class. Once the movie part was over, they turned the lights back on, and I blinked a bit as my eyes got adjusted, as did the rest of my fellow Saints Peter and Paul junior high eighth graders. This was already a banner day at the school, and it was only going to get better.

A big tall guy with broad shoulders and a crew cut strode with heavy footsteps from the back of the room up to the front, turned around and asked if we had any questions. He had introduced himself at the beginning of the session, but to most of us, he needed no introduction: this was Gerard A. "Gerry" Faust, Moeller's head football coach, here to talk to us junior high guys in person. This beat the hell out of algebra class any day.

Faust was already a football legend in our part of Ohio. His father had coached at Chaminade High School in Dayton, just one county over. Gerry played under him there before going on to be the star quarterback at the University of Dayton. He graduated in 1958, and four years later signed on to be the first head coach at Moeller, which had opened in 1960. There he became one of the most successful high school coaches in the country. At Moeller, he put up a total record of 178–23 with seven unbeaten seasons. He later went on to be the head coach at Notre Dame, where his record wasn't as good, but at Moeller his legacy was—and still is—secure.

All of the Catholic high schools in that part of the Cincinnati area drew from different parishes. Before Moeller was built, the Catholic kids from the area would have gone to either Purcell High or Roger Bacon High. I would have ended up going to one of those myself. But when Gerry Faust came to coach at Moeller, that changed the game. Every elementary and middle-school kid playing football wanted to make it to the "big leagues" and play for this real live local hero. I'd been playing football since I was a little kid, mostly defense, but I'd learned to become a pretty good long snapper too. Before Faust had even begun his presentation, I was already sold. So I don't remember paying that close attention when he talked about everything the school had to offer—the academics, the brand-new facilities, and all of that. I'm sure it was nice, but come on . . . that's not what I gave a hoot about. He mentioned something about becoming "Men of Moeller"—it was an all-boys' high school—but I wasn't listening that closely. I just couldn't wait to lace up my cleats and show Coach Faust what I could do.

Imagine how it felt, then, after Faust finished his talk and started to walk down the rows of desks, when he stopped at mine and put his hand on my shoulder. His big broad hand—a quarterback's hand, alright—just rested there for a second. I froze. He looked me right in the eye, man to man, and said: "I sure hope you're gonna come. We're looking forward to having you on the team." I'd never met Faust, definitely had never spoken to him. Why he decided to stop at *my* desk, I still have no idea. Maybe I just looked like a beefy kid who probably played football. But however it happened, it was the highlight of my life up to that point. I was pumped up, and ready to hit the Moeller field right then and there. It was only later that I realized how much I would learn from Gerry Faust that had nothing to do with football—and what becoming a "Man of Moeller" really meant.

Playing for Coach Faust was exactly the kind of experience that would bring a group of guys together. At first, we were united in fear. Faust was tough. His dad had been even tougher—he used to carry around a leather strap to whack his players (his own son included) when they screwed up. That wasn't Gerry Faust's style. He got mad, sure, but I never once heard him use a four-letter word. He sure knew how to make himself understood though. He'd get right in your face, grab hold of your face mask and shake your head when he really wanted to get a point across. But you didn't have to play for him long to realize that he was just as fair as he was tough. He knew how to inspire us, and motivate us to be the best we could be. When you did something right, he let you know it. When you screwed up, he let you know it too.

One practice I got in a great block on Jerry Mouch (another Jerry, I know), a senior linebacker whose family owned the jewelry store across the street from Andy's Café. He and I got along fine and our families were friends, but I was lined up against Jerry, and I had my job to do. Coach Faust saw my block and came over to us after the whistle blew.

"Nice work, Boehner!" he said, and I felt like I was on cloud nine. Then he turned to Jerry.

"Mouch," he said, "get off my field."

Poor Jerry had to go run laps for letting a "reserve" guy get the best of him. But once he got back on the line, for the rest of the practice, Jerry made sure to lay my ass out every chance he got. Two years later, I ended up on the other end of that stick. I was a senior playing pulling guard, and one practice I was lined up against a sophomore defensive end who I guess hadn't hit his growth spurt yet. He was a small guy, and I felt bad for him. When I went to block him I'd hold him at arm's length, to take it easy on him. Faust saw me, blew the whistle, came right over and ripped me a new one. He got right in my face and reminded me that I had one job to do and that was to block—period. If I wouldn't take it easy on the other guy in a game, I damn sure shouldn't do it in practice.

Then he stepped back and hollered, "I wanna run that play again." And turning straight to me he said, "And Boehner, you're gonna block that guy."

The next play I floored that poor little sophomore flat on his back.

"Now that's more like it," Coach said.

Faust's sense of humor would pop up in the most unexpected places. One day my sophomore year I was walking down the hall on my way to class, and from somewhere behind me I heard his voice: "Hey, Boehner!"

I turned around hopefully, thinking maybe he was going to tell me I was getting called up to play in that week's game. Nope.

"Boehner," he asked, "why do you have a wallet in each back pocket?"

I didn't have a clue what he meant. I hadn't put one wallet in my back pocket, let alone one in both. Then it dawned on me. Coach Faust was making fun of me for having a big butt. Great. He walked away chuckling down the hall. Nowadays I guess people would make some big deal about "body shaming" but I just laughed it off . . . although I clearly never forgot it. From that day forward I've never carried a wallet in my back pocket. Not once.

A couple jokes thrown your way were just part of the deal. Nothing could make me disloyal to Gerry Faust. When my junior year came along and I was looking at a spot on the varsity football team, I ended up having to make a tough choice. I'd played basketball my first two years at Moeller, and my junior season was about to start. A lot of guys on the football team played other sports as conditioning. Jerry Van ran track, and was one of the best 4×40 runners in the school. I had a lot of fun playing basketball, and our coach Jerry Doerger was a fine man—yet another great Jerry in my life. It's a common name in our part of the world, okay? Doerger coached high school basketball well into his eighties, and his famous "Doerger Defense" was known to generations of Cincinnati-area athletes.

One day as I was walking down a hallway to class, I heard what sounded like an argument around the corner. As I got a little closer, I realized it was Doerger and Faust, arguing back and forth about some kid. Uh-oh, I thought—I'd hate to be in that poor sucker's tennis shoes. Well, I pulled up short when I heard them mention my name.

Faust wanted me off the basketball team so I could spend more time in the weight room. Moeller was one of the first high school football programs in the country to have a weight training program. And boy was it state of the art . . . one of the assistant coaches just ran it out of his basement. Faust thought I could really make a difference on the varsity football team if I focused on that and got my strength up. But Doerger was telling Faust to back off. He wanted to keep me on the basketball team. For me, it was *not* a hard decision to make. I was closer to Faust and trusted his judgment, so I quit basketball that year and hit the weight room. I was going to stick with football for the next two years. And my two years playing varsity for Gerry Faust were two of the most meaningful years of my young life.

That's not to say I was some football superstar. Far from it. I wasn't even guaranteed to make the varsity team as a junior. We all had to try out again, and Faust made it clear that you wouldn't make varsity unless you were willing to put in the work. He had no time for slackers. For me, that meant sweating it out in the weight room when I would rather have been playing basketball. But I made the varsity team, and that made it all worth it.

Being a starter was a totally different ballgame—literally. Everything changes when you're out there in the middle of the field with the stands full of your family and friends all looking down at you, hoping you don't screw up. I just tried to do the best I could, which, in sports, politics, and pretty much everything else is easier said than done. I played linebacker or pulling guard most of the time, but somehow my long-snapper skills from back in junior high had stuck with me, so I played that position too. That meant I was on the field a fair amount, which meant more chances to screw things up.

In one game against Newport Catholic, we were set up to punt and I was in position, ready to snap the ball to the kicker. As we lined up at the line of scrimmage, I had noticed the linebacker across from me was a giant. That was bad enough.

But as I got over the ball, in the few seconds before the play was called, I made the mistake of looking into this guy's face. Even through the facemask I could tell that he was just about the ugliest son of a bitch I'd ever seen in my young life. And he was looking right at me.

Right before the snap was called—I will never forget this sound as long as I live—he looked at me and growled. He let out this low, guttural sound that basically said "I'm going to eat you alive." That scared the living hell out of me, and I let off a bad snap that sent the ball flying over the kicker's head. After that, my fear of the ugly-as-sin linebacker was replaced by a much more immediate fear—getting reamed out by Coach Faust for flubbing the snap.

There was one time when I decided I just couldn't face Faust's temper at all. It was my junior year, and we'd just been handed a pretty bad loss by Princeton High School in Cincinnati. We didn't lose often during my two years on varsity, but when we did, we knew there was going to be hell to pay at the team meeting the next morning. When I woke up that Saturday morning, I decided I just wasn't going. Wasn't even getting out of bed. After the gut-wrenching loss the night before, I just couldn't take reliving it with Coach, with an extra helping of anger thrown in at the practice afterward. So I stayed under the covers.

My mother was not having it. She came into the room with all the bunk beds I shared with my brothers, all empty except for me firmly planted in mine.

"Get out of that bed, John," she said. "You made a commitment to that team and you'd better be there with them when they take the heat."

I didn't care. If it meant I had to quit, fine. I was not going to face Coach Faust that morning. Then the phone rang out in the hall, and Mom went out to answer it.

"Yes, he's here," I heard her say. There was a pause. "Don't worry, he's coming. He's running a little late, but he'll be there."

She almost had to drag me out of bed, but sure enough, I made it. Coach made me run extra laps for being late, so in the end I missed the worst parts of rehashing Friday night's game after all. But that was the last time I ever thought about quitting. Although something happened my senior year that did make me wonder if my high school football career would end early.

Our archrival was Roger Bacon High School, and we *hated* those guys. That year, we knew the game against them was going to be a bruiser. Their coach, Bron Bacevich, had put together a top-notch team, and our work was cut out for us. We had an intense practice schedule set up for the whole week leading up to Friday's game. On Monday, Coach Faust showed up with a water cooler full of some special kind of drink. It was supposed to give us energy, he said. It wasn't on the market yet—it was some sort of magic formula that had been cooked up at the University of Florida. He called it "Gatorade." Nobody on the team had ever heard of it before, and I still don't know how he got hold of it, but for that week we fueled up on Gatorade, hoping we'd be able to practice that much harder and really hand it to Roger Bacon.

Friday finally came. We were playing as part of a doubleheader matchup of Catholic high schools held at the Xavier University stadium. Playing in a college stadium was a huge deal. In the opening game that afternoon, LaSalle beat McNicholas. Moeller vs. Roger Bacon was the marquee bout. In the end, the secret Florida formula didn't help us much. We lost 45–0 (still the worst defeat in Moeller history), and I ended up getting carried off the field.

I'd gone for a block, and the next thing I knew I was on my

back and couldn't move. On the sidelines, the team doctor—who was an osteopath and didn't seem to always have his shit together—poked around and said everything seemed fine. My back spasms disagreed with him. I'd had some back issues before, going back to the age of 15 when I'd wrenched something lifting a crate of pickles at Andy's Café. I got checked out at the hospital where they found no permanent damage, but my back really hasn't been the same ever since.

I returned to practice only a few days later, and I played through the rest of the season, even when my back flared up. The way I saw it, it was my final season, I'd been with the team all four years, and there was no way I was going to miss the last couple games because of a backache. Besides, by that point I knew that I probably wasn't going to make it as a football player in college. But I'd been playing most of my life, and I wanted to enjoy the game as much as I could before I hung up my cleats for good.

It was a good thing I hadn't concentrated *only* on football in school. There were actual classes I had to attend, after all. I had to do something in the offseason, right? But in academics, like athletics, I wasn't the worst but I sure wasn't the best either. I never got a D or an F in my life, but I didn't get many As or Bs either.

Gerry Faust was my teacher as well as my coach. He taught typing. A bunch of us signed up because we figured Coach liked us, and we'd have an easy time passing the class. Uh-huh . . . we thought we were pretty slick, as so many teenagers do. We should have known that he would be just as demanding in the classroom as he was on the field. He made us attack those typewriters like they were Roger Bacon linemen. He worked our fingers sore just like he worked our legs sore in practice. Somehow I passed, but I'm still not all that good at typing.

Of course, faith was a big part of what brought the Moeller community together. Praying and going to mass had been a big part of my life for as long as I could remember. My family went to Saints Peter and Paul Church for mass together every Sunday. In grade school, we had mass every day before school started. At Moeller, which was run by Marianist priests and brothers, it was only once a week. But if you were on Gerry Faust's football team, you never forgot who was really in charge. We said Hail Marys before and after every practice. On game-day Fridays, we said more prayers than I thought anyone knew. We prayed that morning, we prayed together at lunch, and in the afternoon there was a special mass before we got ready for the game. If it was an away game, we prayed on the bus. We prayed on the sidelines before the game. We prayed at halftime. And we prayed after the game—whether we won or lost. I said more Hail Marys in high school than at any other point in my life—and I still say some every day. Remembering that God has a plan, that it was bigger than you and bigger than a football game, was important. Years later I would remind myself that God had a plan and it was bigger than any House bill or blown-up White House negotiation. And it definitely helped to keep that 45–0 loss in perspective.

Going to Moeller also showed me that there was a much bigger world out there than the little corner of Reading, Ohio, where I grew up. Most of my life up until then had been spent between my parents' house, my grandparents' house, Andy's Café, church, and small parish schools where I knew almost everybody. At Moeller I met a whole bunch of different kinds of people from all over. Some kids dressed to the nines every day, and I realized for the first time that although my family wasn't poor by any means, we didn't have nearly as much money as a lot of the folks in our area. But I also learned how little that really mattered—what mattered was how hard you worked and how you treated everybody.

It was these kinds of lessons that helped set me straight before going out into the wider world, and some of the most important were the ones I learned from Gerry Faust. He taught me to never quit, that the absolute only way to get what you want is by putting in the work, day after day. The simple phrase "never give up" might sound corny, but I'll tell you, when you're in a giant college stadium getting blasted by your rival school in front of everyone you know and that scoreboard is ticking up to 45–0, it's pretty tempting to want to give up. And if you hurt your back during that mess of a game, who in their right mind would go back? Why not sit the rest of the season out?

Coach wouldn't have it. It was that simple. And most of us would do anything we could not to disappoint Coach Faust. More than a coach, he was a teacher, a mentor, and a father figure to everyone who ever played for him. He did more than teach us how to run this play or that one and yell at us when we screwed up. He taught us what it meant to be a "Man of Moeller"—to know what was required of us to become men and become leaders, and to do the right thing no matter what.

Coach Faust loved coaching at Moeller. He once said he'd only leave the job under one circumstance: if he was ever asked to become head coach at his beloved University of Notre Dame. As it turned out, he was asked to do just that. It was unusual, to say the least, for any college football program to hire a head coach from a high school team, who had no experience on the collegiate level. In most cases, a coach like Gerry Faust would be brought in at a secondary post, like an offensive coordinator. And it was unheard of for a program like Notre Dame to take a gamble like this. Coach Faust had to

have felt the risk too. He would be giving up his incredible record at the high school level to take a shot at one of the most-
watched football programs in the country. What if he blew it?

But the idea of walking in the same footsteps as legends
like Knute Rockne was irresistible to him. So he headed off to
South Bend to take the field with the Fighting Irish for the 1981
season. Unfortunately, his record at Notre Dame was nowhere
close to what it was at Moeller. Still, Faust treated every day
spent there as an honor, and left a mark of good sportsmanship
and integrity on every player he met. And he had a view of life
that I tried to copy during all my time in Congress—no matter
the setbacks, he felt honored and lucky that the good Lord had
given him a chance at this dream. After all, most people don't
even make it that far. And he knew he gave it his all.

When he stepped down in 1985, he said, "I had only 26 miserable days at Notre Dame; that's when we lost. Other than
that, I was the happiest guy in the world." I knew what he
meant. So those 26 game days were rough, but all the practices,
all the time spent getting to know and work with fine young
men on a campus where the Catholic faith runs strong—those
days were good for his soul.

And anyone who played for him will tell you that learning
from him was good for theirs too.

There was another guy I came to know, much later, who also
knew a thing or two about what was good for the soul. He
stepped in to clear away one of the biggest shitstorms this
country has ever seen, and in doing so, helped to heal the soul
of the nation. He'd never let anyone say that kind of thing
about him when he was alive, because that's just how modest
he was. But now that he's dead, I'll say it as loud as I want and

I don't care who hears it. This was President Gerald R. "Jerry" Ford. And when I first met him, I thought I was being set up for a presidential-sized smack on the wrist.

At the time, I was a freshman congressman who liked to spend his time throwing bombs at his party's leadership. So then I got invited by the leader of my party to go out and play golf with one of the greatest "institutionalists" the House had ever known. It was 1992, when Bob Michel of Illinois, the leader of Republicans in Congress, asked me to come to the Jerry Ford Invitational, a pro-am tournament that former president Ford had held in Vail, Colorado, every August since he left politics in 1977.

I didn't know what Michel was up to. There had to be some sort of catch. Clearly I was in trouble for something. I had spent my first term making a few friends and a lot of enemies, kicking over rocks like the House bank and the House post office that had been enriching members of Congress but costing the taxpayers dearly. Needless to say, this upset the leadership of both parties—Democratic Speaker Tom Foley and Michel, who was the top Republican. And because I was in Michel's party, it was his job to try to "deal with me." To be frank, I was a pain in his ass. But somehow I still kept up a good personal relationship with Bob and his chief of staff Billy Pitts, always making sure to give them a heads-up when I was up to something with my young hotshot buddies. After all, it doesn't cost anything to be nice.

Bob was a golfer himself, and he liked that I was. That was something we had in common, at least. He had been in Congress since 1957 and served alongside Gerald Ford in the House for many years. Even though he went on to serve in higher office, Ford's true love in politics was the House of Representatives. He knew the institution inside and out. As we got to become closer friends later, I learned how deep that love went. Maybe Bob Michel thought it would be good for this hotheaded freshman to meet the grand old institutionalist. So he asked me to come out to the tournament after we finished nominating President George H. W. Bush to run for reelection at the Republican National Convention in Houston, and of course I accepted. That's when I first met Jerry Ford.

President Gerald Ford is not a name that most people think of these days when considering great Republican presidents. That's not really his fault. Ford's problem was that he was surrounded by two men who were both very prominent for different reasons: Richard Nixon and Ronald Reagan. He also narrowly lost his own election to the presidency to Jimmy Carter in 1976. But none of that changes the fact that Ford was an important leader in the twentieth century. He took over after Nixon resigned in disgrace, and his integrity and decency were essential to restoring public trust in public officials. Prior to his time in the White House, he was a leader in the U.S. Congress and had worked to reform the House in his own day. There were very few people in the world who counted Ford as an enemy—even Carter, his onetime bitter political rival, eulogized him when he died. I had the great privilege of calling Jerry Ford a friend. Over the years I had glimpses of the real Jerry Ford in the sport that truly shows people who they are—golf.

After Ford died, a local newspaper said his drive was "as straight as his character and as true as his word." Yeah, right. As a man, Ford was certainly always straight and true, but the same could not always be said for his swing. Though he got a bad rap over the years as some kind of klutz—as president, he once fell down a flight of stairs—he was a fine athlete, a former football star at the University of Michigan. But golf was a different matter. He loved the sport, mostly as a reason to hang around with his friends and have a good time, but he was not a natural golfer. When he was vice president, he once sent a golf ball flying so far off target that it hit a bystander in the head, sending the guy to the hospital. On that same day, another ball pounded an unsuspecting golf cart that was carrying a policeman. Golf legend Arnold Palmer used to joke that Ford's kamikaze golf balls just barely missed him on more than one occasion. The famed comedian Bob Hope, an old friend and golfing partner of the president, used to say, "It's not hard to find Jerry Ford on a golf course—you just follow the wounded."

There was a great group of current and former members of Congress, lobbyists, professional golfers, and other "celebrities" (most of whom I barely knew) who showed up for these Jerry Ford Invitationals, and everybody had a hell of a time. Days on the golf course were followed by nights with good food and good wine. And you could still smoke pretty much everywhere. In fact, I became especially good friends with a former Ford military aide who had gone on to work for U.S. Tobacco. Given my long-term acquaintance with their product, I figured he'd be a good guy to know.

I had so much fun my first visit that I made a point to come back every year. Once I played in a foursome with country music star Vince Gill, who—in case you wondered how clueless about pop culture I was, and still am—I had never heard of, let alone met. He was mobbed on the course. Everybody wanted his autograph. They hardly seemed to care about Ford, the man who rescued the country after Watergate. It says something a little disturbing about the country, especially our education system, when people recognize a singer more than a president. But Ford being Ford, he took it all in stride.

The last year the tournament was held was 1996. Ford wanted to make that one special—and for me, it truly was. That year, I had brought along one of my longtime friends from my hometown, Al Busemeyer. It seemed like the whole town of Vail had turned out for the last-ever Jerry Ford Invitational. There were huge ads taken out in the local paper telling everyone to come out to the Vail Golf Club. And the people showed up in a big way. There were crowds all over the course. Ford was in demand everywhere, so it was totally understandable that he didn't have time for everyone. And yet somehow he seemed to.

In the middle of this circus, on the first day, Buzz and I ended up in the same foursome with President Ford. Ford had never met Buzz, who was just a regular guy from Ohio and was in awe of all the big-name celebrities all around. About halfway through the course, out of nowhere, Ford said, "Hey Buzz, come over here and read this putt for me." And without batting an eye, up stepped Buzz. He gave Ford his two cents, and the former president sank the putt. After that, Buzz ended up basically being Ford's caddie for the next three and a half days. Ford would barely take a swing—especially not a putt—without getting Buzz's advice. Buzz, of course, was eating this all up. A former president of the United States needed *his* advice to play golf on a world-class course. I got a little choked up at the idea of me and my buddy being lucky enough to be yukking it up with a former president, who treated us like we'd all been friends for years.

On the very last day of the tournament, the crowds *really* turned out. We came around a corner on the eighteenth hole, and there must have been 10,000 people gathered around. That was a lot of pressure, but I kept my head down and played it out. After everyone was finished, Ford and his wife, Betty, took photos with everybody, and when my turn came, he looked around and said, "Where's Buzz?" So the former president told the photographers to wait, and in front of 10,000 people found Busemeyer, brought him out of the crowd, and plunked him right between Betty and himself. Everyone around us had no idea who this guy was, but Ford had gone out of his way to make Buzz feel welcome even though he wasn't one of the big shots at the tournament. That's what I mean about golf showing you who people really are.

That evening, there was a concert at a local outdoor theater to close out the festivities. The guest of honor was the entertainment legend himself, Bob Hope. For readers under a certain age, the name Bob Hope probably doesn't mean as much to you as it does to the rest of us. But trust me, he was entertainment royalty. A natural comedian and jokester, he had a catalog of one-liners like, "You know you're getting old when the candles cost more than the cake." In addition to being a staple of American stage and screen (big and small) for decades, and a friend to the troops through his numerous USO tours, Hope had known every president going back to Franklin Roosevelt. "Of all the presidents," Hope recalled, Ford was "the one I can call a pal." The two pals spent a lot of time playing golf, leading Hope to joke that apparently the Betty Ford Center "can cure anything except Jerry's slice."

Hope, of course, showed up for his friend's last golf tournament. He was 93 years old. I saw him during the first few days of the event, being wheeled around in a golf cart. Old age had gotten hold of him, and the guy I'd seen on TV or in the movies for decades wasn't the same person in front of me. That was a sobering encounter, especially since I can say with some certainty that I was *not* totally sober at the time. He didn't quite look like he had everything together. His eyes were bloodshot, and he seemed to be looking around blankly.

This was a guy who once shot out jokes, on the spot, like a machine gun. Now he looked like he didn't even know where he was. When he took the stage in Vail, nobody was sure what to expect. I felt a little bad about it.

But the joke was on me. Bob Hope stole the show. When he took center stage, it was like a switch flipped and a light turned on in the guy. He had some sort of assistant up there with him who would whisper in his ear to remind him of his cues, and Hope would poke fun at that guy and make him part of the act. He was funny on his own, but the way he played off the other guy really got people rolling. He brought the house down.

When Hope's act was finished, Jerry Ford took the stage again to say a final "Thank you and goodnight." As part of that, he asked a bunch of his friends by name to join him on stage. He called my name, and up I went. Next thing I knew, I was standing next to Bob Hope. We all waved to the crowd for a minute or two, and when it was all over, Hope hooked his arm under mine, and we walked off stage together. As far as I know, that was the last live performance Bob Hope ever gave. And the last time he ever walked off a stage after a show was with me. This was a man who'd been on television longer than I'd been alive, who'd met presidents, royalty, war heroes, and every movie star of the last few decades, who'd traveled the "Road to . . ." everywhere with Bing Crosby—and here he was, walking off the stage with me.

The following November, Bob Hope's last-ever television special aired. Fittingly, it was called *Laughing with the Presidents* and the Fords, along with the Clintons and the Bushes, made a guest appearance. In 2003, he died at the ripe old age of 100.

As I suppose is clear by now, Jerry Ford and I got along right away and became fast friends. He was a warm, easygoing guy—from the Midwest, like me, and a man of the House, like I was too. He was first elected to Congress in 1948, and served in the House for more than 20 years before he was called up to be vice president and then president. He hadn't looked for advancement like that, he was just doing his job—and we needed him to help bring much-needed stability to the country after all the Watergate mess. But as I got to know him, it was pretty clear to me that Ford felt his jump to the Executive Branch was a wrong turn on what he'd hoped, for years, was a road to the Speakership.

It was after that final Ford Invitational that I got to play golf with another leader who was about as different from Ford as anyone could be. Getting to know these two men at around the same time made for quite the contrast, and I tried to learn what I could from that.

I'd gotten to know Bill Clinton fairly well since the Republicans took back the House majority in 1994 and I joined the leadership team as Conference chair in 1995. Clinton was an avid golfer, of course, but we'd never played together. After the last Ford tournament, my wife and I and a couple friends got in an RV and drove from Vail, Colorado, to Jackson Hole, Wyoming. We pulled into Jackson Hole and the first thing we noticed was an abundance of reporters. It turned out President Clinton was in town. *Shit*, I thought. This was not where we wanted to be.

Just a few weeks before, I'd been at the GOP convention in San Diego where we nominated Sen. Bob Dole to try to unseat Clinton after one term. Earlier that summer, I'd played a role in Dole's search for a running mate, in what had to be one of the most bizarre projects of my entire political career.

In June of 1996, as Republicans were trying to figure out how to give Bob Dole the boost he needed to beat Bill Clinton in the fall, my chief of staff, Barry Jackson, came to me with what he said was some big news. He'd been talking with some other staffers and people he knew around town, they'd done a ton of research, and apparently they'd come up with a dynamite pick to be Dole's running mate. Of course, I wanted Dole to win so I was all ears. I met with the team and they gave me the name: Antonin Scalia, who had been sitting on the Supreme Court since Ronald Reagan appointed him in 1986.

This wasn't who I'd expected. But the more I thought about it, the more it made sense. He was not only a brilliant jurist but the son of an immigrant and the patriarch of a large Catholic family himself. He also had a blunt way of speaking that made the poor fool he was up against feel like he'd been hit by a 2×4. I liked Bob Dole but he wasn't Mr. Charisma. Scalia would be the perfect guy to send to the Knights of Columbus or the VFW hall. So now it was my job to see if he had any interest whatsoever in making the leap from law into electoral politics. I didn't know Justice Scalia at all, but I cold-called his office and he accepted my invitation to lunch.

Jackson and I met him at A.V.'s Ristorante, a classic Italian place on New York Avenue that is now, unfortunately, long gone. The older woman who ran the place escorted us into the back room, which wasn't open at lunch, but there was Scalia, sitting at a table by himself in the middle of the room, a bottle of wine and a glass in front of him. We introduced ourselves, and I called him "Mr. Justice."

"Nino," he said immediately. "Call me Nino." That put us at ease right away.

I didn't feel like beating around the bush. "I want to ask you a favor," I said. "And do you think you could avoid telling me 'no' until lunch is over?" He agreed to this condition, and then we looked at our menus. As it turned out, all of us had a fondness for pizza with anchovies. Things were going pretty well.

When I brought up the idea of him joining the Dole ticket, he looked at me like I was crazy. He was concerned about how his leaving could affect the Supreme Court, as well as the federal pension he could risk losing if he left his seat. He had nine kids to support, after all. I reminded him that there would be plenty of Washington law firms ready to hire a former justice for an "of counsel" position no matter how the election went.

Well, he was intrigued, and asked for the weekend to think it over. True to his word, he called me the next week and told me he had his response ready. "You're not a lawyer," he said, "so you need to write this down exactly as I say it." And he dictated to me what turned out to be the same phrase Chief Justice Charles Evans Hughes once used in a similar situation: "The possibility is too remote to comment upon, given my position." This was a classic Washington move, the non-denial.

This was pretty exciting. I'd only been in Congress a few years, and here I was helping to pick the next vice president. And we'd sealed the deal over a pepperoni and anchovy pizza! But we weren't quite done yet. There was still someone else we had to talk to about it: Bob Dole. Nobody had wanted to bring it up to him until we'd talked with Scalia. He'd been on the road campaigning anyway.

As soon as he got back to Washington, Jackson and I rushed over to see him. His first reaction when we told him was, in typical dour Dole fashion, reflexively negative: "Scalia's not going to do this, he's on the Court!"

"Bob," I said, "I took it upon myself to have lunch with him." Now Dole's eyebrows arched a bit. He was intrigued.

I walked him through our conversation and then, triumphantly, handed him the note where I'd written Scalia's response.

"Well, this means yes," he said. Yes, at least, he was interested. So we left Dole with his new running mate all teed up.

"If you need me to do anything else," I told him, "just let me know."

I headed out of there like a conquering hero, a real player, at least in my own mind. And I never heard anything about it again. Never knew what the hell happened. Dole picked his old political rival, Jack Kemp, as his running mate and went down to a big defeat against Bill Clinton. Oh well. Scalia probably would have been a fine vice president, but all in all, America was damn lucky that he ended up staying right where he was for as long as he did. And we got to be friends out of it, enjoying anchovies together in many other forms over the years.

———

So maybe my VP plan didn't work out, but I was still set to campaign full-bore against Clinton all the way up to the elections in November. And I needed this golfing vacation to relax a bit before the tough fights ahead. So you can imagine how I felt when I answered the phone in the house we'd rented in Jackson Hole only to hear a voice identify itself as a member of the White House staff.

"The president would like to invite you to play golf with him tomorrow," they said. *How the hell did he even know I was here?* I thought. I had to find some way out of it.

"Well," I said, "I'm supposed to go fishing tomorrow. How about the next day?"

There was a short pause.

"*Congressman,*" the voice said, emphasizing the word, "the president of the United States"—carefully pronouncing each

When you're managing a bunch of knuckle-heads in Congress, sometimes you have to be the adult in the room . . .

. . . and sometimes you're the happy warrior!

The night of the historic Republican comeback in 2010, just about when it hit me that I was going to become the Mayor of Crazytown—I mean, Speaker of the House.

Even though she could wield a knife (metaphorically speaking) as well as anyone I've ever seen in politics, Nancy Pelosi and I got along . . . most of the time. That gavel was handmade for the occasion by my friend Dick Slagle of Middletown, Ohio. *(AP Photo/Pablo Martinez Monsivais)*

At the 2011 State of the Union, right after the Republicans took back the House, President Obama noted how the American Dream meant that "someone who began by sweeping the floors of his father's Cincinnati bar can preside as Speaker of the House in the greatest nation on Earth." It was a nice moment, especially since I was sitting next to another "working class kid"—as Obama called him—Joe Biden. *(AP Photo/Charles Dharapak)*

Happy to have my buddy Paul Ryan drop by the Capitol during his campaign as Mitt Romney's running mate in 2012. Years earlier, Paul had volunteered on my first congressional race and ended up succeeding me as Speaker of the House. Mr. Health Nut later complained constantly that I'd polluted his new office with cigarette smoke. *(AP Photo/J. Scott Applewhite)*

I usually didn't agree with either of these guys on policy, but they weren't bad people. Photos like this did not endear me to some members of my party— most, really—but somebody had to be the adult in the room, find common ground, and try to get things done. *(Official White House Photo/Pete Souza)*

Meeting the Holy Father was one of the highlights of my time as Speaker and also a sign to me that it was time to get the hell—or maybe I should say "heck"—out of Dodge.

The political situation was so toxic that when I met with President Obama we sometimes had to go incognito.

He took a long, loving look at those cigarettes, but he never touched. The First Lady wouldn't let him!

The portrait now hanging with my fellow Speakers, done by a professional . . .

. . . and another treasured portrait by an enthusiastic amateur artist, George W. Bush.

Deb and I have
been through a
lot together—
and I don't just
mean changes
in fashion.

She's still the
one.

My girls, Lindsay and Tricia. When they were kids I nicknamed them—lovingly—"Bad" and "Worse." But they've been so much fun and made me the happiest dad I could hope to be.

Mom and Dad. They managed to run a business and somehow raise 12 kids in a house with two bedrooms and one bathroom (until Dad built an extension).

word in the full title—"would like to invite you to play golf tomorrow."

I got the message. "Okay, I'll be there," I said.

So the next day I watched, jealous, as Deb and our friends headed off for a day of rafting and fishing on the Snake River. Our tee time had been pushed back because of something much more pressing—a bombing in the Balkans that required the president's attention—and there wasn't much I could do about that. But eventually we met up and teed off. Clinton's close friend and advisor Vernon Jordan was with us as well. Bill Clinton was a guy who liked to have a good time—sometimes too good a time—but he kept pretty focused on the golf course. All in all it was a pretty normal game, and Clinton played decently.

As we finished out the eighteenth hole, I saw Deb and the other two couples standing behind the rope waving to me. To this day I'm not sure how they all got themselves in, but somehow they did. I also saw a bank of photographers and TV cameras getting ready to take pictures of the president coming off the golf course—with me, a member of the House Republican leadership, who was supposed to be making his life harder. Dammit. There was no getting out of this one. I was trapped.

Of course I had to take Clinton over to introduce him to my wife and our friends, and because he's a talker, we all stood around chatting for several minutes. And of course the TV news all over the country aired footage of Clinton yukking it up on the golf course with Boehner the House Republican Conference chair. I got a lot of calls from friends the next day, harassing the crap out of me for spending so much time with my new liberal best friend.

There wasn't a big golfing scene in Hope, Arkansas, but Bill Clinton set out to get good at the game because he figured it would help ease his way into the ranks of the political elite to which he aspired from an early age. Well, he certainly made it to the top rung of that ladder, and he got pretty good at golf along the way. But he didn't always strictly come by it honestly. He wasn't afraid to call a mulligan or two—which became known as a "Billigan"—in an outing. So there was a slightly shady side to his game too. That wasn't exactly a surprise, given the phrase "whiff of scandal" that became attached to the Clintons over time. And maybe, knowing the guy, it wasn't exactly a surprise that he usually got away with it too.

Even after the Ford Invitational formally ended, Jerry Ford and I met up to play golf several times near his home in California. On one of those later trips, about 1999, I saw the funniest thing I've ever seen on a golf course.

Ford went down in history as the all-American suburban dad—calm, mild-mannered, maybe a little clumsy—who wound up in the White House with his pipe and sweater. And while it's true that he was always a perfect gentleman in public, he was also an ex-navy man, and he knew how to swear like any old sailor. That was a side of him that came out occasionally, and on the golf course he wasn't always a saint.

One day at Morningside, I was playing with the 86-year-old former president, and we found ourselves on a par 5 with a fair amount of water hazards. On his second shot, Ford hit the ball over the water, and did the same with his third shot. Now we were onto the fairway, and Ford had the short ball. On his fourth shot, he hit the ball straight into the water. He was not happy, but he dropped a new ball. He hit that one right into the water too. He was getting visibly upset. He dropped a third ball . . . and damned if he didn't knock that one straight into the water too. And then the 86-year-old former leader of the free world began to jump up and down, screaming "FUCK" as loud as he could scream. Over and over again. Up, "fuck!" Down, "fuck!" Up, "fuck!" Down, "fuck!" It was like some crazy exercise routine. I'd never seen anything like it on a golf course, and haven't since. I'll never forget it as long as I live.

I had a lot of fun on the golf course with Jerry Ford, but he could get introspective too, especially in those later years. That was when I really learned a lot from him about the House of Representatives as a body, how all the different committees and caucuses and offices worked together as part of a whole. Ford had a deep love for the House. He used to tell me, a bit sadly, that all he'd ever wanted to be was Speaker.

When I made it to that office, I often thought about Jerry, and tried to follow what he'd taught me. I know I did my best to take care of the institution of the House, like he would have wanted. I just wish he'd lived a few more years, because I would have loved to have shown him into the Speaker's office he'd had his eye on for so long. I know for certain that if history had turned out differently, Speaker Gerald R. Ford would have been one of the finest men to hold the office.

But while I couldn't give Ford a tour of the Capitol as Speaker, I could welcome him there in spirit. I still have one of his White House ashtrays in my office. And in 2011, a statue of President Ford was unveiled in the Capitol rotunda, an event I was proud to preside over as Speaker. That night, after the ceremony, former Ford staff and family members gathered for a reunion dinner in the adjacent Statuary Hall. I had some other event to go to and couldn't make the whole thing, but I stopped by long enough to tell the family the story of Jerry sinking three balls in a row into the water at Morningside and going apeshit. I cleaned it up for them—barely. Still, they roared with laughter.

———•———

Two Midwestern football players with the same name. One devoted his whole life to the game and teaching and molding the young men who play it. One wanted to be Speaker of the House but ended up becoming president of the United States. One helped me grow from a kid into a young man who knew to put his team before himself and God before everything else. One helped me gain a deeper understanding of the House of Representatives, an institution we both loved.

I was very lucky to meet Gerry Faust and Jerry Ford at the times in my life that I did. If it weren't for the discipline of Gerry Faust's football team, who knows what sort of bullshit I would have got up to in high school. If I hadn't learned Jerry Ford's wisdom about the House early on in my career there, I might have spent a few terms as a bomb-throwing Meadows/ Mulvaney-type jackass before burning out and going home. Thinking about either of those alternatives is enough to make me sick.

Some people knock Gerry Faust for not doing so great as Notre Dame's coach. Some people knock Jerry Ford for losing his election to the then-unknown Jimmy Carter. Bullshit. A good man is a good man. Teddy Roosevelt famously said in 1910, "It is not the critic who counts; not the man who points out how the strong man stumbles . . . The credit belongs to the man who is actually in the arena, whose face is marred by dust and sweat and blood." Anybody who's actually been in the arena can tell you that a good man is worth a hell of a lot more than points on a scoreboard or an electoral tally. Faust and Ford are two good men I've been very lucky to know.

There was one time when the lessons of those two men came together for me, at a moment when I needed it most. In 2006, I ran in the House leadership election to become the majority leader. The former leader, Tom DeLay, had stepped down a few months earlier after getting into some campaign finance trouble. Rep. Roy Blunt of Missouri filled in as acting leader, and was running against me to gain the position for himself. Rep. John Shadegg of Arizona rounded out the field.

It was a close race, and naturally I was nervous. But the night before the election, my buddy Tim McKone, who worked for AT&T, called and invited me to go to the 7:00 AM mass with him at St. Peter's Church on Capitol Hill. Well, that was just what I needed. So the next day, a cold February morning, Tim and I went to the early mass and then had breakfast at one of my favorite spots, Pete's Diner, just a short walk away. As we walked out of Pete's, my cell phone rang, with a call coming in from a number I didn't know. For some reason, I picked up. On the other end of the line was Coach Faust, who gave me a classic pep talk from our days on the field together—about stepping up when the team needs you, keeping your head in the game.

So I just stood there, listening to this great man, standing in the cold on the sidewalk in front of Pete's Diner, crying my eyes out. I've never gotten a phone call from God (at least not yet), but that was about as close as I'll ever get. And later that morning, my colleagues chose me as their majority leader. I can credit the race to both of these men. Jerry Ford's love for the House helped convince me to stick with the leadership, and Gerry Faust's encouragement helped give me the confidence to be an effective, helpful leader.

God has a way of bringing the right people into your life at the right time. You can learn something from pretty much everybody you meet, if you know how to listen. I am grateful to have been able to learn from guys like Jerry Ford and Gerry Faust. What they taught me was what helped keep me from leaping off the Speaker's Balcony when it looked like things were spinning out of control. And God knows, in Washington, especially once I became Speaker, I found myself in that situation pretty regularly.

# FIVE

$\Longleftrightarrow$

# Bull Balls and Bailouts

I f you walked into the conference room in the Speaker's office during my time working there, you'd find yourself looking at a curious sight. Smack-dab in the middle of the fine hardwood table was a dark, leathery, shriveled object encased in a clear plastic box. I set it out there one day and periodically watched as people tried to figure out what it was.

Once they determined what exactly was in that box, members of my staff kept trying to move it. So did members with queasier stomachs who came in for meetings. People would stack their papers up in front of it so they didn't have to look at it. Sometimes the staff would hide it in a closet or a cabinet somewhere (the Speaker's suite has all sorts of nooks and crannies for squirreling stuff away). But I would always rescue it eventually and put it right back on that conference table, so that most mornings every member of our leadership team would gather around staring at it.

Whenever people asked, "Mr. Speaker, what the hell *is* that?" I'd tell them.

This, I informed them, was the scrotum of an African Cape buffalo, which I'm told is the nastiest mammal on earth. No,

I'm not a hunter. But I have friends who are, and one of them gave me this unique and touching gift. How I came to end up with a bull's ball sack on my conference table is an instructive story about how governing in Washington really works.

The first thing anyone trying to figure out our government has to understand is that America is a pretty settled country. Except when faced with a truly dramatic event—the Great Depression, World War II, 9/11—we just aren't built for sweeping, breathtaking change. Our system, because it doesn't allow for major swings in policy, has given American businesses of all kinds—everything from huge corporations to one-man home offices—some sense of stability in terms of what to expect out of Washington. They know that one election might shift policies a little bit to the left, and the next election will shift things a little bit to the right. But because they aren't dealing with giant fluctuations, they're able to adjust. And even though that can be frustrating to people who *do* want major change one way or the other, I think by and large the system has served our country very well. It's provided us more stability than, for instance, a parliamentary system like the United Kingdom's, where there are often wild swings one way or the other depending on which party gets the majority.

Hotheads on either side of our political spectrum almost never understand that. Often our presidents don't get that either, especially if they cut their teeth outside Washington. That's why it often falls to the guys who've been around for awhile—like yours truly—to help them figure it out.

I first really came to know George W. Bush in the mid-1990s. House Republicans were trying to build closer relationships with party governors to try to get some things done that involved buy-in from the states, such as welfare reform. I was right in the middle of this as the liaison to the Republican Governors Association, which meant I'd go to periodic meetings where we'd talk and drink and discuss policy. And then when formal discussions were over with, some of us would loosen our ties and play poker.

My regular group of gubernatorial poker buddies included Bill Weld of Massachusetts, George Allen of Virginia, and John Rowland of Connecticut. They were quite a crew. Allen had been a buddy of mine since his days in the House. Rowland ended up going to jail—twice, actually. And as for Weld—I don't know if he really was drunk for all of our games, but I know he had a coffee cup he kept excusing himself to refill, and by the end of the night he could hardly sit up straight. But the son of a bitch could play cards. He walked off with a lot of our money, so whatever was in that cup—or whatever he made us *think* was in that cup—must have helped. Either that or he was just that damn good.

And then there was Governor George W. Bush of Texas. It wasn't long after he started joining our games that we all figured out his "style" of poker playing. Whenever he was in on any hand, we would all fold. "W." wouldn't ever get in unless he had a packed hand. He never bluffed. He seemed incapable of bluffing, in fact. He'll probably disagree with me, but he was not a good poker player. So much for representing the namesake of Texas Hold'em. He is, however, a good friend.

After Bush was elected to the presidency, he very quickly put together a meeting in Austin to discuss what he thought would be his chief policy initiative during his first term: education reform. He planned to summon who he and his team thought were the key players on Capitol Hill on the issue. That included the key Republicans and Democrats on the Senate HELP (Health, Education, Labor, and Pensions) Committee. The Republican point man was Senator Judd Gregg of New

Hampshire. Gregg was a stern, serious guy. If he smiled, it was a headline news event. I dubbed him "Mr. Happy." His Democrat counterpart was Ted Kennedy. Bush knew there wasn't a hope in hell of getting anything related to education passed by Congress without Kennedy, who was the patron saint of the national teachers' unions.

And then there was me, the brand-new chairman of the House Education and Workforce Committee. I still had a lot to learn about education policy. I admit that it had not been one of my top issues during my early years in Congress. As a conservative, I basically felt that education should be run by local communities, not some distant Washington bureaucrats (even me). But a whole bunch of people kept working on me to take over that committee, including Bush. That's probably because he knew whoever was chairman was going to have a big say in his education plans—and he didn't want a nutjob. "Listen, I'm relying on you," he kept saying. "You're the one that's gotta get this done." So, fine. I agreed. I worked overtime to study all the issues that were going to come before my committee.

Before I agreed to come down to Austin for the first big meeting, however, I asked the Bush folks a question. "Hey, do you have George Miller coming?"

Miller was the ranking Democrat on the committee. He was a tall California representative with a big mustache and a reputation as one of the biggest liberals on the Hill, and therefore not a fan of George W. Bush.

"No Miller," the Bush folks told me. "We don't want him." I'm sure someone had told Governor Bush that George Miller was a big waste of time. So right there we had a problem. The absolute worst thing I could do as the new chairman of a committee was to piss off my counterpart from the other party, who, by the way, knew a hell of a lot more about these issues than I did. Contrary to popular opinion, members of Congress who work together a lot, regardless of their political views, like to get along.

"Well, I'm not sure I should be there if George isn't there," I said. "If you guys really are serious about getting this done, he's going to need to be part of this." After some hemming and hawing, they agreed to invite Miller. And we all set off to Austin.

Next thing you know, we were all having lunch at the governor's mansion. Bush got up and gave some opening remarks about what he wanted to do with K–12 education. Then, in deference to the man's near-legendary status, Bush invited Ted Kennedy to stand up and say a few words. Then it was my turn.

And then the governor looked to Miller—who he would soon dub "Big George."

"George, what would you like to say?" Bush asked.

Miller rose and said, "I appreciate being here, and if you're serious about this, I can tell you, I'm serious about it too." Miller, like Teddy Kennedy, was part of the old-school congressional tradition of actually making deals instead of running around trying to stop everything in its tracks. I respected them. As a matter of fact, I loved Ted Kennedy. He was a great man and a great legislator.

Everyone in the right-wing media loved to attack him as some loudmouth liberal with scandals in his past—and believe me, he could be a fierce partisan. You did not want him against you. Later in the Bush years when we were working together, I'd see him go out in front of the press, and he would just say these god-awful things about President Bush. He could be nasty. You just knew the presidential ears were burning somewhere in the White House.

So next time I talked to Ted, I'd say, "Ted, can you just throttle it back a little bit?" He'd just kind of chuckle, because he understood the game. Yes, he played to his base, but then when he sat down to work with you, he turned into a very different guy. There was the public Ted Kennedy, the liberal lion of the Senate. And then there was the private Ted Kennedy, an old-school pol who loved to get things done. A discussion with Kennedy was more than just going through the motions—which is more than I can say about a lot of politicians. This guy wanted a deal. He came to Congress to legislate.

He'd work with you. He'd negotiate with you, and find a way to get to a consensus. Of course, he'd never give up on trying to get more, and his staff was even more aggressive. But he was a workhorse, and once you reached that consensus with him, he would defend it until the end. He was a crucial player—maybe *the* crucial player—in giving Republican George Bush, who was totally loathed by the left, a major legislative victory.

Ted Kennedy was the godfather of the National Education Association. At one point, after we finally came to an agreement on a bill, we got word that they were going to come out in opposition, which could have sunk everything. So I picked up the phone and called Kennedy.

"Ted," I said. "These are your people. You need to stop this. They don't have to endorse this bill, but they can't be out there in opposition to us. The bill doesn't have a chance otherwise."

Of course, I didn't need to explain this to the veteran legislator.

"I understand," he said. "What can I do?"

I never thought it would end up being my job to order Ted Kennedy around, but this was no time to hesitate.

"You go down to their meeting right now," I said, "and tell them this is good for kids. Tell them they may not love every part of it, but they can't get in the middle of this and screw it up."

(Maybe I didn't say "screw.")

Ted got the message and simply said, "I'm on my way."

Later that night, the NEA issued the decision to take "no position" on the bill. That took care of one hurdle.

Now it was my job to take care of the conservatives. Even though we had a Republican president, there were plenty of Republican members in the House who would have been okay with abolishing the U.S. Department of Education. They weren't too excited about passing a brand-new federal education law. More accurately, they had no interest at all. Zero.

A couple members of the GOP decided to put forward an amendment to our bill that would effectively give almost all control over education to the states. Now, as I've said, this happened to be an idea I'd largely agreed with over the years. A lot of conservatives did. But this amendment was not actually trying to solve a problem. It had no hope of being passed by the House and Senate. This was a classic case of people wanting to make a statement versus people wanting to get something done.

I knew it would be a disaster. And then George Miller confirmed it. "You put this into the bill," he told me, "and we're done."

The trouble was that most people in the Bush White House didn't get it at all. They'd say, "What's the big deal with this amendment? We all want to give more education control to states, don't we?" They didn't have a clue that this could blow up one of the president's major priorities.

Sometimes it really seemed like there was nobody in charge. In May 2001, while we were in the middle of negotiations on the education plan and this amendment was threatening to send everything crashing down, I did what I often do when I need to take a step back and clear my head—I went to go play golf.

I was due to head down to South Carolina for a golf weekend but had some free time before I left, so I went to go play nine holes at Burning Tree. One of the guys in my foursome there was David Hobbs, who worked in legislative affairs for the White House. For all nine holes he drilled into my head about how much trouble I was in with the White House *and* the congressional Republican leadership. Somehow this all had to get sorted out. There was going to be a big meeting at the White House on Monday to try and get that done.

So before I left to go to beautiful South Carolina with my friends Saxby Chambliss, Tom Latham, and some other guys from DC and Ohio, I was warned that Dick Cheney was going to call me over the weekend. Cheney was not the biggest fan of these education initiatives, I knew, and he had the power to torpedo the whole thing if he wanted. Still, he knew this was important to the president, so I figured we weren't sunk yet.

This was back in 2001, before everybody had cell phones. I certainly didn't have one. So they gave Cheney's office the number to Saxby's phone. We weren't allowed to have cell phones on the course, but we would check it as soon as we came off. But the call never came. Not Saturday, not Sunday. Finally the weekend was over, and we were getting into our cars for the ride to the Savannah airport when the call came through from the vice president.

I'd rehearsed this conversation with Cheney in my head all weekend. It probably distracted me out on the course. We talked over our plans for the education bill and how this Republican amendment would screw everything up. He made no secret of the fact that he was okay with the bill blowing up. But I knew the president didn't feel that way. The meeting was that afternoon, and as long as I got back in time I figured I had as good a shot as anyone at keeping Bush on our side.

By that time we'd gotten to the airport. We took off and made our first scheduled stop in Winston-Salem, North Carolina, but before we could take off again we got word that there was a line of thunderstorms headed straight for Washington. We were stuck. I knew I was going to be late.

My first phone call was to David Hobbs in the legislative affairs office to tell him we were delayed and ask him to push the meeting back. His response was what I expected: "Are you crazy?" This was a meeting with the president of the United States, and they weren't going to reschedule it for me. And I knew that if I didn't show up, there would be plenty of people in that room who would love to talk Bush into supporting that House Republican amendment that would kill the bill. They would have been just fine if I didn't show up. I couldn't let that happen.

After a few more anxious minutes of chain smoking, we still showed no signs of moving, but I had another idea. I called Hobbs back.

"Can you at least get us pushed up in the lineup once they open up DC?" I asked. And sure enough, someone from his office got to the FAA in time to push our flight to the front of the line to land in Washington. But I was still running late. I had no time to change clothes. I borrowed a jacket from Saxby and a tie from Latham, got mostly dressed on the plane, and jumped out as soon as the door opened. I ran across the tarmac, dodged huge puddles left and right—it would be even worse to show up late *and* soaked—and made it to the car that two staffers had driven over in to pick me up.

I could hardly look more out of place. I'd been playing golf for four straight days, and had a pretty good tan going, and was dressed in borrowed clothes that didn't fit right. When President Bush's father, George H. W. Bush, was a congressman from Texas, he had once been summoned to meet President Nixon at the White House, and instead of heading the short distance down Pennsylvania Avenue he drove all the way to his home in northwest DC to change his shoes from loafers to wingtips, because he just didn't feel that loafers were appropriate for the White House.

I couldn't afford to be that proper at the moment. I would be lucky just to get there. And somehow, by the grace of God, I was only 15 minutes late.

This may not seem like much, but President Bush always made a big stink about being on time for everything. "Mr. Impatient" would probably show up early for his own funeral. So he probably wasn't going to be too happy with me.

Everyone was already gathered in the Oval Office. The congressional Republican leadership was there, and so were Cheney and plenty of White House staff. The president looked up at me with a big frown on his face and immediately gave me grief for being late. I apologized, and while he didn't really seem satisfied, he let it pass. As I sat down, he said, "Alright if I continue?" Ouch.

Apparently some people were glad I had made it just so they could get their licks in. As soon as the president had finished his opening remarks, everyone else who spoke took the opportunity to kick me further and further under the bus.

Even my buddy, House Republican leader Dick Armey, was grumbling about me.

"Boehner's causing problems with the rest of the House Republicans."

"Boehner's trying to kill a good amendment."

"Boehner's caving to the liberals and his new pal Teddy Kennedy."

On and on it went. I hadn't taken a beating like that since I played football.

But the man whose opinion mattered the most, the president, just sat quietly, listening to everyone. Once everyone had had their say, he looked at me and said, in his crisp, to-the-point manner, "Alright, Boehner, what have you got to say for yourself?"

My first thought was, *Well, you're the one who got me into this mess in the first place!* But I couldn't say that out loud. Instead, with the whole room arrayed against me, I went through step-by-step what our bill was trying to do and why this amendment would blow the whole thing up. I was addressing the whole group, but really I was playing to an audience of one. Education reform was one of President Bush's top priorities, and he had to know that the best way to get an actual bill passed was to let me handle it my way despite all the whining from the sidelines.

"Listen," I finally summed up, "you want to get a bill out of the House. We'll get a bill out of the House even with this amendment since we have the majority. But if this amendment goes in, we will never get a bill passed in the Senate to put on your desk." This is a mistake, I said. It will kill the whole deal. We shouldn't do it.

I could feel the daggers from all around the room. I tried to avoid the angriest glares. Cheney in particular looked displeased. But Bush was in decider mode. Time to make up his mind and move on.

"I'm with Boehner," he said, simply. And the meeting was over.

President Bush could have made another decision, of course. It would have been easy. He would have won praise from talk radio hosts and those stuck-up brats who write columns on every issue under the sun who never worked a real job in their lives. He would have smoothed things over with his party in Congress. And then when the bill inevitably failed, he could score another political victory by blaming the Democrats for killing it.

But Bush did not do that. And I was proud of him. Not just because he'd sided with me, but because he trusted me with this initiative that was near and dear to him, and had the potential to help out a whole lot of kids around the country.

Although, as the meeting was breaking up, he couldn't resist giving me one more jab for being late.

Most of the participants bolted for the Oval Office door in a fury, probably rushing to get firewood to burn me at the stake. I had to rush after my colleagues and find some way to calm them down. We all had to work together, after all.

Within a week, the House of Representatives passed our bill by a huge bipartisan margin. The numbers were a bit lopsided though—it was passed mostly with Democratic votes and only a few dozen Republicans. Plenty of people are still stewing about it. Even years later, when I'd pass some members in the hallway, I could've sworn I heard, muttered quietly, "You let Ted Kennedy play Bush."

Bush didn't get played by anybody. He accomplished a goal he'd set out to do when he was first elected. And he got it done early in his term. Oh, and by the way, American kids got a better shot because of it.

After "No Child Left Behind" passed Congress, Bush was so elated—not something we saw often—that he decided to keep the celebration going by holding several different signing ceremonies for the bill. He chose the locations in honor of some of the people who had helped bring the law into being. So we went up to New Hampshire for a ceremony for Judd "Mr. Happy" Gregg, one in Massachusetts for Ted, and one in Ohio, for me, which was nice.

And then, of course, there was another big event in DC where the president's brother Jeb came up from Florida. But to me, the most important guests were the two hundred or so kids that my program had helped get scholarships to local Catholic schools. I figured these kids may never have an opportunity to meet a president again, so I wanted to make sure each and every one of them got to shake hands with Bush. So we stuck around after the event and, sure enough, Bush shook every one of those little hands. It was a beautiful moment.

After that, everyone had pretty much left, so President Bush and I walked out together. Before he got into the limousine to head back to the White House, I said to him, "Mr. President, I've got to remind you of something."

"What's that?" he asked.

"Do you remember that meeting we had in the Oval Office, when you stood up for my plan in front of everybody?"

"Oh yeah, I remember."

"Well, I've got to tell you something. If you hadn't made that decision that day, we would not be here today."

He didn't say anything. I could tell he was thinking back to that moment. And then I started to see tears come to his eyes. And me, I'm always an easy target when that happens. Tears form in my eyes too. In front of all of his staff and Secret Service and all the spectators who showed up for the event, the president gave me a big bear hug. Then he got into his limo and left.

The moment was so moving that I didn't realize for a few minutes that I was now completely alone. The event was over. I didn't have any staff with me. I hadn't driven myself. I was just standing there in the parking lot, and I had to get back to the Capitol to go back to work. So I ended up having to weave through the crowd to the street and hail a cab.

All the time I see people on TV or read newspaper pundits bemoaning how the two parties can't get anything done together in Washington. Yes, it can be hard. But George W. Bush did it—and he did it with Ted Kennedy, one of the most liberal legislators ever to set foot in the Capitol. Of course, Bush wasn't always like that. And the Democrats weren't always so cooperative—especially as the Iraq War dragged on and Bush's approval ratings went somewhere south of colonoscopies. But for a while there, he got things done. He really worked hard at it.

And when he left office, I had similar hopes for his successor, even though he came from the opposite party. But it turned out that was a whole other kettle of fish.

◆

Barack Obama promised to be different. Of course they all promise that—but a lot of people believed Obama meant it. His campaign was about hope, it was about working together, about having new conversations. It was a pretty compelling message that most Americans rallied behind. I even knew Republicans who voted for Obama. His election as the first black president was historic, and he came in with enormous goodwill. I thought to myself: if he actually governs like he said he would, this is going to change Washington.

Early on, I tried to share with President Obama—who hadn't spent that much time in the Senate, after all—how things worked on the legislative end of Pennsylvania Avenue. I told him that if you want to enact something that lasts, it has to have bipartisan fingerprints. Everyone needs a piece of it, a stake in it. The last Democrat to hold his office, Bill Clinton, understood this, and worked with Republicans to pass initiatives like welfare reform in the 1990s.

Obama had urgent priorities for sure. The economy was still suffering from the Great Recession of 2008, and he had to do something about that. So he pledged to pass a stimulus bill to reinvigorate the economy. But the president wasn't particularly involved in crafting the bill, leaving it instead to the Democrats in Congress, where no taxpayer dollars have ever been spared. The idea was to spend a trillion dollars and boost the economy, by just throwing money at stuff. But one of the things they threw almost no money at was something that should have been hugely popular: infrastructure, meaning repairs to roads, bridges, airports, etc. And these projects were sprinkled through every congressional district in America. Republicans, just like Democrats, love to bring home federal dollars to fix a local highway or whatever needs fixing.

There was a key opportunity here for Democrats to get Republican buy-in with more infrastructure spending in the stimulus. If they had just thrown $10 or 20 billion of that stimulus money into infrastructure, they'd have brought at least 50 Republicans to join them. Obama would have started off with a big bipartisan bill and a big victory against the GOP, who were trying to keep everyone in line against the Democrats. But with the Democrats holding a majority in both the House and Senate, the White House didn't think they had to do any outreach to Republican members.

And for some strange reason, at this same time, the new president was claiming that he wanted to work closely with us. At one point during these deliberations, he said to me and some other Republican leaders, "Listen, you guys that have got ideas, give them to me." So we outlined some ideas and a few days later I presented them to the president.

Obama looked at the list and bristled. I never got the sense that he was a particularly warm guy, but today he was cooler than ever.

"Don't like this," he said as he went down the list. "Or this." "We're not doing that." And so forth.

"Mr. President," I said, "you said you were going to try to work with us." I assumed he knew that he wasn't going to like everything Republicans proposed any more than we liked everything he proposed. George Bush would have figured that out. He was smart about that sort of thing.

But Obama just looked at me, and in his too-cool-for-school way, he said, "Well, John, you have to remember, I won."

I'd never been sucker punched like that in my life. It was like he'd kicked me in the stomach. The arrogance of that comment combined with my own personal embarrassment after thinking he had meant what he'd said was huge. I certainly didn't need to be reminded that he'd won the election. I'd just lived through three months of being reminded of his great victory. I'd read about it every day. He was sitting in the White House. I sure wasn't.

But even worse than my personal discomfort over Obama's attitude was my bewilderment. It was as if they had no idea what they were on the verge of accomplishing. Republicans— and by that, I mean the reasonable majority of the GOP, not the screwballs—saw the power of Obama's vision. They saw how the country responded. They knew it was in their interest to try to work with him, at least in those early days, because he was popular.

If that administration had worked with us at all on the stimulus bill, there's a bunch of Republicans who would have voted "yes." They would have hardly had to do anything, except throw a few bones out there. That would have reshaped the politics of America. But he didn't do it. His rhetoric didn't help, and the Democrats on the Hill had no interest in getting Republican buy-in. That would have meant the left wouldn't have gotten exactly everything they wanted. They would have had to be urged by their president to do it, and he wasn't interested.

The people around Obama were pushing him to talk to the far left instead of talking to America, so they squandered what I thought was a pretty big opportunity for them. Hubris will kill you in politics.

After getting shut out on the stimulus, it was easy for Republicans to turn on Obama. The stimulus got labeled a big money throwaway that hurt him with voters, since it didn't have bipartisan support. And then there was the Affordable Care Act, his next big initiative that came to be called "Obamacare." Then, too, the White House took a backseat and let Democrats in Congress call the shots in putting the bill together, and of course they shut out Republicans again. The law that finally passed ended up being something that was popular on the far left but less popular with most of America.

Today, there's not much left of Obamacare. When I was Speaker, we passed a dozen bipartisan measures to change various parts of it. It's been falling apart ever since.

By the time Obama's first midterm elections came around in 2010, the shine had worn off. The electorate hadn't embraced a one-sided rewriting of our health code or the generally arrogant attitude of the Obama White House. And another unintended consequence of Obamacare: House Speaker Nancy Pelosi strong-armed moderate Democrats into voting for a bill that was extremely unpopular back in their districts. In 2010, lots of these folks were thrown out and replaced by Republicans.

Voters from all over the place gave President Obama what he himself called "a shellacking." And oh boy, was it ever. Across the country, Republicans picked up seven hundred state legislative seats. You could be a total moron and get elected just by having an R next to your name—and that year, by the way, we did pick up a fair number in that category.

We won six seats in the Senate, picked up six governorships in the Rust Belt, including Ohio, and retook control of the House of Representatives. That put me in line to be the next Speaker of the House over the largest freshman Republican class in history: 87 newly elected members of the GOP. Now I was able to deal with Obama from a much stronger position—with a majority in Congress behind me. I decided I was going to try to get him to work with us after all. This would lead to the defining moment of my Speakership. And it was also one of the most defining moments of all my years in Washington, DC.

Since I was presiding over a large group of people who'd never sat in Congress, I felt I owed them a little tutorial on governing. I had to explain how to actually get things done. A lot of that went straight through the ears of most of them, especially the ones who didn't have brains that got in the way. Incrementalism? Compromise? That wasn't their thing. A lot of them wanted to blow up Washington. That's why they thought they were elected.

Some of them, well, you could tell they weren't paying attention because they were just thinking of how to fundraise off of outrage or how they could get on Hannity that night. Ronald Reagan used to say something to the effect that if I get 80 or 90 percent of what I want, that's a win. These guys wanted 100 percent every time. In fact, I don't think that would satisfy them, because they didn't really want legislative victories. They wanted wedge issues and conspiracies and crusades. To them, my talk of trying to get anything done made me a sellout, a dupe of the Democrats, and a traitor. Some of them had me in their sights from day one. They saw me as much of an "enemy" as the guy in the White House. Me, a guy who had come to the top of the leadership by exposing corruption and pushing conservative ideas. Now I was a "liberal collaborator." So that took some getting used to.

What I also had not anticipated was the extent to which this new crowd hated—and I mean *hated*—Barack Obama. By 2011, the right-wing propaganda nuts had managed to turn Obama into a toxic brand for conservatives. When I was first elected to Congress, we didn't have any propaganda organization for conservatives, except maybe a magazine or two like *National Review*. The only people who used the internet were some geeks in Palo Alto. There was no Drudge Report. No Breitbart. No kooks on YouTube spreading dangerous nonsense like they did every day about Obama.

"He's a secret Muslim!"

"He hates America!"

"He's a communist!"

And of course the truly nutty business about his birth certificate. People really had been brainwashed into believing Barack Obama was some Manchurian candidate planning to betray America.

Mark Levin was the first to go on the radio and spout off this crazy nonsense. It got him ratings, so eventually he dragged

Hannity and Rush to Looneyville along with him. My longtime friend Roger Ailes, the head of Fox News, was not immune to this. He got swept into the conspiracies and the paranoia and became an almost unrecognizable figure.

I once met him in New York during the Obama years to plead with him to put a leash on some of the crazies he was putting on the air. It was making my job trying to accomplish anything conservative that much harder. Roger went on and on about Benghazi, which he thought was part of a grand conspiracy that led back to Hillary Clinton. Then he outlined elaborate plots by which George Soros and the Clintons and Obama (and whoever else came to mind) were trying to destroy him.

"They're monitoring me," he assured me about the Obama White House. He told me he had a "safe room" built so he couldn't be spied on. His mansion was being protected by combat-ready security personnel, he said. There was a lot of conspiratorial talk.

And it was clear that he believed all of this crazy stuff. I walked out of that meeting in a daze. I just didn't believe the entire federal government was so terrified of Roger Ailes that they'd break about a dozen laws to bring him down. I thought I could get him to control the crazies, and instead I found myself talking to the president of the club. One of us was crazy. Maybe it was me.

Another person in that world was a golfing buddy of mine named Donald Trump. Trump has had a longtime habit of talking about this conspiracy or that conspiracy, and he really seems to believe in at least some. He spent money to send people to Hawaii to investigate Obama's citizenship. That's how I knew he believed there was something to it. Because there was no way Donald Trump ever spent a dime on anything unless he was serious about it. He was not the kind of guy to throw around money unnecessarily.

In January 2011, as the new Republican House majority was settling in and I was getting adjusted to the Speakership, I was asked about the birth certificate business by Brian Williams of NBC News. My answer was simple: "The state of Hawaii has said that President Obama was born there. That's good enough for me."

It was a simple statement of fact. But you would have thought I'd called Ronald Reagan a communist. I got all kinds of shit for it—emails, letters, phone calls. It went on for a couple weeks. I knew we would hear from some of the crazies, but I was surprised at just how many there really were.

All of this crap swirling around was going to make it tough for me to cut any deals with Obama as the new House Speaker. Of course, it has to be said that Obama didn't help himself much either. He could come off as lecturing and haughty. He still wasn't making Republican outreach a priority. But on the other hand—how do you find common cause with people who think you are a secret Kenyan Muslim traitor to America?

Still, my job as Speaker wasn't to just sit around in an elegant chair all day, smoking cigarettes and planning my Fox News contract. I had an obligation to try to get something going on issues I cared about. And so I tried with Obama yet another time.

Ever since I'd been in Congress, and long before, a major conservative priority has been reducing both government spending and the national debt. We shouldn't be spending more taxpayer dollars than we brought in. This is a pretty clear consensus among the Republican Party.

Of course, like any Republican "consensus," this one was turned on its head by the far-right knuckleheads that came to

Congress radicalized by blind Obama hatred. Most of these types wouldn't really support a balanced budget plan if I put one up for a vote, because that would be backing "leadership," the number-two enemy after Obama. Those chickenshits would have run a hundred miles an hour in the opposite direction. They didn't really want to cut spending. They didn't want Washington to work. They wanted chaos. And they wanted to go on TV complaining about spending without actually solving the problem, and then watch the money from outraged viewers flow into their own fundraising coffers.

Meanwhile the country would still be stuck under crippling debt. It was tragic more recently to watch the Republican Trump administration abandon the debt crisis altogether, with many Republicans in Congress following their lead. By May of 2020, the Trump administration had added more than $5 trillion to the national debt. Not all of that was his fault—some of it was due to the stimulus package needed to fight COVID-19. But Trump had been running up the debt well before the pandemic hit. The point is, we will be buried under red ink as far as the eye can see.

That makes it even harder to remember that we had a real shot at fixing this back in 2011. I was serious about rescuing our kids and grandkids from being crushed under the weight of the national debt. I still am. And I thought, with a new Republican majority in the House, I might just be able to make a deal with a president who claimed to be interested in bipartisan cooperation.

Barack Obama ran for president by promising to be everything George W. Bush wasn't, but golf was one thing they had in common. When he took office in 2009, I was the House minority leader. As soon as President Obama arrived, there was chatter around town about him inviting me to a "get to know you" round. Eventually the chatter made it into the press. But 2009 came and went without an invite from the White House to play golf. I guess playing nice with Republicans took a back seat to passing the Affordable Care Act legislation on a party-line vote. And 2010 went by without an invite, too, but when Republicans took back the House that fall and they knew I was going to become Speaker, the talk started up again in a big way.

The president and I spent the first months of my Speakership publicly going after each other, but finally in late May of 2011, my office got the call from the White House. The president wanted to schedule a round for Father's Day weekend. That was fine with me. After the official scheduling work between our offices, I got a follow-up call from President Obama himself. "I've invited Biden," he told me. "Bring somebody."

*Shit.* He wanted a full foursome. That meant he was taking this seriously. The political and optical stakes of this game were high enough. But I knew Obama and Biden were both good golfers and I did *not* want to lose. But who was I going to bring?

I mulled this over as I headed back to Ohio for a fundraiser, an annual event put on by a major Columbus utility company. The night before the event itself, the news leaked out that Obama had invited me to play golf. They even included the detail that Obama was bringing Biden, but my partner had not yet been named. When I arrived for the fundraiser, who did I see right away but my old friend Jack Nicklaus, Ohio's own "Golden Bear" and one of the best professional golfers ever. It seemed like fate. But I also noticed he had a stricken look on his face as soon as he saw me.

Naturally, everyone else at the event started teasing us about playing golf together against the president and the vice president. Jack said *nothing*, and faced it all with a frozen smile. Finally, when we had a quiet moment he said, "Boehner, I need to talk to you," and took me aside. We found a secluded corner.

"Listen, man," he said urgently, "I'd go anywhere in the world to play golf with you. You want me to help raise some money? That's fine, just say the word. But please, do not ask me to play golf with you against the president." I admit, the thought *had* crossed my mind. But Jack was crystal clear, so I just said "Yes, sir" and that's all there was to it. He wanted to stay well away from the political spotlight, which I could understand.

But being back in Ohio gave me another idea: *How about I invite John Kasich?* Kasich and I had been friends for a long time, and he was then serving as Ohio's governor. When I say we'd been friends for a long time, I mean a *long* time. And you know how you have some friends that are always easy and fun to be around? Then you've got *other* friends—the kind who require some effort on your behalf because they can get wound up a little tight. Well, John Kasich requires more effort than all of my other friends put together. But I still love the guy.

I called Kasich and he was excited to be part of it. The news that I was bringing a moderate Republican governor of a swing state went over well, too. We made plans for him to fly to DC the evening before the match, and we would meet for dinner at the home of some mutual friends, Bruce and Joyce Gates, in northern Virginia. Kasich showed up with the Ohio state policeman who travels with him everywhere, and I could already tell this was going to take some effort. John Kasich would have a hard time relaxing on a beach with a cocktail and a massage. But this time, I knew he was wound *really* tight. He didn't want to make a fool of himself before the president, vice president, and the global press corps.

"John," I told him over dinner, "calm down, for God's sakes. They're going to be a hell of a lot more nervous than we are."

I seemed to be getting somewhere with that.

"We can play golf, they can play golf," I assured him. "It's just a game!" By the time we left, he seemed to have calmed down somewhat.

Apparently it didn't last long. By the time my SUV picked him up at his hotel the next morning, he was a basket case yet again. He was jittery the whole ride over.

"Listen," I said, "I told you, they're going to be a lot more nervous than we are. I guarantee you Biden's been out there for an hour hitting balls. I *guarantee* it." Biden, I knew, did not want to be the anchor on President Obama's golf game. Sure enough, we pulled up at the course and the first thing we noticed was that Biden's shirt was wet. So were his socks. He'd been out there just pounding away in the heat for at least an hour. Yet again, I could see the relief come over Kasich's face.

When President Obama arrived, they brought the carts over and we got ready to go putt a few before teeing off. I got ready to go with Kasich, but before we got in, the president said: "Alright, Boehner, you and I are going to take these two guys on." I looked over at Kasich—this whole time we had assumed it would be the two of us playing against Obama and Biden! Kasich did not adapt quickly to a change of plans. I thought he was going to start crying right there on the spot. Somehow, he kept it together.

So I rode with the president to go putt a few, and while we were in the cart I leaned over to him and said, "Mr. President, let's just keep this about golf, alright?" And President Obama agreed. Well . . . that wasn't quite how things turned out.

We teed off in front of the press—a huge gathering of them had come out to see this—and off we went. Since it was

Father's Day, that meant it was the Saturday of the U.S. Open, being held just on the other side of DC at the Congressional Country Club. They broke into coverage of the pros at the U.S. Open to air footage of four amateurs—the president, the vice president, the governor of Ohio and the Speaker of the House—sweating it out on the course at Joint Base Andrews.

It was a good day out. The president had the highest handicap of all of us at 18. Kasich and I both played at nine. Biden . . . well, Biden told us he was a seven, but I wasn't so sure. President Obama and I won, beating them handily on the last two holes to get the match. We bet a grand total of $2, and I have a picture of Biden handing me the two bills. There was no way I was going to give Kasich the embarrassment of handing them over.

Obama may have had the highest handicap, but I think he worked harder than any of us out there. His approach to golf was very focused—he stared down every shot with an intense gaze. I figured it was this same intense focus that was able to propel somebody through the academic rigor of Columbia and Harvard Law, then shoot up the rungs of the Democrat ladder and win a presidential campaign after just a few years in the Senate. As I saw how carefully and critically he approached the strategic side of the game, not to mention how relatively well we got along playing together, an idea started to take hold.

By the time we got back to the clubhouse, I knew how I was going to end this day. We shook hands with the current and retired servicemembers at the base clubhouse and then the four of us had some time to ourselves before everyone went home. I turned to the president. The day wasn't just about golf anymore.

The debt ceiling was due to expire in a month and a half, at the end of July. I had made clear to him before that I was not going to raise the debt ceiling without doing something about the out-of-control spending and debt problems the country was facing. I had been working on him in the weeks before, trying to convince him that big things could be done, big things *had* been done in our nation's history when there was bipartisan will behind them.

After President Obama and I worked together to beat Biden and Kasich, I thought maybe we could work together to get the country's finances in order. "I think you and I can get something done," I said to him. "But it's going to have to be you and I, or we'll never make it work."

The president responded positively, and wanted to set up a meeting. Staff work would be necessary, of course, but we had to have absolute trust and absolute good faith between the two of us if anything was going to move forward. When we left Andrews that day, I firmly believed I had that.

But soon the problems started. Right as our conversations kicked off, they ended up getting leaked to the press. And it came from "my side"—the House majority leader, Eric Cantor, had some staffers who were upset that they weren't involved in the discussions, and so out came the leaks—drip, drip, drip.

I tried to talk with Eric about this personally. He had two major concerns: he thought I was putting myself out on a limb, and he was upset that he wasn't in the loop himself. I could understand both of these. For one thing, I *was* putting myself out on a limb. I knew that. But I thought this effort was worth it. And for that reason I wanted to deal with President Obama myself, man to man. So there was no "loop" for Eric or anyone else to be in. You can't really have a loop when it's just two people involved—there are only two points.

Naturally I had to meet with Obama in secret. We'd drive up the south drive and I'd get dropped off at the diplomatic receiving door. If I'd been filmed coming out the main entrance of the White House, the right-wing news would have decided I was selling out yet again. Maybe they'd start questioning my place of birth. Plus, Obama had his own problems with the left-wing crowd who thought he wasn't radical enough for them. I kept thinking—how on earth did we get to this point in our country?

We kept the teams for the discussion pretty small. With me in the meetings were Barry Jackson, my chief of staff, and my top policy advisor, Brett Loper. On Obama's side, it was usually his chief of staff Bill Daley and White House Legislative Affairs director Rob Nabors, along with the administration's top economic guys like Treasury secretary Tim Geithner and OMB director Jack Lew. My goal was to get government spending down and get a long-term fix for the entitlement programs that were running out of money. As the Baby Boomers (like me) got ready to retire, the Medicare and Social Security funds would dry up even faster. I didn't want to kick the can down the road yet again and drop this problem in the next generation's lap.

Of course, to get there, we would have to make sacrifices. In any good deal, everybody has to give up something they want. For us on the conservative side, that meant revenue—taxes. The Obama administration wanted more revenue coming in, and it was up to us to find ways to get there that didn't put the hurt on average American taxpayers.

All of us in those meetings understood the bigger issues, so we didn't waste time lecturing each other on the power of the free market versus the power of government. We all knew where the other was coming from. So we spent most of our time haggling over what was actually possible in order to reach a real compromise. For instance, the White House wanted the debt limit raised immediately by $1.6 trillion, but we got them down to $1.2. They wanted a minimum of $800 billion in new revenue, but we got them to make that the maximum. They agreed to spending cuts, but wanted to earmark some of the money saved for unemployment benefits—hardly a conservative priority, but in the spirit of compromise, I went along with it. And so we went back and forth for about five weeks.

There were lighter moments, too. There was that warm summer Sunday night, July 3, 2011, and we were outside the West Wing taking a break. Obama was drinking iced tea and chomping on Nicorette gum. No matter how stressful things got, he never once asked to bum a cigarette. My theory was he was afraid of what his wife would say. But she couldn't stop him from giving my pack of Camels longing looks.

The last meeting at the White House was Sunday, July 17. I'd brought Eric with me this time, and he brought some of his top staffers. I knew it was important, as we reached the end stages of the agreement, that Cantor be brought in to feel some ownership of the deal. We would need him to sell the proposal to our members. A deal was very, very close, and I didn't want to take any chances.

All in all, the framework for the deal we came up with was highly favorable for Republicans, and for the American people. In order to raise the debt ceiling, a Democratic administration had agreed to give up $1.2 trillion in government spending. They would get a smaller amount, $800 billion, in revenue. But there were key components of tax reform worked into the deal that would give taxpayers a break in the long run. We would simplify the tax code to make just three tax brackets, with a top tax rate of no more than 35 percent and a reduction in the corporate tax rate, too.

After Cantor, our staffers, and I spent the morning going over the details with the White House aides, President Obama himself came back from church and asked to speak to Cantor and me alone. We talked about how tough this would be to sell to our respective parties, and that we would need each other's help in getting the votes to get it done. Obama understood the challenges, but he was confident. He reassured me personally, taking me by the arm and saying: "I have great confidence in my ability to sway the American people." Well, that was enough for me. Good faith was good faith. At the end of that meeting, we shook hands, and I thought the deal was done.

Then came a giant wrench flying right into the gears from the other side of the Capitol. Two days after our final White House meeting, a group of senators calling themselves the "Gang of Six," which included my buddy Saxby Chambliss from Georgia, released their own debt reduction plan with a big to-do. And the Republicans in that group had given up more money in revenue increases—over $1 trillion—than the $800 billion I'd dragged Obama into agreeing to. The president was positive about this new development. "The framework is broadly consistent with what we've been working on here in the White House," he told the media, "and with the presentations that I've made to the leadership when they've come over here." Well, it was a little different than the discussions he'd had with me.

I still expected him to stick to our agreement. After all, we had shaken on it. But with the senators now putting more revenue on the table, the opportunity for new leverage was apparently too good to pass up. A couple days after the Gang of Six bombshell, President Obama called me up to alter the deal. He wanted $400 billion more in revenue.

"Mr. President," I told him, "we've been having the conversation for a month now, and you know there isn't a dime more on the table."

But he was insistent. "I've got to have $400 billion more," he repeated, several times.

"Mr. President, that's just not going to happen," I said.

We went back and forth on this for a few minutes, and President Obama kept asking me to "think about it." I finally said that I would, and we hung up. But there wasn't much to think about. It would have been hard enough to get Republican votes for the limited revenue increases in the deal as it was. I knew we were going to have to get Democrat votes to help it pass, and I expected the White House legislative operation to deliver those—helped along by the president's personal promise to "sway the American people." But adding more revenue on top of that would have made it impossible to get enough Republicans on board. So the deal was basically dead. That handshake on Sunday seemed a hundred years ago.

To this day, I still don't understand why Obama chose to make a last-minute alteration to the deal I thought was done. I know he was under pressure from his base, and I sure as hell was under pressure from mine. But I had made my peace with the possibility that this deal could be the end of my Speakership. I knew it would piss off enough shortsighted Republicans that they just might be able to get together and boot me from office if it passed. And if our deal *had* passed, fixing these constant problems before our kids and grandkids had to deal with them, I wouldn't have minded losing my job over it. Not one bit. I remember telling one journalist that the House Republicans could have thrown me out of office the day after this deal passed, and I'd still be the happiest man in the world. We had everything agreed, and we could have got the package through Congress—with plenty of Democrat votes, sure—and onto Obama's desk.

In the end, it didn't work out that way. I couldn't dwell

on it though. There were plenty of other fights ahead. But there was one, shall we say, "distinctive" consolation prize that came out of the whole thing.

When you shoot a Cape buffalo in parts of Africa, the locals who butcher it will also eat the testicles, which they consider a prime delicacy. Then they present the leftover scrotum to whoever brought the bull down. This is what happened to my friend Jim, who kept the leathery sack encased on his desk. Until, that is, he sent it to me, as a gift after I went toe-to-toe with the president. Apparently, he thought to himself, "Boehner's got bigger balls than I do."

I wasn't going to argue.

# SIX

# Mayor of Crazytown

A lot of people sling around ideas to "fix Washington," and most of them are bullshit. But there's at least one thing that every single American citizen, no matter where they live, can do to help set things right in the nation's capital. You can vote to send people there to represent you who actually want to get things done instead of hucksters making pie-in-the-sky promises or legislative terrorists just looking to go to Washington and blow everything up.

Pick an issue you care about. It doesn't really matter what it is. Whether it's the economy, or healthcare, or immigration, or national security, no meaningful progress will ever be made unless we elect serious people who truly want to make that progress. Some may say that's surrender, and that if we just elect enough people to office who think like us, eventually we'll be able to do everything our way. Well, if you think like that, chances are you're part of the problem.

As polarized as this country is, there are plenty of hard-liners on both sides, from the Jim Jordans on the right to the Alexandria Ocasio-Cortezes on the left. And the reason the House of Representatives has been swinging back and forth between Democratic and Republican control in recent years is because the key to getting a majority lies in a few dozen "swing districts." So no, we are not going to see some massive Republican or Democratic majority storm into Congress ready to usher in a conservative or liberal utopia anytime soon. And that means whoever is in charge is still going to have to find common ground with the other side to get things done. I always tried to remember that "common ground" and "compromise" were very different things. You can find common ground with others without having to compromise your own beliefs. That's how you actually get things done.

I get it. It's fun to vote out of anger—"Let's send this clown to that capital with a pack of matches and some gasoline"—but it's also dangerous. There are people we are electing who will destroy this country if we aren't careful. It doesn't matter whether they call themselves "conservatives" or "progressives." Many of them are actually neither.

Trust me, I know. I worked with a lot of these people, and fought them plenty. Sometimes they were just annoying, but sometimes they were downright destructive. Lots of people think that they only started showing up in Congress in 2010, products of the "Tea Party"—a so-called grassroots conservative movement (more like a payday for Washington fundraisers, but more on that later). Anyway, these folks were around for years before. They'd already come damn near close to destroying the American economy. They thought it would be fun to play kamikaze pilot in a plane in which our economic growth—including your job and wages, as well as those of your family—was strapped in the backseat.

It's one hell of a scary story.

You may recall that in 2008, when George W. Bush was in his final year as president, America experienced the worst financial crisis since the Great Depression. There were a lot of reasons for this, which I could get into, but plenty of others have already done that. The point is that many major American companies along with our entire banking system were on the verge of collapse. As the House Republican leader, I was one of the first in Congress who was clued in early on to what was happening. I got updates directly from Treasury secretary Hank Paulson and Ben Bernanke, the chairman of the Federal Reserve. I'll never forget the scene as long as I live. Paulson was telling us we were facing a worldwide depression. Meanwhile, as he was talking, I kept glancing over at Bernanke. His lips were trembling. That's when I knew this was a major deal. You don't often get to see well-heeled Wall Street types shaking in their boots.

What the administration wanted from Congress was a massive bailout bill. The price tag was monumental—$700 billion—to bail out some of these banks. And that was just for starters. The Treasury secretary was in effect asking for a fat blank check to do pretty much whatever he wanted with the money.

I knew my people in the House. This wasn't going to smell right to them and, to be honest, I wasn't very excited about it either. I was one of the biggest evangelists for fiscal discipline there was. I'd been fighting for a smaller, less costly, more accountable federal government for years, alongside many of them. Republicans, generally speaking, didn't do bailouts of failing industries, and certainly not with that kind of price tag.

But President Bush was determined. He didn't want to be this generation's Herbert Hoover, and who could blame him? Paulson and Bernanke were scaring the hell out of all of us, talking about people going to ATMs and not being able to get money and major companies shutting their doors. Nancy

Pelosi, who was then the Speaker, seemed like she could get her people in line, as usual. So did Senators Harry Reid and Mitch McConnell. Those two guys always seemed to have the numbers they needed. Now it was all up to me—and that was just great. These guys had no clue what kind of clown car I was trying to drive on the Republican side of the House.

This plan was going to be DOA on our side of the Capitol, and I knew it. But I still had to give it a try. So I made the case to the Republican members and of course got it all thrown back into my face. Some of them said bluntly that if companies and banks are failing because of their own dumb mistakes, we should let them. Others didn't like just giving Paulson—a Wall Street guy before he came to Treasury—a ton of money for him to kick back to his old Wall Street pals.

Frankly, I could see the logic in these arguments, and I said so. I shared their hang-ups, and in a normal situation I'd probably have been on the same side. But we were not facing any normal situation. This was a full-blown crisis, and it was only going to get worse if we didn't act. I kept trying to conjure all the images from the last Great Depression—a run on the banks, people not being able to buy food, all these companies going out of business—and trying to make clear that instead of this happening to people in old black-and-white newsreels, this would be happening to their constituents back home.

It's unusual for such a divide to exist between the member of one party sitting in the White House and the members of the same party in Congress. But by this point in his administration, my friend George Bush had pretty much lost all credibility with conservatives, who hated his view on immigration, and the rest of the country, who were tired of the war in Iraq. I remembered fighting hard with him to get education reform past many of these same cranks back when he first came to office.

So much had happened since then, and now he was in a tough spot. I really felt for the guy. Every time he went out to speak about the urgent need to address the financial crisis, the stock market plummeted by hundreds of points. They even sent Dick Cheney over to the House to try to talk people into supporting the relief plan. A former Republican Conference chair who made it all the way to the vice presidency, Cheney had conservative credibility that nobody could question. But the members still weren't buying it.

Then almost out of nowhere, Senator John McCain decided to pop in. This was the last thing anyone needed—including, as it turned out, John himself. McCain was, at this point, our party's nominee for president. He was in a tough race against his fellow senator, Barack Obama, and had been spending most of his time away from Washington and out on the campaign trail looking for votes. That is where he should have stayed.

I loved John McCain. He was a war hero, a tough SOB, and funny as hell. But he was never a favorite among the far-right crazies. They remembered his support of immigration reform and cooperation with Democrats on a few too many issues for their liking. He'd been too much of a maverick—to use his own word. Plenty of people in the party had less charitable words to describe him. But John didn't care. When you'd been where he'd been and seen what he'd seen, petty insults and political bullshit couldn't faze you.

Still, the man wanted to be president of the United States, and he was a skilled politician. He knew that in order to win he had to energize the conservative base. And so he picked one of the chief crazies as his running mate—an Alaska governor no one had ever heard of named Sarah Palin. I had met her some time earlier with some other members. Nobody had come away exactly impressed by her deep knowledge of government. A few of the other members had commented on her looks. But she did energize the base—which may or may not have been a good thing.

I'd never figured John as an expert on economics. National security was more his ballpark. But that didn't stop him from announcing he was "suspending" his presidential campaign—whatever that meant—to come to Washington at once to help deal with the financial crisis. It was a dramatic move and got a lot of attention. I guess it was meant to show that he was a leader who put the country ahead of his own interests. At least, I figured, he was going to come to DC with some kind of plan. Republicans in the House may not have liked him all that much, but he was going to be on the top of the ticket that fall. Most of them would probably get in line with whatever he was going to propose, if only because it might impact their own elections. And believe me, if anyone else wanted to take charge of the asylum for a while and give me a break, they were welcome to the keys.

So I was a little surprised when John, freshly arrived from the campaign trail, walked into the middle of my Daily Management Meeting on the day we were due to go to a meeting with congressional Democrats at the White House. He walked in, plopped down on the couch, and looked at me. He was alone, as far as I could see, and he wasn't holding a folder that said "Miracle Solution" on it. As a matter of fact, he wasn't carrying anything. Maybe he had it all in his head.

"So what's the plan for today, John?" I asked him.

"That's why I'm here," McCain replied. "What's the plan?"

*What's the plan? Is that what he just asked me?*

At first I thought he must have meant the logistics—when we were supposed to be at the White House, who else was going, and so on. He couldn't have meant what it looked like he meant. So I clarified: "What do you plan on saying at the White House today?"

"I don't know," he said. I tried to keep my mouth from flopping open. "What do you think I should say?"

Now I was a little troubled. If I'd had a cigarette in my mouth, I might have swallowed it. "Where are your staff?"

"I don't have any staff with me."

Oh Lord. Now it was clear: there wasn't anybody who was going to get us out of this mess. No cavalry was coming. And though I didn't think it was possible, the mess had somehow gotten worse. When I woke up that day, all I had to do was turn around a stubborn Republican Conference, cut a deal with the Democrats they hated, help save our economy, and stop a global depression. Now I had to find some way to help the nominee of our party look like he knew what he was doing. And it was still morning.

I turned to Mike Sommers, my top policy staffer. "You're staffing McCain today," I said, and Sommers nodded.

Later we all headed over to the White House to meet with President Bush and the House and Senate leaders from both parties. The Democrats brought their own last-minute addition to the party—the junior senator from Illinois, Barack Obama. The Democratic presidential nominee decided that if McCain was going to get in on this action, he ought to be there too. The whole thing was a disaster from start to finish.

The Republicans showed up early to meet with President Bush and strategize for the bigger bipartisan showdown. I'm using the term "strategize" loosely. As I've said, George W. Bush was—and still is—a friend of mine. I like him and respect him. But sometimes even a friend, even a president, can tick you off. One thing you have to understand about Bush is that he likes to dig at you when he senses you are vulnerable about something. And he knew I was having a hell of a time corralling Republican votes. So he started to complain that I couldn't get it done and went after me in front of all these other guys in the room.

I had seen this needling from him before. Guys do it all the time. It's usually not a big deal. But at that moment we had the national and probably the world economy hanging in the balance, and he *still* wanted to trot out this frat-house trash-talking bullshit. Nobody had time for that. So I admit, I snapped. Looking at Paulson, who kept telling House Republicans to give him a blank check, I said something like, "Mr. President, if Paulson had any fucking ears, we wouldn't be in this position."

That pissed off Paulson, understandably. Let's just say tempers were frayed. So Bush wisely decided our pregame meeting had come to an end.

Now it was time to meet with the Democrats. And they were coaching their MVP from the beginning. Senator Obama was front and center. I saw him huddling before our meeting in the Cabinet Room with Pelosi and Reid, scheming about how this was all going to go down. I felt for John McCain. He wanted to do something to help. He wanted to show leadership. He truly was the kind of a guy who tried to put country before party. But, as I said, he would've been better off out on the campaign trail. As we took our seats, I sat next to McCain and told him to keep quiet. As far as I was concerned, the less he said about this mess, the better. He wasn't going to fix it anyway. No single politician could.

But apparently nobody told Obama to keep quiet. He led off for the Democrat side and sounded, at least, like he knew what he was talking about. Bush decided he had no choice but to call on McCain to go next, and did so. But our nominee just shook his head and said, "I'll wait my turn."

I don't know why he did that. Maybe he thought Obama looked arrogant speaking for the Democrats, and wanted to set a better example himself by deferring to the more senior lawmakers in the room. That may have been noble, but it didn't exactly show a take-charge attitude from the guy who had suspended his campaign to come back to Washington and figure this out.

So I started talking, in part to help John, and started going over what we would need to do in order to deliver enough votes from House Republicans for the relief package. Other people started to chime in about the House situation, and it looked like we might be getting somewhere, when all of a sudden Obama pipes up again. Probably sensing McCain's discomfort, he said, "I'd like to hear what McCain has to say."

Uh-oh. In just a moment this had gone from a discussion on how to save the world economy to a political pissing match. Obama knew exactly what he was doing.

McCain stepped up to the plate and tossed out a word salad positive-sounding generalizations that might have sounded good to people who weren't really following along, but didn't have much actual substance. Unfortunately, everyone in the room was following along closely. I saw Obama sort of smile. I think he knew at that moment he'd won the election. I think John knew he'd lost it.

Even President Bush, whose relationship with McCain after their nasty 2000 primary battle had thawed but wasn't exactly warm, seemed confused by the current nominee's contribution to the meeting. "What the hell was that all about?" he asked me afterward.

I've heard since that it was bad staff work on McCain's campaign team that pushed him to suspend his campaign and left him unprepared to discuss the nuts and bolts of the looming crisis. It was his top political hands who wanted him to make the grand gesture of suspending his campaign to hopefully grab some good headlines. At the same time, these same political aides had frozen the campaign's top economic advisor out of key meetings, leaving the candidate without the critical information he needed to make a plan after announcing the suspension.

In any event, McCain took a risk in suspending his campaign, and while that action may have helped him capture a news cycle, he didn't have a plan to follow through. We saw that in the White House meeting, and unfortunately the American people saw it too. Never make a move without knowing your next one. John and I were friends until he died, but I don't think he was ever quite the same after his loss in 2008.

Things only got worse for me as I tried to rally Republicans in my Conference to salvage our economy. McCain's efforts hadn't helped anything. His endorsement of the bailout bill—which became known as the Troubled Asset Relief Program, or TARP—moved few votes. The vast majority of Republicans voted against the bill when it came up for a vote. One congressman, Michigan's Fred Upton, started updating us on the collapse of the Dow Jones Industrial Average as the vote looked doomed to failure. It was dropping by one hundred points, then three hundred, then five hundred. I said a prayer. I truly feared our economy was going to move to a very dark place, and there was little I could do but let it happen. Too many Republicans in Congress cared more about what Sean

Hannity thought than the secretary of the Treasury or the Speaker of the House or the president of the United States. They were ready to destroy the economy for decades rather than come up with any realistic alternatives—just as long as it looked as if they were standing up to the "establishment." We were, to put it bluntly, screwed.

Some of the more reasonable members were panicked. But the nuts were even more emboldened. They were proud to send this bill to its death, and they didn't give a shit if the economy collapsed. Various outside groups—such as the so-called Senate Conservatives Fund, headed by Jim DeMint—egged them on. This was all being done in the name of conservative purity, they claimed, so that we could finally elect real, honest-to-goodness defenders of fiscal discipline and a balanced budget. That was supposedly what the Tea Party movement was all about.

But I knew the truth. It was a story I would see played out over and over again in the next few years. It wasn't about any so-called principles—it was about chaos. But it was chaos that developed in a predictable pattern: the far-right knuckleheads would refuse to back the House leadership no matter what, but because they were "insurgents" they never had the responsibility of trying to actually fix things themselves. So they got to "burn it all down" and screw up the legislative process, which of course allowed them to continue to complain loudly about how Washington's spending problem never got solved. That kept their favorite straw man alive to take more hits. And every time they punched him, they got another invitation to go on Fox News or talk radio, or they got another check from their friends in outside groups like DeMint's outfit. It was their own little private stimulus plan.

Now they were willing to let every business in America

collapse, every bank fail, ATMs stop working, just so they could pretend to be budget cutters. It was pathetic. It was irresponsible. But it was only the beginning.

We ultimately did scrape together a sufficient number of sane Republicans to side with a sufficient number of sane Democrats and pass a bill. Things leveled off. The crisis passed. But none of the so-called conservatives who were willing to blow up our economy ever paid any price. And they never acknowledged that the plan they vilified actually worked. In fact, TARP turned out to be one of the more successful economic measures ever passed by Congress. All of the money spent was paid back, with interest, by the companies we saved from collapse. Not to mention, it stopped another Great Depression across the world. But none of that mattered to people who had already decided that everyone in Washington was corrupt, that their leaders were liars, and that the system was rigged against them.

All this happened under a Republican president, George W. Bush, who had once been praised as the most conservative president since Reagan. Now he's generally considered a liberal sellout failure by many of these same people who glommed onto Trump, who, as I've mentioned, ballooned the national debt. Things got even worse, as noted, when Barack Obama—immediately identified by this crowd as a mysterious closet-Muslim who wasn't born in America—came to power.

I was living in Crazytown now. And when I took the Speaker's gavel in 2011, two years into the Obama presidency, I became its mayor. Crazytown was populated by jackasses, and media hounds, and some normal citizens as baffled as I was about how we got trapped inside the city walls. Every second of every day since Barack Obama became president I was fighting one batshit idea after another. The first one, as I mentioned, was that Obama wasn't a citizen. Then I couldn't even play golf with the guy without looking like Public Enemy Number One.

I tried not to let craziness and personal attacks against the president get in the way. I knew we had serious work to do. We'd campaigned to take back the House in 2010 by asking the American people a simple question: "Where are the jobs?" Between Obamacare and weak economic growth, there weren't many, and Americans deserved better. I wanted to do my damnedest to help create the conditions that would let businesses create more jobs and put more Americans back to work. That's what I vowed to do from the moment I took the Speaker's gavel.

I'll never forget the moment Nancy Pelosi passed me that huge oversized gavel we were using for the ceremony. That gavel had been made for me by a woodworker buddy back in Ohio, Dick Slagle, after I'd won the Conference election to be Speaker. The recess before I was sworn in, I got together with some friends—Pete Dobrozsi, Tom Hazelbaker, and Dick—for breakfast at the Bob Evans in West Chester, and they presented me with this gavel. It looked oversized then, but by the time I was taking it from Nancy Pelosi at the podium, it seemed to have grown ten times bigger. But Dick made a fine piece of woodwork.

So I was standing up there with this gigantic gavel and I was supposed to make a speech, but there, sitting in the front row, I caught sight of my three best buddies—Richard Burr, Saxby Chambliss, and Tom Latham—all sitting together. We'd been friends since our early days in Congress, and there they were, Burr and Chambliss having come over from the Senate to wish me well. That was it. The waterworks opened. I had to go through a lot of tissues that day.

But then it was down to business. It was our job in the leadership to keep the conference focused on what we could actually do with our power—at that time Republicans controlled one-half of one-third of the government—to help as many Americans as possible. A big part of how we did that was helping our members do their job well, especially the new folks. And there were a lot of new members taking office in 2011.

One thing we consistently advised on was how to set up a good staff. Congressional staff usually get overlooked or sometimes even picked on, but they're the ones who keep America's representative government going. The average population of a congressional district in America in 2010 was 710,767 people, which is a lot for one person to handle on their own—or even a dozen people, which is about how big most congressional staffs are, give or take.

The top person in an office, right under the member, is the chief of staff, who makes sure everyone is doing their job and is usually the member's top advisor. The scheduler is the one who really keeps everyone—boss and staff—running on time. On the legislative side you have a legislative director and a few legislative assistants, who keep an eye on the House floor and handle certain policy issues for the boss. Then there is a communications director who writes everything from press releases to tweets. Legislative correspondents answer mail from the folks back home. And then the staff assistant and interns answer the phones and do what they can for everyone else, to try to gain experience. Most folks move up the same way. And in my experience, a member is only as good as the staff they have around them. That was something we tried to impart to every new member as they tried to get their offices set up: make sure you hire the best.

Of course, plenty of members have to do things their own

way, especially (as we noted early on) in the Class of 2010. Every once in a while one of the kooks would even argue that we should impeach the president, which I never took seriously for a single second, and, to their credit, neither did the vast majority of the Republican members. But every time we went up against the administration, I knew there was someone else in the Republican Conference who was looking at me and thinking they could do a better job running the show. They thought they would be smarter, tougher, more determined, and if only it was them in charge instead of that softy Boehner then we'd be able to roll over the Democrats like a bulldozer. So there were coup plots against me, but only occasionally. Much more constant were the leaks to the media.

I tried not to let things like this bother me too much, but it's still a kick to the gut when someone on your team actively throws a wrench in the gears. Rep. Eric Cantor of Virginia was the House majority leader when I was Speaker, and it was our job to work closely together with the rest of the leadership team to follow through on the promises of limited government the American people voted for when they helped Republicans take over the House in 2010.

Eric and I were about as different as you could imagine. For one thing, I was a blunt Rust Belt Yankee, and he was a smooth southern gentleman. But the two of us got along just fine. Some of our staffers never meshed, and the friction between them often came after somebody gave away details of internal House leadership discussions that had been kept private so that people weren't afraid to speak their minds. Those leaks almost always ended up making it harder for everybody involved.

But leaks ended up not being the worst thing Eric had to deal with. He and I had been through some bruising fights together, and I had worked hard to help get him ready to take over as the next Speaker, when out of nowhere, to everyone's surprise (especially his own), he lost in the 2014 Republican primary to a Tea Party radical. The House majority leader position was created in 1899, and in the 115 years since then, no sitting holder of that office had ever been booted in a primary. Cantor's Tea Party replacement, by the way, didn't last long—after just two terms, he lost in 2018 to a moderate Democrat, flipping the seat from red to blue. Cantor's loss was a waste, a good member and a good leader taken out of the House just when he was most needed.

Knocking off Cantor, of course, only emboldened the radicals to come after me. It was bizarre. I came to Congress as a conservative reformer, going after supposed pillars of "the Establishment"—like the private bank that let congressmen pass bad checks and the private restaurant that let them skip out on their tabs. I pushed for spending cuts and entitlement reforms when they were unpopular topics—when the "get along, go along" mentality prevailed. Now I was being denounced by the talk show circuit as if I were a hippie with flip flops and beads plotting a socialist takeover of America. I didn't get it—I hadn't changed. I was still the same guy, and still am today. But I didn't give a damn what anyone said about me if at least we could get something done. But that wasn't happening either.

The fight over immigration reform was a classic example from my time as Speaker. This was a major issue the parties had been arguing about for decades, and in 2013 a bipartisan group of senators dubbed the "Gang of Eight" came out with a major immigration bill that passed the Senate with bipartisan support and then got dumped in our laps in the House.

I knew that the Gang of Eight bill was dead on arrival at the House. And part of that had to do with certain House Republicans who had made a name for themselves as demagogues on the immigration issue. One of the worst was Steve King of Iowa, who famously said that young immigrants brought to the United States illegally as children had "calves the size of cantaloupes because they're hauling 75 pounds of marijuana across the desert."

It was an awful thing to say, and he got ripped for it, rightly. People would deliver actual cantaloupes to his office. I called him an asshole, and then sometime later he stopped me in a hallway and asked, very seriously, "Why did you call me an asshole?"

"Because you are," I said, and kept walking. He was, and probably still is—his constituents saw fit to get rid of him in a primary in June 2020.

While the Senate Gang of Eight was getting all the press attention on immigration, there was a bipartisan group of House members who had been working quietly for years trying to come up with our own immigration deal. And they'd come damn close. If they'd been literally standing on either side of a line, they would've only been about an inch apart. And I knew that if we wanted serious Democratic buy-in on the House plan, it didn't make sense to go talk to the Senate. I needed to go to the president. And I was convinced that two of the three areas of disagreement between Republicans and Democrats in the House immigration bill could be resolved in a one-hour meeting between President Obama and myself.

I had wanted to make an immigration reform deal for a long time, and I'd made that clear to Obama. This was a festering issue that wasn't going to solve itself, and it was stirring up some pretty nasty rancor. But I knew that the way to get it done wasn't with one giant bill but with five or six smaller ones. That was how to get it through the House. It would be a nightmare to try to get enough House members to agree to everything all at once, with so many facets, but if you broke the measures up, I thought, there would be a solid coalition of three hundred or so members—Republicans and Democrats—who would vote for each one. Maybe they all wouldn't vote for the same ones, but the votes would be there for each. You would still end up with "comprehensive" immigration reform, just in more digestible pieces.

I ended up getting stymied from both sides. I would say to Obama, "Mr. President, if you're serious about this, here are the things I would do and here are the things I would not do." And I'll be damned if he didn't always do the exact opposite of what I suggested. This was a different kind of interaction than when we would discuss economic issues. President Obama was a serious negotiator when it came to fiscal matters. But with immigration reform, I don't believe he was really interested in a solution. He just kept poisoning the well with things he knew we would never agree to. He would politicize everything to no end.

I'm not sure how to account for the difference in the President Obama who worked on serious fiscal deals with me and the President Obama who seemed to phone it in on immigration reform. Maybe he thought it was more politically advantageous to leave immigration unsolved so that Democrats could continue to campaign on it as a wedge issue. That might have been bad policy, but it could still be good politics. God knows there were plenty of Republicans who felt that way. I had to deal with them too.

The chairman of the House Judiciary Committee, which had jurisdiction over immigration, was Rep. Bob Goodlatte of Virginia, a friend of mine going back to the days when we served together on the Agriculture Committee. But Bob was very much a hard-liner on immigration, and he refused to budge from his hard-right position. Nothing would get him to move an inch toward compromise. I don't know whether it was his committee, his staff, his district, or just him. But he never moved. And I just couldn't drag him with one hand and President Obama with the other.

The failure of our Grand Bargain on spending and entitlement reform is my biggest regret from my time in Congress. In that case, though, everyone seemed to make their best, honest effort—at least until things fell apart at the very end when, I maintain, they really didn't have to. But my second biggest disappointment was seeing the unwillingness—in both parties—to seriously fix our immigration laws so that they actually work for real people. That was just stubbornness, plain and simple.

———◆———

Early on in this book, I talked about power. I thought it was important for any book that deals with Washington antics to make clear that power, especially in that city, doesn't stick around. As I've said, a dog that shits quick doesn't shit long. Nobody can hang on to power forever. And even if you look like you're in charge, new centers of power can pop up and destabilize everything.

For instance, when I became Speaker of the House, I got a fancy new office where I could make any rule I wanted. Finally, I could smoke in my office, and nobody could say shit. That was nice. I held an important constitutional position, and was second in line to the presidency. Big deal.

Under the new rules of Crazytown, I may have been Speaker, but I didn't hold all the power. By 2013 the chaos caucus in the House had built up their own power base thanks to fawning right-wing media and outrage-driven fundraising cash. And now they had a new head lunatic leading the way, who wasn't even a House member. There is nothing more dangerous than a reckless asshole who thinks he is smarter than everyone else. Ladies and gentlemen, meet Senator Ted Cruz.

Ted was one of those guys you meet who has all the answers. You know the kind of person I'm talking about. We've all met them—at work, in the neighborhood, on your rec league softball team. They've always got a solution for everything, they're very sure of themselves, and they're very calculating when it comes to making sure their pronouncements are followed.

I don't trust people like that, but they are out in force in Washington, DC. Time and again I've seen people get elected to office, and after 15 minutes they decide they know how to run the place better than those of us who scraped and scrapped our way to the top over decades by putting in the work. The capacity for politicians to snatch defeat from the jaws of victory, and do it happily, will never cease to amaze me. And it's hard to think of a better example of that than the 2013 government shutdown.

Since Obamacare had become law a few years earlier, Republicans had been working on a strategy to repeal and replace it. I had worked damn hard to keep the bill from passing, reminding my Democrat colleagues with strong language that there was no way they could claim their bill was written with the openness and transparency necessary for good government. "Hell no you can't," was how I believe I put it at the time. Once the bill passed and was signed into law, I campaigned damn hard to help elect more Republicans, take back the House, and work to get rid of it. And when we took back the majority in 2010, I promised to work damn hard to make good on that pledge and repeal it.

Easier said than done, of course. By 2013 the law was still

on the books, and a lot of people were understandably frustrated. Hell, imagine how frustrated I was. I wanted to rip up Obamacare more than anybody. But I also knew what our efforts were up against. Ted Cruz may have known what we were up against too, but like his knucklehead pals on the House side he had ginned up his voters with a black-and-white promise to get rid of it, come hell or high water. Well, that might sound good to people who are pissed off and, because they have real jobs and better things to do, don't pay that much attention to how Washington really works.

The dirty little secret of Obamacare was that parts of it were popular, especially protecting people with preexisting conditions from getting bounced off of their healthcare by some insurance company. The other little secret is that as hard as it is to pass a law like Obamacare in the first place, it can be just as hard or harder to repeal or "unpass" it. The way to do it is to dismantle key components bit by bit. And we were actually able to do that to Obamacare during our 2011–19 majority, not that Hannity and Levin and company gave us any credit. We got rid of provisions like the medical device tax to bring the burden on companies and individual Americans down to a more manageable level. And now, there really isn't much of Obamacare left.

But Cruz and his buddies didn't understand any of that. They didn't care. Ted Cruz didn't come up to veteran legislators who shared his priorities and ask our advice on how to get something like this done. He wanted it done in one fell swoop, and it was his way or the highway. And the rest of us, who opposed Obamacare but didn't kill it immediately, were just stupid or lazy or worse—traitors. We weren't as noble as he was (not that anyone could be). And he convinced a lot of the crazies in my House Republican Conference that this was true, so they followed him.

That brings us to the fall of 2013, when the federal government had to vote on whether to raise our debt ceiling—the amount of money the United States is allowed to borrow to keep the government functioning. I hated this vote. Anyone who cared about fiscal responsibility hated it. Nobody was proud of the fact that we had to keep voting to raise the ceiling because we couldn't control government spending. But not voting to raise the ceiling meant that government would stop running. The country wouldn't be able to pay its bills and would risk going into default on the money we owed. Over time that meant parks would close and essential services—getting out the mail, processing tax returns, paying the members of the military—would be imperiled. Government agencies would eventually run out of money.

That didn't seem to bother the crazy caucus (not that they realized that it was their constituents, along with everyone else, who would feel the pinch of a nonfunctioning government). So Ted Cruz and a couple of other accomplices came up with the idea to put a price tag on Republican support for raising the debt limit, which the Obama administration needed because we were the majority in the House. Their price tag was killing Obamacare. The strategy was to make the White House destroy their prized legacy legislative accomplishment in exchange for Republicans taking a routine vote to keep the government running.

This was a dumbass idea. Not that anybody asked me.

In the first place, it was bad messaging. The Obama administration was just starting to launch enrollment on the Obamacare healthcare exchanges, which was turning into a PR disaster. The website wasn't working right, it was confusing, and the Obama team looked like amateurs. It was the best unforced error we Republicans could have hoped for. But that was all going to be overlooked if Republicans decided to launch a stunt like this. The press had actually been covering problems with the Obamacare rollout because they were real news. But I knew, if given the choice between covering Democrats' screw-ups and Republicans' screw-ups, the press would shine the bigger light on Republicans any day of the week.

More practically, I also knew there was no way in hell President Obama would ever give in on his signature achievement just to appease Ted Cruz and the radicals. Obama was open to making deals, yes, but this wasn't a real deal. This was insanity. He would blame us for putting the economy in peril by refusing to vote for the debt limit, and the media would be only too happy to push that narrative. We'd end up looking like a bunch of fools.

It never made sense from the beginning. But Cruz, who was already stacking up "Cruz for President" yard signs in his garage, had started ginning up the Tea Party knuckleheads in July 2013. At least twice before everyone left town for the August recess, I had talked to our members to try to convince them that this was a bad idea. But Cruz and company took advantage of the recess to convince Republicans around the country that this suicide mission was the only way to get rid of Obamacare.

I tried to do the opposite. Like I did every August, I toured around the country in a bus, raising money for Republican members (and maybe playing some golf here and there along the way). That month I did two conference calls from the road, with as many members as we could muster, trying to convince them that this just wasn't going to work.

When the House came back into session after Labor Day, I kept at it. I tried talking to members informally, which had worked in the past on all kinds of issues, laying out to them in plain if salty English that this would just end up playing right into the hands of Nancy Pelosi and Harry Reid—not to mention the White House. They were all sitting on their sides of the Capitol and down Pennsylvania Avenue just waiting for us to step in a big pile of our own shit.

At our Conference meeting on September 9, in the basement of the Capitol, Cantor and I tried to put up a compromise plan. We would force votes in the House and in the Senate to strip Obamacare of its funding, but without hitching those votes to funding the government. Our House Republican majority would make its stand and force the Democrat-run Senate to make theirs, but without tying it to funding the rest of the government, we couldn't be blamed if the government shut down or ran out of money. Or at least it would be harder for the Democrats and the media to blame us. Suffice it to say, that plan was not well received by the members. I seem to recall there was booing.

It was then that I saw how far the chaos campaign had gone. When we got to the open-mic portion of the meeting, member after member, including some of the practical, down-to-earth folks I had known for years, were speaking in support of this fight. To have Tim Huelskamp from Kansas and Ted Yoho from Florida pushing for this was expected, but when guys like Chris Stewart from Utah joined in, as reasonable and levelheaded as they came, I knew this had truly become the will of the Conference. And as I've often said, a leader without followers is just a guy taking a walk.

I knew the crazies in my Conference. There was no talking to them. They were being urged on by the talk radio crowd and the cable news know-nothings. Many of them came from deep-red districts with no viable Democratic challenger, so there was no real pressure on them back home. Besides, their idols in the "upper chamber" like Ted Cruz and Mike Lee were telling them this was a genius move. Some House members have a bit of an inferiority complex when it comes to the Senate. Sometimes it can seem like the senators are the seniors in high school, and the House members are the juniors. When seniors give juniors the time of day, the juniors don't ask why, they just go along with it. I never bought into this, but I saw it a fair amount. A member is more likely to fall for this if they don't take the time to get to know and respect their own institution, the House of Representatives—which most of the crazies, as staunch "anti-institutionalists," did not.

And thus the great prophet Ted spoke unto the people and told them President Obama would cave. He'd show us all. At the very least, he and his acolytes promised, this would force the president to the table to give Republicans something to cut a deal. Of course, none of them had met Barack Obama for any length of time, or had ever tried to negotiate with him. As I said, he was open to making deals, but at the negotiating table he was the coolest customer God ever put on this earth. But that didn't matter. Ted Cruz knew everything and could outmaneuver Obama. Just wait and see.

Remember, Ted Cruz may have been the leader of this effort in Congress, but there were plenty of forces at work pushing him from outside. These would be the so-called conservative outside groups, and that was where the big payday came in. There was Jim DeMint's Senate Conservatives Fund. Another was FreedomWorks, which used to be headed by my old colleague Dick Armey until he quit after they went totally nuts. One of the worst was Heritage Action for America, an arm of the once-venerable Heritage Foundation. It was as if the respectable conservative scholars at Heritage had decided to set up a JV team of whiny campaign operatives and pay them to attack . . . other conservatives.

These groups knew how to do one thing well—raise money. And they loved to fundraise by attacking "the Establishment" (whatever that was) and the House leadership, which was me. We did our best to push back. I remember Jeb Hensarling, a conservative whose right-wing credentials were unquestionable, who had served in the leadership as Conference chair and was then chairing the Financial Services Committee, stood up dramatically in one of the member meetings and reminded everyone that nobody, not Heritage Action or anybody else, could tell them how to vote. Hensarling combined brains with Texas toughness, but even he couldn't sway the crazies.

So, finally, I was the one who caved. Sometimes you have to let people blow themselves up to make a point. Besides, I didn't really have much choice. I either had to strap the dynamite to them or to myself. OK, I said, I'll go along. At least they wouldn't be able to call me an Establishment asshole anymore. And sure enough, when I did come on board I was treated like a hero. I was finally a "true conservative," whatever that meant to them—never mind that I had been fighting for real conservative values in Congress while most of these clowns were still in law school. What kamikaze stunts like this had to do with conservatism, I never quite figured out, and I don't think they did either. I knew how this was going to end. We were on the *Titanic* playing chicken with an iceberg—and a loudmouthed jerk from Texas was at the helm, grinning like a damn fool, as the water started filling up the boat.

By September 18 I was committed to going along with this. And once I was committed, I made the case as forcefully as I could. To most outside observers, I looked like I was totally on board. I went on the talk shows. I held press conferences. No one could say—and to their credit, no one did say—I wasn't in this fight. The conservatives were beside themselves that

House Republicans were finally "united"—united in insanity, but sure, whatever. As dumb as I thought this was, I was the leader, and this was my job. And I went into the trenches every single day.

That meant going in front of the TV cameras pushing our cause. It meant coming up with proposals to try to get the Senate to negotiate. I was constantly in touch with President Obama and Harry Reid, trying to find some common ground, some fig leaf to get us out of this mess. Over the last two weeks of September we tried to make the deal more palatable to the Democrats. We walked back our demand to kill Obamacare entirely and instead tried to get them to delay its full rollout for a year—a request that wasn't *that* ridiculous considering the problems they'd already had with the exchange websites— plus get rid of the tax on medical devices, which was still on the books. No dice.

I still hoped that we could somehow avoid a shutdown. At the last minute, we offered to let the Democrats keep the medical device tax if they would hold off putting Obamacare in place for a year. I just needed some bone to throw to my members, some tiny scrap from the Democrats we could spin as a "win." But the Dems turned down every offer. Forget the fig leaves—Obama and Reid never even gave me a twig. Nothing, zero, nada. They knew they didn't have to. They knew that we were the ones who would get blamed, whatever happened. And of course, they were right. Bastards.

And by the way—what was Senator Cruz of Texas doing while I was scrambling around trying to keep the government running as September ran to a close? He was listening to himself hold forth during a 21-hour speech, which for some technical Senate reason couldn't be called a "filibuster." It was yet another stunt, during which he read the Dr. Seuss classic *Green*

*Eggs and Ham* on the Senate floor. But you can't govern by stunt, and eventually we couldn't govern at all. The government shut down on October 1.

The meetings went on, as did our attempts to make our case in front of the TV cameras. Our serious members and those dedicated staff who had been declared "essential"—other federal employees had been furloughed—still came to work to diligently try to negotiate a way out of this. The crazies were desperate to get something, anything, out of this standoff so they could go back home and claim some sort of victory. That made sense, I suppose, except for one thing: Obama knew that too. And he still had us by the balls. In case anyone was keeping track, the idea that a Democratic president was going to stand by and give Republicans the power to screw with his legacy of enacting a longtime liberal priority was, yep, still insane. But we were in it now. I gave it my very best with Schumer and Reid and Pelosi and Obama. They all looked at me like I was crazy. I'm sure Mitch McConnell felt the same way, but at least he was a little more polite about it.

The first week of October came and went, and suddenly we were looking down the barrel at October 17, the day the Treasury Department had declared the government would run out of money unless we raised the debt ceiling. Obama showed zero signs of caving. He blamed Republicans for trying to hold America hostage to score political points. Most people in the media agreed. This was the narrative that dominated the opinion columns and newscasts. Another blow came on October 15, when Fitch, the credit ratings agency, publicly threatened to downgrade the nation's excellent AAA bond rating, which would have been another nasty gut-punch to the economy.

As the Treasury deadline got closer, our House crazies went even further out to lunch. I didn't think it was possible, but they found a way to lose even more touch with reality. They started to claim that the October 17 deadline didn't mean anything, that somehow the Treasury could just wave a magic wand and prevent a default. Maybe this was the "denial" stage of grief, I'm not sure. One of the loudest voices pushing this was Mick Mulvaney, who later, as head of Trump's Office of Management and Budget, presided over dramatic growth of the national debt and the budget deficit.

By this time I had started to hear from some of the other folks in my Conference—the non-crazy ones. They were, to put it politely, freaking out. These were the people from tougher districts who actually had to worry about fighting for reelection. Not everyone had Cruz's luxury of throwing bombs from the comfort of (then) ruby-red Texas. We had plenty of members from lighter-red or purple districts, and they were starting to get shit from back home. They quickly started to loathe Cruz and company for getting us into this mess in the first place.

It wasn't just my House colleagues who felt this way. In fact, the reaction from some of Cruz's Senate colleagues was even more, shall we say, pointed. Unlike House members who generally—with some exceptions like Delaware and the Dakotas—represent a particular area within a state, senators represent the whole state. They have to respond to a more diverse population, and because of that they tend to be more moderate, on average. Senate races are often more competitive. So the Senate is not a natural home for bomb-throwers. Most Republican senators didn't like Ted Cruz from the beginning—Mitch McConnell *hated* him with a passion I didn't know Mitch had in him—and they all gave his crazy plan about ten minutes to fail, knowing (and hoping) that it would do so in spectacular fashion.

So naturally, these folks became Cruz's targets too. He railed against anyone in his own party that wasn't as "pure" as he was. They were creatures of "the Swamp," or some such nonsense. At the time I remember thinking it seemed a little strange that Cruz was concentrating so much fire on his Republican colleagues, since it was also obvious that his turbo-charged ambition would lead him to run for president at the first opportunity. Anyone in Washington who had two peas between his ears knew that those colleagues he savaged regularly in the press would be delighted to return the favor just when it hurt him the most.

That turned out to be exactly what happened—when Cruz ran for president in 2016, my buddy Lindsey Graham declared, "If you killed Ted Cruz on the floor of the Senate, and the trial was in the Senate, nobody would convict you." Around the same time, I called him a "miserable son of a bitch" and "Lucifer in the flesh" in front of an audience at Stanford University. I figured, in an academic setting, it was better to be polite.

After a little more than two weeks of shutdown, the act had started to wear thin. The momentum had shifted to the "Mod Squad"—the more moderate Republican members—who were leading the calls within our Conference to end the shutdown. So I walked into another emergency all-Conference meeting in the Capitol basement and announced, "This fight is over. Today."

I could never have guessed what would happen next. The place erupted into cheers. I got a standing ovation from every member in the room, including the knuckleheads. They all—God only knows why—were happy we'd fought the fight, no matter how much credibility with the public and leverage with the Democrats it cost us. The media scolded us, of course. But then, on November 1, the Obamacare exchanges opened for business with a disastrous, glitch-filled online rollout. It was a mess. And so we moved on to the next crisis—the DC press had another story to cover, and we had something to hit the Dems back with.

If reading this story now doesn't make sense to you, congratulations—I didn't understand it either. I still don't. That's got to be one of the most bizarre events I've seen in politics, and given what I've seen in my career, that's saying something. But maybe that's the most consistent lesson I've learned from the political game: weird shit is just going to keep happening, so you might as well give up being surprised.

Even though we didn't win on the debt limit, did I think it was a noble fight on principle? Did I think it made an important point to the nation? Nope. It made the Republicans look weak, ineffective, and more interested in stunts than in getting stuff done for our voters. Was it worth it? Not at all. But at least I could console myself with the fact that for a moment we were all on one team. For a moment my party was sane again.

For a moment.

I suppose I should have seen it coming. The year that ended with a crisis had begun with one too. And that time too I had ended up leading a fight I knew we couldn't win.

—◆—

Barack Obama was reelected to the presidency in November of 2012, defeating our nominee, Mitt Romney. Romney was a straight shooter who ran a good, honest campaign—and I was especially proud that he chose my House colleague (and former campaign volunteer) Paul Ryan to be his running mate. Yes, Romney got in trouble for pointing out—pretty much correctly—in a private setting that Obama had 47 percent of the voters locked up because they "pay no income tax" and are "dependent upon government." Never mind that according to the Tax Policy Center, 46.4 percent of households did not, in fact, pay any federal income tax in 2011. The media saw a chance to jump down a Republican's throat for being insensitive, and they did it with relish. If only they could have imagined the kind of stuff Donald Trump would say on the campaign trail in 2016 . . . Romney would have sounded like a choirboy.

Obama still faced some headwinds going into the election. The economy was barely limping along. The disastrous attack on our consulate in Benghazi, Libya, that left four Americans dead hadn't done any favors for his image as commander in chief—or the credibility of his secretary of state, Hillary Clinton. My House Republican colleagues and I campaigned hard for Romney—and our buddy Paul—but Obama won fair and square. Oh well. We still held the House majority but were still the opposition in Washington, just as things had been in Obama's first term. At least things hadn't gotten any worse . . . right?

No such luck. Obama had made the bold promise during his reelection campaign to raise taxes on anybody who made over $200,000 a year. But that wasn't the only tax threat Americans were about to face. December 31, 2012, was the point when a whole lot of tax cuts—from those enacted during George W. Bush's administration to temporary measures we negotiated with Obama in 2010—were set to expire. They called that the "fiscal cliff," and we were barreling toward it. Going over the cliff would mean that significant cuts in government spending would go into effect, which was a good thing. But Obama, cleverly, was counting on the fact that the expired tax cuts, something individual Americans could see and feel and understand, would make a bigger political splash.

Between Obama's drive to raise taxes and the other tax cuts

set to expire, lots and lots of Americans were about to take a hit in their paychecks. We knew this could kill small businesses too. Republicans weren't about to just let that happen. So as 2012 came to an end, we spun the negotiating wheels into gear. And Obama, to his credit, offered to raise his limit on the tax increases to people making over $400,000. That wasn't great, but it was better than $200,000, and the president had a lot of leverage—the mandate of a recent election, not to mention the media in his corner.

But I thought we could do better. I thought we could protect more Americans from more hurt on their tax receipts. So I came back to the White House with $1 million. I was tired of Republicans—and especially poor Mitt Romney, who had done well for himself—being blasted by the left and by the press for only caring about "millionaires and billionaires." Well, here we were offering a tax hike on millionaires and sparing a huge chunk of the American middle class. I hoped Obama would take that as a show of good faith, a sign that we were serious.

And who showed up to torpedo everything? The so-called conservatives in the House Republican Conference, of course. They wouldn't budge on any tax increase under any circumstances. Most Republicans, when they came to Congress, signed a pledge put out by Grover Norquist's Americans for Tax Reform group never to raise taxes in office. Even Grover, to his credit, announced that this deal wouldn't count as violating the pledge, but I guess even he was now "too establishment" for these kooks. They didn't listen. They refused to back the plan to raise the limit to $1 million.

What was so "conservative" about their argument I still don't understand. Why would any self-proclaimed anti-tax warrior *choose* to put the hurt on more Americans when they had the option to put the hurt on fewer, who would better be able to absorb it? There were masses of American taxpayers making between $400,000 and $1 million, including small-business owners, who all could have gotten a break. Yes, we still would have had to get Obama and the Dems to agree to it, but at least the House showing unity behind the $1 million plan would have given us a better hand. But no, that was too much to hope for. As it happens, we just played right into the left's argument—now it looked like Republicans cared so much about millionaires they were willing to screw over all Americans making between $400,000 and $999,999 just to protect their super-rich friends. That was just great.

This was pure, blind, knee-jerk ideology, and it reflected the mood on the right at that time. So many of the members who were elected to the House in 2010 had gotten there by challenging more sane politicians from the right in primaries, and they were terrified someone was waiting in the wings to do the same to them. Live by the sword, die by the sword. "Primary" was now widely used as a verb, as in "if I don't vote with the crazies, I'm going to get primaried." And even if Grover Norquist had stood this one down, there were plenty of our other old pals in the outside "conservative" groups ready to eat their own—running ads and funding challengers attacking normal Republicans for "raising taxes." We were trying to prevent an even bigger tax hike at the bottom of the fiscal cliff, but of course that didn't matter.

Once again, I was at the negotiating table basically naked. My own party had taken away my boxer shorts. With about two weeks left in 2012 and the cliff approaching, I had no more leverage with Obama and Harry Reid. We just had to accept whatever they offered now. I remember I recited the Serenity Prayer live on TV: "God, grant me the serenity to accept the things I cannot change, the courage to change the things I can, and the wisdom to know the difference." It seemed like the right thing to say.

I admit, this fight took a lot out of me. Anybody who knows me knows I don't do angry—especially not at work. You hear stories about some representatives or senators throwing staplers or shoving all the papers off their desk in a rage. I knew plenty of angry people. But that wasn't me. I never got mad at my staff—ever.

Colleagues were a different story—I'd get mad at them *very* rarely. But at one of these meetings at the White House toward the end of the fiscal cliff negotiations, I lost it on Harry Reid. He'd been talking all kinds of shit on the Senate floor, calling the House "a dictatorship of the Speaker." I'm sorry, but fuck that. I never ran the House like a dictatorship. If I were a dictator, do you think I'd let all these members get away with screwing me over all the time? Hell no! And Reid, who was a ruthless bastard, knew exactly what he was doing. That speech was aimed right at the House crazies—he was trying to gin them up even more and make my position even worse.

So when I saw him at the White House the next day, talking quietly with Mitch McConnell before the meeting, I went over, got in Reid's face, and said, "Do you even listen to all that shit that comes out of your mouth? You can go fuck yourself." I guess he wasn't used to people getting in his face like that. He couldn't think of anything to say back to me. I guess he was taken aback that someone had called him out on his bullshit. Weirdly enough, our relationship got a lot better after that. Poor McConnell, though—Mr. Decorum was a stunned and horrified witness to this angry encounter. I thought he was going to keel over from cardiac arrest then and there.

There was another outburst a few days later, when the House voted on the Senate's bill to solve the crisis on New

Year's Day 2013. The final version kept the tax increases for everyone making over $400,000, but everyone below that level got a break with the extension of the Bush tax cuts. The bill passed in the House with majority-Democrat support, but a little more than a third of the Republicans joined in—all that was left of the sanity caucus.

A couple high-profile defections really pissed me off—Eric Cantor was one, and the majority whip, Kevin McCarthy, was the other. These were the guys who were supposed to have helped me build support for the $1 million plan, and to see them lose their faith at the end was something I couldn't stand. When I learned about it I said something like, "Are you shitting me?" which I really shouldn't have done on the House floor. I went to go talk to the boys to try to figure out what they were up to—and maybe to knock their heads together— but they both scurried out of the chamber before I could catch them. But you know who did decide to cast a grown-up vote in favor of the deal? Paul Ryan. That was a moment where he showed he was ready to lead, and make the tough calls often required of a good leader. I had that in mind when I worked, a couple years later, to convince him to take over the Speakership, even though he didn't really want the job.

Anyway, it wasn't a great way to start a new year. And it was a preview of the shutdown nonsense to come in a couple months.

But here's the real point of these stories. Most of these guys who poke their heads up in these crises and vote "no" on every compromise and claim they're doing it all for "conservative principles" don't actually give a shit about fiscal responsibility. If they did, you'd think they would be slap-happy excited when a Republican president came to Washington who, with a House *and* Senate majority, could make serious progress on getting our national debt and entitlement spending under control.

Guess what? None of these guys said anything when the Trump administration added $1 trillion to the federal budget deficit by the end of 2019—*before* a single dime was spent on COVID-19 relief. They were rubber stamps for it in Congress. Many of them who raised huge stinks about TARP were only too happy to let Trump bail out farmers hurt by his trade war with China. These are the same people who were willing to destroy our economy to make their point but went on to suddenly abandon this core principle.

And why? Because it's not really about the money. It's not about principle. It's about chaos. If it were about principle, they'd have stuck to their principles no matter who was in power.

The numbers don't lie. In its first three years in power, before the pandemic, the Trump administration grew our national debt by $3 trillion. COVID-19 relief spending brought the growth total up to $5.2 trillion by May of 2020. As I've said, that's not all Donald Trump's fault—the coronavirus pandemic was an unprecedented situation, and Congress and the administration did the right thing spending money to address it. Still, the U.S. Congress, which allocates government funding, was controlled by Republicans up until the start of 2019, before the pandemic became a spending priority. You would think that folks like Mulvaney and Cruz and all these others who were willing to destroy our entire economy to hold the line on spending would have kept their hard-line views, fighting spending programs every step of the way. Nope. Not a peep from any of them. Mulvaney, as I mentioned, even went on to work as the head of Trump's Office of Management and Budget, which oversees federal spending. He didn't say a word, even as his administration way outspent Barack Obama, even when he became Trump's "acting" chief of staff. Guess who succeeded him as chief, by the way—Mark Meadows, who tried to kick me out of the Speaker's chair for not being fiscally conservative enough. I guess those trillions in Trump debt didn't bother him a bit.

No, most of these guys weren't about principles. They were about chaos and power. Don't get me wrong—the Democrats are far from guilt free in all of this. They never seemed to care much about controlling federal spending when I was in Congress. Now the far-left lunatics have become the center of gravity in their party. What Nancy Pelosi and other sane Democrats—the ones who've been around long enough to know how things work—are dealing with from AOC and her Squad reminds me a lot of what I had to deal with during my days as Speaker from the far-right kooks of the Tea Party or the Freedom Caucus or whatever they were calling themselves. The difference is that the Freedom Caucus usually shared the same policies as the rest of the GOP conference. The disagreements were mostly over tactics. They always wanted to get into a fight with somebody. Which is pretty screwed up, if you think about it.

"The Squad" on the left, meanwhile, has a policy agenda—a radical one that smart Democrats know is (a) unrealistic, (b) unworkable, and (c) alienating to the rest of the country. Democratic socialism just isn't going to play. But these people command a large social media and press following, so Pelosi has to argue with them about tactics *and* policy. Which is a hell of a spot for her to be in. By the way, I can tell you with absolute certainty she knows they are a bunch of kooks. Unlike them, Nancy lives in the real world. I will say I don't know anyone else on the Democratic side who can keep them in line as well as she can, or keep them from destroying themselves with some batshit scheme. They are all screwed when she is off the scene.

She handled the failed effort to impeach Donald Trump about as well as she could. I guess she did get the impeachment, but there was no way the Senate was going to convict him. And Pelosi knew that, no question about it. It was painful having to watch her give in to the far left. When Obama was president, as hated as he was by the GOP base, impeaching him might have been broached once or twice by one of the nuts in our Conference, but never by anyone with half a brain.

I'm pretty sure Nancy knew that a partisan impeachment of Trump was a political loser. As several polls reflected, it drew people who don't like Trump into his camp and lurched the Democrats further to the left. But she eventually had to give in, because she knows a leader without followers is just a person taking a walk.

I'd have pointed the same thing out to Trump himself if he'd asked me. He would call me fairly often when he first took office for advice or conversation. I was never afraid to tell him when I thought he got it wrong, and give him encouragement when he got it right. But the calls came in less and less as his tenure went on. That's probably because he got more comfortable in the job. But I also suspect he just got tired of me advising him to shut up.

# SEVEN

# Deep State Delusions

I was out of office when Donald Trump was inaugurated as our nation's forty-fifth president. That was fine by me because I'm not sure I belonged to the Republican Party he created. Don't get me wrong. Of course I wished him well as president, and supported him on a number of traditionally conservative issues like cutting federal regulation, keeping taxes low, keeping our military strong, and putting constitutionalists on the federal bench.

But while he made a lot of progress on these and plenty of other conservative priorities, he also spent a lot of time—and mouth-flapping energy—on stuff that really comes out of left field. From my perch, out of the fray, it was always a little puzzling to watch. I know times have changed and every president has to adapt. There's one thing, though, that never made any sense to me: Trump's obsession with the so-called Deep State.

Not only was this obsession misguided, it betrayed a lack of understanding of how government really works. I don't really blame Trump for that. The guy spent his entire career building apartments and office buildings—plus some truly wonderful golf courses. He's had other stuff to worry about.

And the Deep State as a boogeyman is not an idea the Trump Republicans invented out of whole cloth. As long as I've been in politics, politicians have railed against this group or that group in Washington as the villains standing in the way of whatever they're trying to do. I too railed against "the establishment" as a young hothead. Then some hotheads railed against me. It's often good politics. Every good story needs a couple of bad guys, after all.

It's true that within the federal agencies of the Executive Branch, there is an entrenched bureaucracy that likes to protect the status quo. Republicans in the past have portrayed them as stuffy and resistant to change, and especially anxious to protect their patch from conservative efforts to shrink and streamline government.

But this took a nastier turn in the Trump era. Bureaucrats went from cranky obstructionists to Deep State villains engaged in a massive conspiracy against America as a whole—and Trump in particular. In his telling, they were nothing short of traitors. "Unelected Deep State operatives," Trump told a rally crowd in 2018, "who defy the voters to push their own secret agendas are truly a threat to democracy itself." But who are these "operatives," exactly? He didn't make that clear. They're whoever he wanted to point a finger at that day, I guess.

There is something very destructive—not to mention delusional—about the notion that there is some plot deep within the nation's capital—in the FBI, in the federal courts, in the intelligence community—to undermine democratically elected officials and, as Trump often charged, "undo" his election in 2016. Let me be diplomatic here: that's horseshit.

To show you why, let me try to explain what, near as I can

tell, I think Trump means when he talks about the "Deep State" and his other favorite term, "the Swamp." The Swamp is Washington—that's not a new term either—and the Deep State is made up of people who've been there for a long time in nonelected positions of power.

Within this crowd of unelected Washington veterans, there are two main groups: bureaucrats and lobbyists. Bureaucrats have been in Washington since, well, the Washington administration. Yes, they can be annoying as hell, but many of them actually do important jobs. They keep the machinery going— getting out Social Security checks and tax refunds, putting together scientific studies, paying and caring for servicemembers, tracking the weather—and we need them. Republicans would like to make some cuts here and there, yes, but even most on the right would admit that some sort of bureaucracy is needed to run a country of hundreds of millions of people. And when people in that bureaucracy have been there a long time and have institutional knowledge, they usually make things work better rather than worse.

Lobbyists are a little harder to defend, I admit, but let me take a crack at that one too.

I know what most people think when they hear the word "lobbyist." I can see it now: some fat guy in a $5,000 suit, puffing a cigar, hundred-dollar bills bulging out of his pockets, plotting to light the world on fire just so he can offer "hose consultation services" at a premium. I guess there are a few people who vaguely fit that description. There are some lobbyists, yes, who have bad agendas. But you can suss those guys out pretty quickly if you're smart and make sure to avoid them.

What most people don't understand is that lobbyists are not, on the whole, a bad thing. In fact, though the word "lobbying" does not appear in the Constitution, the right to lobby does. The First Amendment guarantees Americans the right "to petition the Government for a redress of grievances." That means if you don't like something the government is doing, you can make your case about it. And if you don't have time to do so yourself, you join with other like-minded people—in a trade association with others in your industry, for instance— and hire someone to make your case to the government on your behalf. If you're doing that, wouldn't you want that person to have the right connections to make sure your views get heard? That's all lobbying is, at its best. And when it's done right, it actually makes government *more* accountable.

Lobbyists also provide an essential service to lawmakers. Since lobbyists tend to focus on one particular issue, over time they become subject-matter experts with invaluable expertise. In fact, our democracy can't work without these creatures of the Swamp. Every capital city has them—not just Washington, DC, but Sacramento and Denver and Columbus. They go where laws are made, and lawmakers need them. Sometimes they save us from ourselves.

I was new to the Ohio state legislature when I was approached about supporting a seemingly simple bill: to get rid of the front license plate required on all cars in the state. At the time, many other states didn't require license plates on the front, just on the back. Some still don't. Why did Ohio have to have both? Like a small-government conservative, I figured that cutting by half the number of license plates on cars would save the state money. We'd need to buy half as much metal and make half as many plates. I decided to cosponsor the bill. It seemed simple enough. Not a big deal, right? Wrong.

Very quickly I became an unpopular person in Columbus. First, folks from the Ohio school bus drivers' association showed up in my office.

"You can't support this bill," they said.

"Why not?"

"You know those flashing red lights that school buses switch on when they stop? When a car runs past one of our buses with its light flashing, we have a better chance of getting their license plate number, and then we can notify the police."

Well, I hadn't thought about that. Nobody wants to make it easier to put little kids in danger getting off the bus.

Then I heard from every law enforcement group in Ohio—the state sheriffs' association, the highway patrol, and the state chapter of the Fraternal Order of Police.

"No, Boehner," they said. "We've got to catch criminals. If you've got two plates on a car, then we have twice as good of a shot at catching them. You want to fight crime, right?"

Well, yes, I did. I hadn't thought about that, either.

Then the good folks from the 3M Company showed up at my office. It turned out 3M made the reflective material that goes on all the license plates.

"If this becomes law," they said, "we're going to lose half of our business in the state." Which meant people would lose their jobs in Ohio, including people in my district. For good measure, they repeated all the things I'd already heard from the school bus drivers and the state police and the sheriffs and all the rest.

Meanwhile I wasn't just hearing from groups but individuals too. I got letters and phone calls to my office all day. *God Almighty.* All I'd done was cosponsor some simple bill. What was going on? I got one of those twitches again. Something wasn't right here.

So I decided a little investigation was in order. As it turned out, the people behind this seemingly harmless piece of legislation were members of the Ohio Car Wash Association.

When Ohioans took their cars through an automatic car wash, the scrubbing mechanisms would occasionally bend or beat up the front license plate. Customers would get pissed and yell at the owners. The owners preferred that that didn't happen, of course. So instead of the expense of fixing their machines or paying for the damage to these cars, they decided to change the law and ruin my life.

I've remembered that story over the years because it makes a couple of points. The first is that nothing in government is simple or easy. When you try to change one thing for one group of people, it can upset a whole bunch of other groups you never even thought about. The second is that lobbyists have an expertise on various matters that a legislator cannot hope to have.

The percentage of your elected officials who read each and every law they're voting on might surprise you: other than a couple of nerds with a lot of time on their hands, it's zero. People act like this is some massive outrage, but it really isn't. We are a big, complicated country, and changing federal laws is a big, complicated deal. You'd have to be a skilled lawyer to understand some of the language of these bills—"amending Section 283(d) of The Whatever Act, which amends IRS Code 433.6, which deletes paragraph 3 of something else"—and even then, you'd have to examine a whole bunch of different codes and existing laws to check all the references for any of it to make sense. Members of Congress don't have the time or the expertise to do that. Some people on their staff do, but they're overwhelmed as it is. Lobbyists make a living knowing what all these laws say.

In that sense, lobbyists aren't just influencers, they're educators. When you're dealing with complicated bills on the Hill, you're going to hear from lobbyists on one side and lobbyists on the other (like the car wash owners vs. the school bus drivers). Sometimes you'll hear from lobbyists who aren't particularly on one side or the other but understand the issues and can help explain the pros and cons. By the end of the day, if you listen to the lobbyists, you're going to know exactly what that language you are voting on actually does, and how it affects real people. Who's going to win and who's going to lose? Who's going to benefit and who's not going to benefit?

You could not have a city council, a state legislator, or Congress without people who lobby. Most of the lobbyists that I dealt with also were my constituents. I'd talk to farmers in my district about a corn bill or about soil and water protections. The local doctors would talk to me about healthcare issues. What may be good for this part of a state or that part of the country may not work elsewhere. If you didn't have these ongoing conversations with lobbyists from your district, you wouldn't really have a clue.

None of which is to say that lobbying, which has become an industry in itself, can't be regulated or reformed in various ways. Lobbyists aren't all superheroes. They're capitalists like the rest of us, and sometimes their agenda to make a buck isn't in our best interest. But government is run by pitting competing interests against each other and, hopefully, coming to a compromise. That is far easier said than done.

One of the most controversial things I did as Speaker was to eliminate earmarks. Earmarks were a long-standing tradition in Congress, as cherished by members as free lunches or Christmas. What this tradition allowed was for members to carve out sweetheart deals for their districts—a post office, a federal building, a bridge, whatever—as part of large federal spending bills. If it worked, it meant Congressman X could send out press releases claiming credit for bringing taxpayer dollars back to their communities. It was, as you would expect, very popular.

The problem was that a lot of these projects either took advantage of taxpayers or just plain didn't make a lot of sense. Among the more notorious examples was Senator Robert Byrd's effort to basically dismantle the federal government in Washington and bring it back, piece by piece, to his home state of West Virginia. Another was my old friend Don Young—the guy who pulled that knife on me—who infamously supported money for a project that became known as "the bridge to nowhere," which was pretty much what it sounds like. Okay, it didn't go literally "nowhere," but it was an attempt to spend hundreds of millions of dollars to build a massive bridge between mainland Alaska and an island with a few dozen people on it that already had its own airport and a perfectly good ferry service.

There was an entire industry here in Washington, DC, built on these earmarks. Former members of Congress and other groups would shake down everyone from universities to hospitals, museums, states, cities, and counties and convince them to hire them to lean on current lawmakers to get earmarks put into various bills. The firms had armies of lobbyists whose only job was to get earmarks inserted into legislation benefiting their clients. And usually whatever amount they got in there (of taxpayer dollars) they would get some percentage from the client in payment.

When we got rid of earmarks, we destroyed that little cottage industry. Conservatives generally cheered this move—at least at the time—but it did not make me a hero to everyone. I remember running into a former member of Congress not long after earmark reform passed. As it happened, he had just recently retired and gone to work as an earmark pusher. Before he even had time to get his business going, we had turned off the tap. When he saw me, he cussed me up one side and down the other. You'd have thought I'd made a pass at his wife.

Since then, and still to this day, there are covert and overt efforts to bring earmarks back into Congress, often pushed by very powerful industries. Some industries demonstrate how a particular lobby can be allowed to grow so powerful that it holds everyone hostage for no real good reason.

Take ethanol, for example—gas made from ground-up corn. It's supposed to be more environmentally friendly or something. Baloney. Ethanol doesn't work, and it's expensive to produce. But most of the production goes on in major corn-producing states, the largest of which is Iowa. So a government mandate to use a certain amount of ethanol in fuels means, in practice, a major giveaway to Iowa corn producers. See where I'm going with this? Every politician thinks they can be president. Everyone starts their presidential campaigns in Iowa. And nobody wants to show up in Ames and piss off farmers by telling them ethanol stinks. So ethanol subsidies live on.

Another industry that's done a good job of keeping everybody's balls in a vise? Sugar. The sugar people have had a very effective lobby going for over 140 years. For instance, sugar beets need a lot of water. So where do we grow them? We grow them where we've built reclamation projects and dams in the driest places in America. They drain all this water up because, as I said, beets take a lot of water. And why do we grow sugar beets in these dry places? As usual, because there's lots of money involved.

The sugar lobbyists spend their entire waking day making sure that there's a minimum price on sugar and a limit on how much sugar comes into the United States from overseas. It's protectionist and, frankly, a bit socialist if you ask me. I think

Bernie Sanders would approve. The thing about Bernie, by the way, is that he is probably the most honest person to ever run for president, ever. We came into Congress together, and I can tell you, he genuinely believes all the crazy shit he says. So he may be nuts, but at least he's not cynical—and a non-cynical politician is rare no matter how you slice it.

Anyway, sugar prices in the United States are, by some estimates, twice as high as everywhere else. In fact, the sugar industry receives about $4 billion—billion with a b—a year from American taxpayers to support some 4,500 sugar farms, protect their industry, and keep other players out. Not so sweet when you look into it, is it? More like a disgrace.

Sugar was never really my fight, but I always thought it was a little silly that the sugar industry has all this power in Washington. But I liked to spend my time on issues I might actually be able to change, and I knew the chances of winning a fight with Big Sugar was basically zero.

At one point in the mid-1990s, I got fed up and decided to yank their chains anyway. I was on the Agriculture Committee and we were getting ready to put together the 1996 farm bill. I walked into my office while this was going on and found a sugar lobbyist hanging around, trying to stay close to the action. I felt like being a smart-ass so I made some wisecrack about the sugar industry raping the taxpayers. Without another word, I walked into my private office and shut the door. I had no real plan to go after the sugar people. I was just screwing with the guy.

My phone did not stop ringing for the next five weeks. The guy must have walked straight out of my office to the nearest phone booth (or maybe he had a cell phone even then—these guys were loaded) and called his office and announced: "Boehner, Ohio 8th—Code Red." I had no idea how many people in my district were connected to the sugar industry. People were calling all day, telling me they made pumps or plugs or boxes or some other such part used in sugar production and I was threatening their job. Mayors called to tell me about employers their towns depended on who would be hurt by a sugar downturn. It was the most organized effort I had ever seen.

And that's why you don't fuck with sugar.

———

People underestimate the power of the status quo. Changing the status quo is typically a monumental exercise because people get invested in the status quo. I don't care whether it's a line item in the tax bill or a particular regulation, there is someone somewhere who has become vested in what the law is or what the regulation is, and they typically don't want to see it changed. I'm not saying it can't be done, or that you shouldn't try for real change if you're doing it for the right reasons. I'm saying it's stupid to go in thinking you'll be able to change everything—or anything—in Washington by waving some magic wand.

I got a tough lesson in that working on that same farm bill in 1996. I was in my third term then, and for some reason I was picked to be the guy from the House Agriculture Committee that was sent across the Capitol to talk through this bill with the key senators to negotiate a few points of disagreement. They probably picked me because nobody else wanted the job. But at the time I was feeling pretty proud of myself, a third-termer already in the Republican leadership, walking over there to tell these senators how things were going to go with a big bill and give them the word from the House, where the *real* power was.

As soon as I walked into that conference room, I thought to myself, *I'm not shit.*

There at the head of the table was the legendary Sen. Jesse

Helms of North Carolina. He had been chairman of the Senate Agriculture Committee back in the 1980s and still held a lot of sway. Next to him was my old buddy, Sen. Howell Heflin from Alabama. I believe he was allowed to smoke in this meeting, unlike in the Clinton White House. These two, Helms the Republican and Heflin the Democrat, were the go-to guys on tobacco and peanut farming, and nothing was going to go into the farm bill without their nod.

Helms was every inch the man in charge. He leaned back casually in his big chair and looked at me as I took my seat across the table.

"John," he said, "nice to see you. Welcome to the United States Senate."

I was on his turf, and he was making sure I knew it. I thought we were going to get down to business then, but he wasn't done.

"I think the best way for us to resolve these issues," Helms continued, "is for you to talk with Senator Heflin. Whatever you and Senator Heflin work out will be fine with me."

And with that, Helms got up and, followed by his staff, walked right out of the room. Well, shit. That was a power move I hadn't been expecting. And there was Heflin, just grinning at me. He was in charge now.

Over the next few hours, I did my best to push for the House version of the farm bill with the help of the team of House ag staffers I'd brought over. We had binders and notes and all kinds of facts and figures to make our case. Through it all, Heflin just sat there like the sphinx. He was a tall, broad guy, filling the whole chair and dominating his side of the table—a big immovable object, never giving any hint to what he was thinking while we went on and on. The final verdict on all of our suggestions was always the same.

"I don't think so."

That was it. No negotiation, no back and forth. We kept trying and trying, but all we got was, "I don't think so." We were there all that day, half the night, and went back to it the next day. All we ended up doing was going through a lot more cigarettes and a lot more "I don't think sos." I didn't get rolled that bad in a negotiation until I went up against Obama.

Sometimes you win and sometimes you lose, but when you're trying to change the status quo, chances are you're going to lose. If you want to change something that's been the same way for a long time, you'd better have some forces working along with you to push the momentum in your direction. That's what I didn't understand. I was operating on my own, trying to take charge of writing this part of the farm bill. Helms and Heflin, on the other hand, had states full of peanut, tobacco, and other farmers with vested interests that their senators were damn sure going to protect.

The major force was with them, and so they got what they wanted. When you go out and try to make big changes on your own, like I did, you aren't going to win. To put it in a way that would probably make Heflin chuckle—it's kind of like playing with yourself. It might feel good, but it doesn't really get much done, does it?

Still, sometimes you win—even up against especially formidable forces like the school lunch ladies.

You think I'm kidding? When I was chairman of the Education and Workforce Committee I learned that these gals were no joke.

Early on I was trying to put a bill together that made some modest changes to the federal school lunch program. Honestly, I can't even remember what they were at this point, but they really aren't all that important to the story, as you'll see.

Naturally, for a bill like this we worked with the experts—the representatives of the school cafeteria workers' association. Yes, lunch ladies have lobbyists too. And they were some of the toughest in town.

They weren't too happy about our bill to begin with. The cafeteria was their domain, and they did not like the idea of some guy in DC—especially a new guy running the committee—trying to horn in. And every congressional district in America has schools—and every school has lunch ladies. They were everywhere, and when the call went out from their organization, they showed up. I had four or five of them from my district come to my office one day. When I went home and held events, there they were. You could always tell—lunch ladies, God bless them, look the same everywhere, don't they? They showed up in packs, glaring and scowling at me like I'd just been caught stealing an extra brownie.

In the end, we made a deal with them, and everything turned out okay. But it demonstrated again that you tread into changes like this at your peril. You have to know all the interests involved and what they need to work with you. Railing against them—calling them "the Establishment" or the "Deep State" or whatever the preferred term of the day is—doesn't get you anywhere.

That said, sometimes in order to get things done you *do* have to shake things up. You might even have to threaten entrenched interests. But there is a strategic way to do that.

That's what happened when we decided to mess with Head Start—another popular program that most Americans do not know much about other than that it sounds good. That could be because most Americans don't pay attention to things that help low-income communities, but that's another problem. Head Start is a federal program that provides early childhood education and services to low-income parents and kids. In some places, it works great and does a wonderful job for people who need help most. In other places, it's an easy employment program where "teachers" are hired as glorified babysitters and don't actually do anything to help these kids.

The program is run by the Department of Health and Human Services, and everyone knows who the good and bad Head Start operators are around the country. But they don't want to push too hard on the bad players, because that can make the whole program look bad.

I wanted to do something about that, so I started the process off by setting out simple goals. I wanted to make changes to Head Start to make the educational standards stronger and everyone involved more accountable. My point was simple. This program exists, and there are kids involved, so shouldn't we expect that these kids are actually going to learn something?

You would have thought that I was the devil himself showing up at these meetings. At first the Head Start people absolutely kicked our asses, rhetorically. You could probably write the media story yourself: evil Republicans trying to hurt poor kids, valiant Head Start leaders trying to protect them. Well, I took that one more personally than usual. I've worked my whole life to help poor kids get better access to education all through their schooling. You don't tell me I'm trying to make life tougher for them. Back off.

I wasn't going to let the Head Start lobbyists walk all over me. I knew there were problems in their programs even if they would never admit it. I didn't want to give them billions I was afraid would be wasted when it could actually go to helping kids. So I played rough. Our committee staff dug up a whole bunch of stories from around the country about just what some bad Head Start apples were doing with taxpayer dollars. Some of these guys were driving expensive cars with money that could have bought new teaching materials for classrooms. This changed the whole dynamic of the fight. We got them to the table, and we were able to work things out.

So, yes, playing hardball or "creative disruption" or whatever you want to call it can and does work sometimes. Knee-jerk defenders of President Trump would often say that's what he was up to whenever there was some new pronouncement or action that didn't make sense. Well, they may have been right in some cases. I don't know. I'm not in the middle of it all anymore.

But having to constantly point to the Deep State as this boogeyman responsible for all these problems just seems . . . weird. We still don't know exactly who he means, but the likely suspects, bureaucrats and lobbyists, can actually be responsible for making government work better and stay more accountable to the people.

That's when they do their jobs responsibly, which not all of them do. And when bureaucrats sandbag regulatory change or lobbyists try to flex too much muscle, it's a problem—and that's when you have to get tough. I get that. But even in those cases, it's a far cry from the massive government conspiracy that Trump liked to say was bent on unseating him. It almost seems like an attempt to deflect responsibility, but as every leader knows, the buck stops with him.

All of this, it's worth remembering, can be seen through the various lenses of the media. What we see and hear in print, on TV, on the radio, and on the internet has the power to shape our understanding of what's going on around us.

That's just a basic fact. President Trump was hardly the first Republican to struggle with a media he was convinced was out to get him. God knows I felt that way plenty of days. But the truth about how the American media works is more complicated—far more complicated, certainly—than many conservatives think.

A college degree, a good job, active in church and community, a beautiful family—not a bad life! What the hell was I thinking throwing in politics on top of that?

Getting sworn in to the Ohio House of Representatives, where I learned a lot of the ins and outs of politics.

When you come from a big family—I had 11 brothers and sisters—there are a lot of people to keep track of. It's even possible to forget everyone's name from time to time.

The look on my face says my coach, the legendary Gerry Faust, wasn't in a good mood that day.

On a high school class trip to Washington, DC, in 1967. If only I'd had the sense to stay away. (In case you can't spot me, I'm in the top row, fourth from left, in the cool coat.)

My first desk at
the State House
in Columbus.

Getting an early education in legislating from State House colleagues.

One of my
biggest
challenges
during my
time in public
life—getting
people to stop
pronouncing
my name as
"BONER."

My first congressional race—campaigning with the good kind of pork. I didn't realize I was going to be knee-deep in mud for many years to come.

I got a little emotional the night I was first elected to Congress, one of the greatest honors of my life. Luckily Mom and Dad were there with some encouraging words.

Busy with some committee work during my second term. *(CQ Roll Call Photograph Collection, Library of Congress/ Photo by Laura Patterson)*

Comedian Chris Farley impersonating Newt Gingrich. He made one mistake: Newt would never have worn that nice a tie.

To those who think the two parties can't get anything done, we proved them wrong. Standing proudly with Ted Kennedy as President Bush signed No Child Left Behind in Hamilton, Ohio. Getting it passed was a wild ride that I won't ever forget. *(AP Photo/ Ron Edmonds)*

The tense, disastrous meeting during the 2008 financial crisis. That worried look on my face was *not* an act for the cameras. *(AP Photo/ Pablo Martinez Monsivais)*

He was a terrible poker player, and impatient as hell, but he turned out to be a really great friend.

Gerald Ford was a man of great dignity and decorum— but not when you got on the golf course. President Ford taught me a lot of lessons about leadership, and I'd need them all.

Trying to help President Clinton figure out where his ball went. He may have called one of his infamous "Billigans" on this one.

President Clinton was nice enough to sign an autograph for Deb—but I didn't let him turn on the famous Clinton charm for too long.

A bad day on the golf course is better than a good day at the office, or anywhere else.

I learned a lot during my dinner with Clint Eastwood, including why he got into acting ("chicks") and why he learned to play the piano (also "chicks").

When I first met Donald Trump, the absolute last thing that came to my mind was that I'd just met a future president of the United States. What a country! Yet here we were, also with memorable former colleagues Mick Mulvaney, Mike Pompeo, and Mike Pence—and former staffer Johnny DeStefano. *(White House Photo, provided by the author)*

On the Speaker's Balcony, my last day as Speaker. While we were out there, Caleb Smith, my staffer who took this photo, asked me if I'd miss the view. "I'll remember it," I told him. I've never forgotten.

# EIGHT

## Alligators, Not Enemies

It's a time-honored tradition in Washington for politicians, especially Republicans, to spar with the media. The gentlemen and gentlewomen of the press have long been accused of liberal bias, and with good reason, as I'll explain shortly. But right up there with the Deep State is another phrase in the vocabulary of the Trumpian Republican Party that puzzles me as an outsider: calling journalists the "enemy of the people."

Of course, the press reaction to this ill-advised line was characteristically overblown. Journalists do love to be the heroes of their own narrative. You would have thought Trump was actually throwing reporters in jail left and right like a tin-pot dictator in a Soviet republic. Some of us, myself included, are old enough to remember all the way back to 2013 when Barack Obama's Department of Justice, led by Attorney General Eric Holder, actually spied on reporters from the Associated Press, secretly obtaining months' worth of their phone records. This included tapping the AP's phone line in the House of Representatives press gallery. As of this writing, the Trump administration has not been accused of anything like that.

Still, it was a dumb thing for Trump to say, as it just gives the media another reason to jump down his throat. Deliberately antagonizing the press is not the way to deal with them, as most veteran politicians know. There's an old saying, "Never get in a fight with people who buy ink by the barrel." These days they're buying something digital—I don't know, bandwidth?—but you get the idea. Yes, the press can be annoying, even adversarial. I dealt with that plenty. But the way to handle that is to work with them, not against them.

I called it "feeding the alligators." There's nothing inherently bad or evil about an alligator. They're just another one of God's creatures. They hang out in the water or on the shore in the sun. Most of the time they don't bother you unless you bother them. But, like all God's creatures, alligators have to eat. And if you're going to be around them when they're hungry, you'd better have something to throw their way.

Like a lot of things over the course of my career, this was something I learned the hard way.

———

Thinking back, it was not a good day to get in my way.

A major Republican bill had just failed on the floor of the House. It was the mid-1990s and we were in charge, with Newt Gingrich holding the Speaker's gavel, but even then we couldn't always get our shit together enough to get things across the goal line. I would understand that frustration a lot better as Speaker myself, years later—and by then, I knew how to take it in stride—but at that particular moment I was just a pissed-off member ready to get the hell off the floor.

As Conference chair at that time it was my job to keep the hundreds of rank-and-file Republican members on the same page as the top House leaders, and somewhere along the line, on this particular bill, we hadn't been able to keep the team together. I don't even remember what the bill was about, but I do remember what happened in the minutes after it failed.

I stormed off the floor pretty mad, which, as I've said, is rare for me. Most of my "angry" moments are notable enough that they've ended up in this book. At that moment, all I wanted to do was leave the mess of this floor fight behind me and get somewhere where I could have a cigarette and relax (there were a lot more places you could smoke in the Capitol in those days). But I should have known it wasn't going to be that easy. Before I crossed that river, I had to make it past the alligators. The members of the congressional press corps were waiting to pounce.

As soon as I got out into the hallway just off the floor, one of them rushed me. It was Karen Tumulty, the congressional correspondent for *Time* magazine, and she was known for asking tough questions. She zeroed in on me like a hawk spotting a limping jackrabbit from a mile away. Some reporters will try to joke around and act friendly at first to try and disarm you before they throw you the real questions. Not her. She hit me with a curveball before I knew what was happening.

That one question just set me off. I was tired, I was pissed about the bill that had just failed, and I still needed a cigarette bad. So I took it all out on Karen. I got in her face and chewed her out. I might have used some colorful language that probably wasn't appropriate for the halls of the U.S. Congress. And I was right in the middle of refusing to answer this woman's question in the most belligerent way possible when I happened to look down and realize that she was pregnant.

Needless to say, I felt like a real asshole, acting that way to a nice Catholic girl like her too. I apologized to her right then, and I apologized pretty much every time I saw her for the next ten years. From then on, I could hardly have been nicer to a reporter than I was to her. She has two fine sons, by the way.

It's funny what sticks in your head and what doesn't. I don't remember the bill that failed and put me in such a sour mood, but I sure do remember the exchange that followed. It's true that no matter how long you've been in Washington, you're more likely to remember the people than the politics. Legislative fights come and go, but personal relationships stick around. And there are few more interesting types of Washington relationships than those between politicians and the reporters who cover them.

Some people call it a "delicate dance," with each partner making subtle movements and indications in a discreet game of give-and-take that balances a reporter's search for information with a politician's effort to put their own spin on the story. It all sounds very sophisticated. And it's all bullshit.

There's nothing sophisticated or high-minded about dealing with the press. Like I said, it's just about "feeding the alligators." Before most press conferences, when I huddled with my staff and other members who might be joining in, I'd say, "Time to go feed the alligators." And my main goal was always to feed them without getting myself bit.

When I first came to Congress, I didn't make a habit of talking to the press. I wasn't used to being around a bunch of reporters. Back in Ohio I would talk to a few local reporters now and then, or some of the folks who covered the state house in Columbus, but these Washington reporters were a different breed. I *did*, however, make a habit of smoking, and that's how I ended up right in the middle of the alligator pack.

In those days, you could still smoke in the Speaker's Lobby, an ornately furnished area just off the House floor where portraits of former Speakers look down on you. Nancy Pelosi shut that down during her Speakership, and though I may have considered bringing it back when I took over, I thought that would be opening one can of worms too many. I stuck to smoking in my office, which, as I've mentioned, apparently drove Paul Ryan crazy when he moved in in 2015. Tough luck, Paul.

But in the 1990s, the Speaker's Lobby was a great place to duck off the floor for a quick smoke break. So I spent a lot of time out there, and soon a few of us, including Tom Latham from Iowa, who became my best friend in the House, started hanging out there together. But reporters with House press gallery credentials would hang out there too, hoping to stop members as they came in and out of the chamber for a quick chat.

Most of the time they were respectful and didn't try to interrupt our private conversations, but we knew they always had one ear cocked in our direction. And eventually I spent so much time out there, and saw the same press people hanging around, that sooner or later I would strike up a conversation and get to know them one by one. Sometimes I'd catch them off guard by pointing out a sloppy shirt or a crooked tie. That was fun. I made 'em jump a bit. Reporters are not known to be the best dressers in Washington (except the TV folks, obviously). I struck up a good rapport with some of them and tried to help them out when I could.

It seemed pretty simple to me. They had a job to do, and I had a job to do. So why shouldn't I just make it easier for them to do their job? That way they might make it easier for me to do mine. As I said—toss something for the gators to chow down on so they don't come after you.

I came to have a very good relationship with the press just by being myself, and not posturing or trying to play games with them. Too many members tried to do that—to plant news tidbits or play different people off against each other. Most good reporters can sniff that shit out a mile off anyway. I was as open with them as I could be. Of course, I couldn't always tell them everything, but I told them enough. I was always honest and answered their questions, but I always tried to get it done in as few words as possible. The more words you say, the more chances you have to get yourself in trouble. Remember that old line from Sen. John Tower: "You never get in trouble for something you don't say."

But I never misled a reporter, or tried to play one off against another. I told them what I could, and I was straight up about how much I could say. And when I'd said what I had to say, that was it. I didn't try to string them along and make them beg for more, I just let both of us get back to our jobs. In many ways, I dealt with them just like I dealt with other members—just by being me. Maybe there were times when some of them—members and reporters—wished I'd given them more, but at least they knew I would never bullshit them.

I would give the gators a snack here and there when a reporter would call my office or stop me in the hallway to talk. But the big feeding frenzies were the press conferences. We could call press conferences for special events, but they were also built into the regular schedule. As Speaker, I usually held two a week, with the first one coming right after the Conference meeting where the leadership team discussed the week's agenda with all the members.

We'd go across the hall from our big meeting room in the Capitol basement to a much smaller room where the press was corralled and waiting for us. They'd been gathered outside the meeting room trying to hear what was going on inside—and some members inside were known to text or email live updates to reporters—but if they were patient, they knew they'd get their feeding.

I would take the podium and deliver the House Republican message for the week, which would then be echoed by the majority leader, the majority whip, the Conference chair, and another member or two we'd brought along to help highlight specific agenda items. And then came the real alligator feast— the question-and-answer period. This was a few minutes of controlled chaos. And it was controlled only because I made sure to control it.

I saw too many press conferences in my early years in Washington that were like scenes from a movie or a TV show. There was no organization. The reporters weren't even silent, methodical alligators—they were more like a pack of jabbering hyenas. They just shouted their questions over one another. It was total pandemonium.

I never liked that, and I knew that was not the way I was going to do things. As I moved up in the House leadership and spoke at more and more press conferences, eventually I imposed a rule: no more shouting. We were going to raise our hands. If children in elementary school can discipline themselves to do that, so can full-grown adults.

I remember standing in front of the assembled press corps on one of those early occasions. "Alright," I said, "the first thing is, we're going to have some order here. If you want to ask questions, put your hand up and I'll be happy to call on you. But we're not having everybody screaming and yelling anymore." And believe it or not, they got the message.

Putting that simple rule in place helped keep my conversations with the press running smoothly, no matter which direction they went in. There was one reporter, for instance, who would often ask a question about LGBT issues, whether or not they were related to the agenda we'd been discussing. I always called on him and tried to answer as best I could. That was his beat, and he had a job to do.

Every now and then, some knucklehead reporter from one of the TV networks, who wasn't usually a congressional correspondent, would show up to one of these things. They stuck out like sore thumbs because they didn't know the rules, and kept shouting their questions. And they were usually there to play some game of "gotcha." Jesse Watters from Fox News used to pull that stunt. Well, I rarely ever called on those types. You know why? Because they never raised their hands. They never stood a chance.

There was a reason I decided to try to bring some order to the chaotic Hill press conferences that had become the norm. It wasn't just to make it easier to hear the questions. Somewhere along the way, around the time I became majority leader, I realized I was dealing with the press more frequently than I had been before, so I sat down and thought about a strategy. What sort of image did I want to present? I wasn't going to change who I was—no question about that—but I did have to think about how I wanted to come across and what I wanted to accomplish each time I went before the press.

The answer that came to me was pretty simple. I was going to be the reasonable, responsible adult in the room. That, I figured, was what the American people wanted and needed to see. I wasn't going to be a firebreather—at least not most of the time. There were plenty of other members that did that reliably. Before every press conference, after I made my typical joke to my staff and colleagues about "feeding the alligators," I'd give myself a silent, second reminder: "It's your job to be the reasonable, responsible adult in the room." And that's the last thought I would have before I walked up to that podium.

Over the years, I got to know some reporters pretty well. After all, we went to work in the same place every day, even though we had different jobs to do. Some of them, I wish, had done their jobs a little differently—a little more fairly—but most were straight shooters. Julie Hirschfeld Davis, for instance, covered DC for a number of outlets and always played fair. Lynn Sweet, the veteran Washington reporter for the *Chicago Sun-Times*, on the other hand, didn't even try to hide her bias—at least from where I was sitting. It got to the point where there really wasn't any point in trying to spend time with her.

Most of the TV reporters had a bit more flair for drama than their print colleagues did, but I guess that's to be expected. On TV, it's all about the personality. When you go on one of those shows as a guest—the famous Sunday talk shows in particular—it's not just a simple matter of answering questions. The personality of the host is going to set the tone for the whole experience. It didn't matter which show or network you went on. They were all defined by the manner and style of their particular host.

NBC's Tim Russert, for instance, was probably the classic example of "tough but fair." Maybe I'm a little biased because, I admit, I always liked the guy. We got along well, and he even helped me raise money to give scholarships to DC kids. But that didn't mean he ever went easy on me on *Meet the Press*—just the opposite.

I remember going on his show just a few days after I became House majority leader in 2006. I'd spent nearly a decade trying to work my way back into leadership, I'd finally made it, and here I was ready to face the national Sunday morning television audience. I was playing in a bigger league, and boy, did Russert let me know it. Each question came at me like a missile aimed right between my eyes. He'd clearly done his research, and pulled up clips of me from years ago that of course I had to respond to.

He even brought up the famous "handing out checks on the House floor" story—which at least gave me a chance to clear that up. That was from back in 1996, when I was helping raise money for some colleagues, and I brought a few checks written out to them by a PAC down to the House floor because I knew that was where I could hand them to the members directly. That just seemed easier than mailing them to all the different campaign offices. It was all legitimate fundraising—there was nothing illegal about it, and it wasn't even against the House rules. But people called me on it, and I could see why it didn't look great. So I never did it again. It probably didn't help that the checks were from Brown & Williamson Tobacco Corporation . . . but 1996 was a different time.

Anyway, Russert gave me a rough reintroduction to the dicey media environment that awaits a House leader. But all in all he was a good man who did his job well, and both the media and political worlds suffered a serious loss when he passed away too young.

One of my favorite Sunday morning show hosts, both as an interviewer and as a person, was John Dickerson of CBS's *Face the Nation*. Dickerson and I talked not long after it was announced that he was going to take over that slot. I gave him one piece of advice: "Keep being yourself. Don't let them push you into being somebody you're not." He was one of the straightest-shooting reporters I ever dealt with, and he had absolutely the right personality for a Sunday morning talk show. And I've spent a lot of time on Sunday morning talk shows.

Dickerson was genuine and incisive, and could carry on an honest conversation while still getting good answers out of his guests.

I didn't want any network higher-ups to pressure him into changing his style, and I told him so. "Who wants to hear all this banter on a Sunday?" I said. "Just have a conversation, which you're already really good at doing." I'm proud to say he took my advice. And clearly it worked, because he was promoted to anchoring CBS's daily morning show, and from there went to the flagship *60 Minutes* program.

I had a lot of fun doing *60 Minutes*, but well before Dickerson's time. I was lucky enough to be interviewed by the great Lesley Stahl. I went in expecting a total nightmare and came out with a few lovely minutes of television that my family still treasures.

It was mid-November 2010, and I'd just been elected Speaker. Right after that, my press team told me they'd heard from *60 Minutes*, who wanted to throw together a profile on me. My first reaction was a firm "no." I didn't want anything to do with it. We were riding high after taking back the House majority, and I didn't want to give the media a big opportunity to beat up on me before I'd even taken the gavel. But my staff was pretty insistent. They all thought it was a good idea, and they worked me over pretty good.

After a couple of days of dragging my feet, it became clear I didn't really have a way out of this. We couldn't turn down *60 Minutes*. They wanted to spend four hours with me and my family back in Ohio and then another four hours with me in DC, all for 12 minutes of television that would be watched by more than 20 million people.

"Well," I asked, "who's going to do the interview?" The answer came back: "Lesley Stahl." I went back to thinking this was a terrible idea. I knew she leaned to the left, and I was convinced she was just going to turn this into a hit piece. At the same time . . . Lesley Stahl has had a long and distinguished career in TV journalism. She'd even hosted *Face the Nation* in the 1980s. And, I admit, there was a time when I'd had a little bit of a crush on her. It would hurt if she burned me on this *60 Minutes* piece, so I had to figure out how to play this.

I would meet her first in Ohio, when she showed up to interview my family the Monday before Thanksgiving 2010. We were all going to meet at Saints Peter and Paul Church, and when I arrived the CBS crew was already in place. There were lights and cameras all set up in front of the church I'd grown up going to, where my parents were married, where we had their funerals, and where I'd married Deb. If that wasn't surreal enough, there in the middle of it was Lesley Stahl.

When we introduced ourselves, I told her right off the bat, "Lesley, I've had this crush on you for 30 years, and I can't tell you how excited I am about this."

It didn't matter that I'd fought this whole idea earlier. I was in it now, and I had to play it through to the end. And besides, Lesley *was* awfully nice. They filmed us inside the church, talking about my childhood. She got me crying, and I got her crying too—although her tears never made it onto the air, and of course mine did.

Later we moved the whole production over to Andy's Café, where my family all gathered and where Lesley was supposed to interview me while we were sitting on bar stools. She went off to get her makeup adjusted for that part of the segment. During the break, Deb came up to me and told me, "I don't know what's going on, but this lady is smitten with you." Women can tell these things a mile away. I figured, at least that meant things were going okay.

The rest of the shoot in Ohio went great, and so did the four hours or so we spent together in DC. When it was all over, as we walked through Statuary Hall in the Capitol, I turned to Schnitt—Dave Schnittger, my top communications staffer, who'd set the whole thing up—and told him, "There's no part of this I wouldn't mind seeing on TV." My gut was right—the segment turned out great.

Not long after, a package arrived at my office from Lesley. It was a tie from an online clothing store run by her daughter, one she'd picked out for me as a thank-you for participating. I was touched, and I proudly showed it to my staff, announcing then and there that I was going to wear the tie from Lesley on my first day as Speaker. Jo-Marie St. Martin, my legal counsel, immediately spoke up.

"You can't take that as a gift," she said, "you've got to pay for it!"

She was right, of course. So we figured out the tie's retail value, and I made sure to send Lesley Stahl a check for $87 before I was sworn in as Speaker. I still like that tie.

Dealing with the mainstream media had its challenges, but the so-called conservative media, from Fox News to Rush Limbaugh and the other radio and TV talking heads, was a whole different sort of circus whose acts ran all the way down the line from responsible journalists to fire-eaters, sometimes jumping around and taking different roles throughout their careers.

Chris Wallace is and always was a straight shooter. If anything, he would grill Republicans twice as hard as he would Democrats just to avoid any appearance of favoritism because he happened to be on Fox. Megyn Kelly, when she was on that network, overcorrected in a more dramatic way. It was as though she thought she wouldn't be seen as a serious journalist unless she was tough and aggressive, even angry—which sometimes came off as not quite genuine.

On the radio, Rush Limbaugh is still the king. We were buddies in the 1990s, when I would feed him scoops occasionally. We even played golf together. I'd stop by and see him when I visited Palm Beach. But somewhere along the line, Rush and some of the other conservative commentators changed their model. It wasn't just about getting a message out and countering bias from other media outlets. It became a numbers game—building the biggest audience possible and making the most possible money from the advertisers who profit from that audience. Bigger audiences made for more ad money, and when they found out that ginning up anger tuned in listeners, that was it.

To me, the change seemed to happen around 2010 or 2011, when Mark Levin first made a sharp turn to the right. Rush and Sean Hannity (who balances the TV and radio worlds) were afraid Levin was going to cut into their audience share, so they lurched far to the right too. That was when Ted Cruz emerged as the alleged "conscience" of the conservative movement, and he was a darling to these people. They could wind him up and get him to do anything—like, say, talk a handful of House Republicans into shutting down the government for no real purpose. But of course the switchboards at Rush's, Sean's, and Mark's studios lit up like the Fourth of July whenever something crazy like that happened. That's when these shows went from real commentary pushing conservative ideals to just pissing people off and making money off the anger.

Clearly it's not just right-wing media that chases ad revenue though. It's a problem across the spectrum, and it's part of why the United States is so polarized today. Americans are getting a firehose of information shot at them, and before they know what's going on, they figure they've got to be angry about something.

The changes I've seen firsthand in the last few decades have been striking. The press used to strictly report the news, with less commentary. That was the case for mainstream print, TV, and radio news. Now these outlets offer a lot more opinion pieces alongside the news, because people click on opinion pieces they agree with, and clicks mean ad money. But sometimes it's hard to tell the difference between reporting and opinion. Legitimate journalists go on cable TV as guests or "contributors" but don't just stick to the facts, they speculate and offer their opinion as "pundits." In that way, the media has gained more power than ever before. But when you have people on TV talking and talking for hours on end, they have to come up with things to say, and that means more chances for outrage or bias to color the facts.

A lot has changed since there were only a few radio talk show hosts that most people hadn't heard of, one cable TV channel that just did news, no internet, no Facebook, no You-Tube, and no Twitter. Today, Americans are being inundated with information from all kinds of sources, some legitimate and some not. Some of what's out there is true, and some isn't.

And it's certainly gotten worse since the 2016 election. I know plenty of people have said that already, but I'll say it again. There are huge chunks of the country that don't trust the media at all. Or they only trust certain outlets and are convinced that all the others except their favorites are peddlers of dangerous, anti-American propaganda. It's ugly.

I'll say this for the Trump vocabulary: "fake news" is more than just a catchphrase, it's a real problem. But it doesn't help when people use that term just to refer to a story they don't agree with, as both Republicans and Democrats like to do since the term became popular. Unfortunately, that's going to keep happening as opinions compete with facts and people get pulled more and more into separate camps.

I don't have all the answers we need to fix this situation. I thought the media environment was tough when I was Speaker, but I never expected anything like what it has turned into since 2016. Americans should be smarter than this. If there's one thing no American likes it's being taken for a ride. And when someone on television or radio or elsewhere in the media is trying to gin you up to get mad about something—that's exactly what's happening. They're trying to profit off your anger by selling ads. So maybe it's time to stop looking at every new day's headlines as a chance to prove your political point's right and the other guy's is wrong. If the news becomes fully weaponized, we're in big trouble. The alligators may end up eating all of us.

# NINE

✦

# America, from Inside and Out

It was a long and bumpy ride, and when we stopped, I still wasn't sure exactly where I was. The terrain didn't give too many clues. It was rocky and mountainous as far as the eye could see in all directions. This was wild country, ragged and rough. As I looked up into the mountains, I wondered if there might be some other guy looking down at me, through binoculars or even through a rifle scope. If he was up there, he was probably none too friendly toward Americans. And if he happened to catch the current Speaker of the House in his sights, he could be sure of a handsome reward.

Luckily, I didn't have much to worry about. The guys with me had much bigger guns, and much better training.

The trip had started in Kabul, Afghanistan, where I had traveled with several other members of Congress to meet with Afghan government officials, as well as the American civil and military personnel working to help put the country back together after the defeat of the Taliban. The Kabul meetings were informative, but they were stiff, formal, and full of bureaucrat-speak. Some of us wanted to go where the war was. If we were going to take an accurate picture of the Afghan situation back to Washington, we had to get a real frontline perspective.

So I was taken from Kabul with maybe half a dozen other members to a forward operating base. The farther you get from the city, with its sprawling bases and diplomatic compounds, the more your view of things changes. You appreciate what it's like for these young Americans to leave their homes and families and fight for freedom in a place so alien to them it might as well be Mars. We talked with them at their posts and in their mess hall, and we spent the night out there, on what most people would assume were the front lines of the War on Terror. Not quite.

The next morning, to my surprise, I was approached by a group of our "operators," as I'll call them. I can't say much more about who they were, what unit they belonged to, or what they were doing there. They asked me to come along with them, and I did. We headed east, and went about as far to the east as you can go in Afghanistan until we came to the Pakistan border.

In that corner of the world, a "border" is a pretty gray area. Eastern Afghanistan borders what the Pakistanis call the Federally Administered Tribal Areas, or FATA for short. It's a tough place, home to some of the toughest mountain fighters in the world. Their people have been in that territory for thousands of years, long before anybody drew lines on maps to create nation-states around them. They continue to roam freely over the area, coming and going with ease on the winding mountain trails between Afghanistan and Pakistan, not giving a damn for what both governments admit is basically an unenforceable border. The men up there are formidable fighters. Some of them are on our side, and some of them aren't.

That's how I found myself in the middle of a mujahedeen camp. Strictly speaking, it was hard to tell whether we were in Afghanistan or Pakistan—and strictly speaking, I wouldn't be able to reveal the exact location anyway. There were about forty local tribesmen in the camp, all in traditional dress with thick beards, cradling their AK-47 rifles and rocket-propelled grenades with bandoliers of ammunition slung across their chest. Some of the oldest ones might have helped kick out the Soviets decades before, or at least their fathers had. Their ancestors further back had similarly thrown out the British.

They were looking at me funny, and I could hardly blame them. They were no friends of the Taliban, and that made them our allies, but generations of dealing with Westerners had made them suspicious. Clearly they weren't used to seeing civilians out there, as far out as the front lines could possibly go. Frankly, I agreed with them—I wondered what the hell I was doing there myself.

The operator who'd been showing me around went over to talk with some colleagues, leaving me alone for a moment in one of the strangest spots I've ever been in in my life. So I sat down on a rock—there were a lot of rocks around—and just tried to take it all in. I was surprised when one of the mujahedeen fighters casually walked over and sat down on a rock next to me. Uh-oh. What could this guy possibly want? Before I could say or do anything, he leaned in close and said:

"I went to Moeller High School too. Go Crusaders."

I damn near fell off my rock. He was one of our guys—an American, from Cincinnati no less. I came to find out that about half the fighters in this camp were American operators, providing training and support to the mujahedeen. They'd adopted the local dress and grown out their beards. They were not only fighting but also eating, sleeping, and living alongside the local tribesmen. Both forces had earned each other's respect and learned to work together effectively as a unit.

It was an eye-opening experience, to say the least. And meeting a fellow Man of Moeller out there was a little ironic, given that terrorist propaganda often called American troops "crusaders." I guess in the case of the Moeller grads, they were technically right. But I imagine that any terrorist who came in contact with that particular Moeller Crusader—or any of his friends I met that day on the mountainside—would not be around long enough to appreciate the irony.

If I hadn't been elected to Congress, I'm sure I'd have had a nice life with my wife and kids in our corner of southwest Ohio. I would have stayed in business, and probably made plenty of money. I would have still played golf, smoked cigarettes, drunk red wine, and cut my own grass, and I probably would have ended up the same old jackass. But I would have seen a hell of a lot less of that big, wide world out there.

Nobody says "join the Congress, see the world," as the old navy slogan used to. Congressional travel was the farthest thing from my mind when I first ran for the House. Some people catch the travel bug at a young age. Not me. I didn't really leave home until I was out of high school.

The Vietnam War was going on, and rather than wait around to get drafted, I decided to sign up. I'd worked construction jobs before and had a pretty good handle on things, so I figured I'd put that experience to use for Uncle Sam and join the Naval Construction Battalions, called the "Seabees" for short. They helped build bases all over the world.

So I joined the navy, but I didn't exactly get to "see the

world"—just Gulfport, Mississippi. After a few weeks of training down there, part of which was spent cleaning up the devastation caused by Hurricane Camille—I remember seeing a big ship that had been plopped right in the middle of a highway—my old back injury flared up and I could hardly move. The doctors took one look and sent me home with a medical discharge. Leaving home, I figured, was overrated.

I didn't leave the country until 1978 when, after we had a little more money, my wife and I decided to take a vacation to the Bahamas a month or so before our first daughter, Lindsay, was born. When they learned that Deb was eight months pregnant, the immigration officials on the island almost didn't let us in. They didn't like the idea of American tourists going down there to give birth. We were both disappointed, and the look on Deb's face was especially sad, so the guy took pity on us and approved our entry. But he gave Deb a stern warning: "Not too much dancing!"

If I'd stayed out of politics, a few pleasure trips to the islands now and again would probably have been the extent of my world travel. But as a member of Congress, I got to go all over the world on official travel. Yes, these CODELs are fun, but they also serve an important purpose. If someone is going to serve in Congress effectively, they have to understand America's place in the world and how our foreign relations actually play out on the ground.

The Senate likes to claim that it's the foreign policy hub of the Legislative Branch. Well, the Senate can eat it. Foreign policy initiatives need taxpayer money, and whether it's a war or a trade subsidy, the appropriation of that money is going to come from the House. That's why it's important for House members to get out there and see how this money is actually being spent. And especially if we're going to authorize our young Americans to go fight in foreign lands, we need to see what they're up against for ourselves.

Not only that, by serving with and getting to know my fellow members from all over the nation, I found myself with plenty of reasons to go visit all the different states of our union. A great way to help out my fellow members was traveling to their districts to help them raise money, and before long the "Boehner Bus Trip" was born. Every August, for several years running, I would go on a road trip with some of my staff and friends, stopping in various districts to help my colleagues raise a couple bucks. And we had a lot of fun along the way.

Somewhere between getting to know our own country and the wider world, somewhere between Boise and Benghazi, the guy who'd never left southwest Ohio turned into a bit of an adventurer. I'm not exactly sure how or when it happened, and I was as surprised as anyone when it did. But I'm certainly grateful for it. I'm grateful that I've been able to see as much of God's creation as I have. I'm grateful that I realized a simple truth before it was too late to act on it: if you don't go to the end of the road, you're never gonna know what's there.

I didn't travel at all during my first few years in Congress. Between learning the ways of the institution and getting into scraps about things like the House bank, I had my hands full. But in 1996, Speaker Gingrich asked my wife and me to come along on a trip to Asia with a big group of members. I guess they thought we'd fit in for some reason. I was Conference chair by then, with an eye on higher leadership, so I figured it was about time I broadened my horizons.

We had no idea what we were in for. This might have been the worst slog through the Pacific region since the Bataan Death March. We were up every morning at 7:00 and didn't get back to the hotel until 11:00 at night. Every minute in between was packed full of meetings, tours, and working meals. If we wanted to actually take anything in, we had to do it in a few stolen moments of reflective time. But I'm glad I made time to do it.

Our stops on the journey were South Korea, China, and Japan. I may have been the number-four House leader accompanying the Speaker on an official visit, but I was still a guy from Cincinnati who'd only been outside the country to go to the Caribbean beaches. The Asian capitals were like nothing I'd ever seen before. They were huge, sprawling cities crammed with millions of people. The sidewalks were so crowded you could hardly move. I'm not the biggest guy in the world, but I felt like a giant. The cities themselves may have been huge, but everything in them was built on a smaller scale—even the hotel beds were a little on the small side for us beefy Americans.

In those days, Shanghai was a totally different city than what it's transformed into since. It was still the old city that had grown up over centuries, with little shanties all over the place. Nothing had been fancied up yet. It wasn't long after, though, that all the new money pouring into China led to the creation of a brandnew city from the ground up. The shanties were bulldozed, and in their place is a version of New York City on steroids. I'm glad I got to see old Shanghai before it disappeared.

In Seoul, we met with members of the South Korean parliament and were received by the president at the official residence, called the Blue House. Things were a bit tricky in South Korea. They were just starting to allow some democratic reforms to go ahead after a period of more authoritarian rule. But they remained a key ally, so we wanted to see firsthand how these efforts to modernize their government were getting along.

When we got to Japan, I had a special call to make that was a personal priority of mine. Honda had a large presence in my congressional district and elsewhere in Ohio, so I made a point to visit their offices in Tokyo. They sent a car over to get me—I can't recall if it was a Honda or not—and I had to skip one of the other meetings on our "official" itinerary. But meeting the people my constituents did business with face-to-face was well worth it.

The Japanese leg of the trip also allowed some of us to make another "unofficial" stop. Encouraged by California representative Chris Cox, a dedicated Cold Warrior who used to distribute translations of *Pravda* back in the Reagan years so Americans could see what the Soviets were up to, some of us made a side trip to Taiwan. Mainland China, of course, had claimed Taiwan as their own for decades, and Cox felt—rightly—that it was only fair that we visit Taipei after getting the ruling Communist Party line during our stay in China. So we flew three hours out from Japan, spent two hours in meetings with Taiwanese leaders, and then flew three hours back to Japan—just in time to join our spouses and the rest of the delegation for the long flight home.

I may not have traveled much before this trip, but I'd always been an adventurous eater. I was not what you'd call picky, mostly because I could never afford to be, growing up with eleven brothers and sisters. If you put something in front of me, I ate it. That wasn't going to change just because I found myself in another country. I was familiar with the standard egg foo young, lo mein, and other "American Chinese" dishes, and I was especially looking forward to trying actual Chinese cuisine in China.

I was not disappointed. In Beijing, at a grand banquet with members of the National People's Congress, they served shark fin soup, a delicacy usually reserved for special occasions in China. It's also a controversial dish, inspiring protests around the world over the treatment of the sharks—but I have to say, it was delicious. I can see why someone would fight for their right to eat it.

Another soup they served in China had little roasted chicks floating in it—or at least they were some sort of poultry. All I know is, they were tiny. I drew the line there. It was impossible to cut meat off of them, and I wasn't about to eat them bones and all.

One Shanghai delicacy was as surprising as it was tasty. At a brunch with local officials, I ended up in front of a plate of mushrooms. At least, I thought they were mushrooms. I tried one, and it had a little crunch to it, not like any mushroom I'd ever had before. But I liked it, so I had another, then another. Finally I asked the Chinese official next to me what exactly this was.

"Duck foot," he replied.

Duck foot wasn't even the strangest thing I tasted on any congressional trip. That honor goes to fermented horse milk, which was served to us in Mongolia on another trip years later.

I was always curious about Central Asia, and it did not disappoint. It's like another world, unlike anywhere else I visited. To imagine Kazakhstan, for instance, you have to picture Kansas, but flatter. That is, at least until you get to the shiny new capital, Astana. When we drove from the airport through the flatlands, they kept telling us excitedly about the new capital. We nodded politely, but there was nothing around us to indicate any city anywhere nearby, let alone the paradise they were talking about.

But soon, sure enough, out of nowhere, a dazzling city with gleaming ultramodern towers appeared. It was like Disneyland or Oz had been stuck right there in the middle of a desolate plain. The architecture was cutting edge. It was a breathtaking city of the future. That's what oil money free of Communist shackles can do, I guess.

In Mongolia, on the other hand, it appeared that not much had changed in decades, except the Mongolians were now in charge instead of the Soviets. Ulaanbaatar seemed like a stagnant city, stuck in a Soviet-era time warp. But that was nothing compared to the time warp you enter once you get *out* of the city.

We took a bus up into the mountains—the steppes, as they're called in that part of the world—to visit some nomadic herdsmen. They lived in traditional portable tents made of skins called "gers"—the more familiar term "yurt" is actually a Russian word for the same type of dwelling. Out there they raise sheep, goats, and horses, staying in one place until the animals have eaten all the grass; then they pack up the whole family and the gers and drive the animals to find more grass somewhere else. That's the way they've lived for thousands of years.

In fact, some of them looked like they actually *had* been alive for a thousand years. The patriarch of the family we met was old and wrinkled, a shell of a man, but he still had an air of command around him. He was surrounded by five generations of his family, and he was very clearly in charge. He'd lived a tough life, and you had to respect that. I remember there was one sign of the modern world around him though: stuck on the top of the animal-skin tent was a satellite dish. Maybe the old guy liked to catch *Baywatch* when he could.

But then we were back to the age of the horseman. There was a leather sack hanging just inside the door of the ger, with a ladle sticking out. I looked inside and saw what looked like chalky water. It turned out that this was horse milk, drawn from the mares in the herd by the women of the group, mixed with yeast and left in this bag to ferment into a kind of Mongolian moonshine liquor. We were all encouraged, as we entered, to stir the brew and ladle ourselves a sip. It tasted just like it looked . . . like chalky water. I have no idea how intoxicating it was. There was no way I was going to drink enough to find out.

Back on the bus after this visit, a doctor traveling with us opened his bag and took out a handful of the biggest pills I'd ever seen in my life. He said they were antibiotics, to counteract whatever germs might have been fermenting in the leather sack along with the horse milk. Not only did he demand we take the pills, he made us each swallow as he watched—I suppose so that he could say he'd done his job if anything unfortunate happened. Luckily, nothing did.

Horses (not just their milk) were of great value to the Mongolians. The local government officials presented me with my own as a gift, a white pony. He had a brand on him already—an "A" with a circle around it. Naturally, I named him Andy after my grandfather. I didn't get to take him home, but I was assured, "When you come back, he'll be here waiting for you." I never did make it back to Mongolia. Sometimes I wonder how Andy is doing.

Traveling in the former Soviet Union is always interesting, but present-day issues are more immediately pressing in some places there than in others. The Mongolian herder patriarch, sitting in his ger watching *Miami Vice* on satellite TV with a mug of fermented horse milk, likely doesn't have to worry about Vladimir Putin invading his goat pasture to feed modern Russia's imperial ambitions. Estonia, on the other hand, is a different story.

This small but feisty and dynamic nation is one of the three Baltic states, along with its neighbors Latvia and Lithuania. The West likes to keep an eye on these three to make sure they don't become a flashpoint of Russian aggression. Estonia has a population of just 1.3 million—less than the Cincinnati metropolitan area—and about a quarter of those are ethnic Russians. Just like Hitler invaded Czechoslovakia in 1938 claiming to protect the local ethnic Germans, Putin invaded eastern Ukraine in 2014 claiming to protect the ethnic Russians. The Estonian leaders know that they and their Baltic neighbors could be next. And they know it could have already happened if it weren't for the United States and our NATO allies guaranteeing their security.

This was clear to the Estonian prime minister when I met with him in the late 2000s. A young, passionate politician, he spoke forcefully about how much American support meant to him and to the people of his country. This Estonian was a more patriotic American than a lot of native-born Americans I've met. Before he was through, I had to get out my handkerchief. His gratitude and love for a country thousands of miles away from his own brought me to tears.

On the same trip, we stopped in St. Petersburg. It's a nice town. But I won't be going back to Russia anytime soon. I've been on their "no-fly list," banned from entering the country, ever since I called Putin a "thug." Well, he was, and still is. And if he's pissed enough about it to ban me from his country, fine by me. The golf courses there are all shit anyway.

I may never have the opportunity to meet Putin, but I've certainly met other nefarious characters—or at the very least, people whose relationship to the United States was a matter of debate. Once, in the middle of the Libyan Desert, I came face-to-face with Muammar Gaddafi. He even gave me something to remember him by.

Libya was the last stop on a CODEL that had taken us first to Egypt, then to Tunisia. This was during the George W. Bush administration, after 9/11, and engagement with Arab nations was a critical part of our anti-terrorism strategy. We were even taking steps to normalize our relations with Gaddafi, who had been unfriendly toward America and the West for decades. Colonel Gaddafi—as he preferred to be addressed—had ruled Libya since 1969, under his own homebrew ideology that was part socialism, part Arab nationalism, and all cult of personality. But after 9/11, Gaddafi took a hard line against radical Islamic terror groups, which he saw as a threat to his own power in Libya. The Bush administration saw him as, at least, an enemy of our enemies, if not quite our friend.

As our plane headed southwest out of Tunis, flying over the Mediterranean Sea toward the Libyan capital of Tripoli, we hoped we'd get the chance to meet Gaddafi himself. But he was known to be eccentric and erratic, and whether he'd actually show up would be anyone's guess.

Still, his underlings had plenty planned for us. When we landed, we were shown around their parliament building, called the People's Hall (of course). I couldn't help but chuckle to myself—no matter what the official tour guides told us, there was only one parliamentarian who mattered in Libya, and that was the colonel himself. I also wondered why, despite being supreme leader, he never got around to promoting himself to general.

They took us on an excursion outside of town to see a great man-made river project called, naturally, the Great Man-Made River. It was a huge operation that involved creating a man-made lake in the middle of the desert, from which they pumped water hundreds of miles up to the Mediterranean coast. Most of Libya's population is concentrated in the coastal areas anyway, where they have plenty of water already. The reason for pumping water from desert to coast instead of the opposite direction does not make any sense to me, then or now.

We were glad to get out of the desert for lunch, which was, we were told, being set up for us back at the People's Hall in Tripoli. We piled into the old Mercedes-Benz sedans that were our transports—heavy as tanks thanks to the armor plating—and hit the road. Before we got back to town, though, we were confronted with a roadblock. The diplomatic security agent sitting next to me was nervous, but it turned out there was just a change in plans. We'd been summoned—the colonel wanted to meet with us after all.

We were directed to turn off the highway, into the desert, and drive south. We went 10 miles, then 20, then 30, bouncing and rumbling over the ground in these armored cars. Herds of sheep, goats, and camels whizzed past out the window, the herders with them looking up confused and not too happy about all the dust we kicked up. Finally, I saw a giant tent in the distance, sitting all on its own in the middle of the desert. It got closer and closer until we were stopped at a final military checkpoint. I saw the diplomatic security agent move his hand, slowly, toward the gun he wore. But we were waved through without trouble. We were the colonel's guests.

There was just one problem: the colonel wasn't there. Carpets had been laid out for us in the tent, but our host had not appeared. Nobody wanted to sit down because one layer of carpet wouldn't do much to protect our rear ends from the rocky ground. Meanwhile, we were missing lunch.

And then, all of a sudden, someone pointed out past the tent flaps. We could see him, the colonel, coming out of the desert and toward our tent. He was wearing a military uniform, with a round cap and sunglasses—a trademark Gaddafi look. We introduced ourselves and he asked us to take a seat. Now that he had arrived, they at least served us tea.

It was clear from our conversation that he wanted to work with us against the radical Islamic terrorists, but I had been briefed before we left on a few things we needed him to redress if he wanted to be taken seriously on the world stage. I pressed him on cleaning his chemical weapons dumps and resolving unfinished business relating to the bombing of Pan Am Flight 103 over Lockerbie, Scotland, in 1988. Colonel Gaddafi's top priority, on the other hand, was getting Condoleezza Rice, then the secretary of state, to come to Libya and meet with him. He probably made that request ten times. He was obsessed with the idea—or maybe just obsessed with Dr. Rice.

He also had some blunt advice about how the Saudis should handle Islamic extremism in their own country. "You've got to kill all the Wahhabis," he said. "Kill all of them." I'm not sure he had thought that through entirely. The ultra-strict Wahhabist sect of Islam is the official religion of Saudi Arabia, and the vast majority of Saudis are Wahhabists.

At some point in our conversation, I noticed that it was getting brighter in the tent. There had been cloud cover for most of the day, and now the clouds had broken and the sun came out. Gaddafi may have been expecting this. He had gone through this entire meeting with his sunglasses on.

As he was talking, he turned his head in my direction. Then he did it again, even while someone else was talking to him. I had no idea why he kept looking over at me, but I didn't like it. Finally he called an aide over, whispered a short, sharp order and sent the man scurrying out of the tent. He came back a few moments later with a small box, which he handed to his leader. The colonel then got up from the rug, walked over to me, opened the box and handed me some sunglasses. He was offering me his spare pair.

"Desert not kind to blue eyes," he said.

Well, for the rest of the meeting, I sat there wearing sunglasses. So did Gaddafi. And nobody else. It felt weird, for sure, but I figured it would have been rude to refuse. I've sat in a lot of meetings, and this was by far the strangest.

As the meeting began to break up, I tried to give him his shades back and thank him for letting me borrow them. He wouldn't take them. "You keep them," he insisted. So I did. They're in a junk drawer in my DC apartment. They're an Italian brand called Safilo, in case you're interested. Not really my style.

Things didn't turn out so well for Gaddafi, who was deposed and killed in 2011. Civil war has been raging in Libya ever since. And while I haven't made any return visits—apparently the parliament moved from the People's Hall to a ferry boat offshore for a time—I've spent a fair amount of time in other dicey parts of the world, where a stray bullet zipping past your head is hardly out of the realm of possibility.

In addition to meeting mujahedeen fighters on the Afghanistan-Pakistan border, I've met with Afghan president Hamid Karzai—although that was in an air-conditioned office in Kabul. Elsewhere in Afghanistan, I met a soldier who happened to be the brother of one of my communications staffers. You never know who you'll run into.

Afghanistan and Iraq tend to get lumped together, but they're very different battlefronts. In much of Afghanistan, life goes on the way it has for thousands of years. Not far from our embassy compound there are still outdoor meat markets where fully skinned goats can be found hanging from outdoor stalls. Out in the countryside, people live in mud-brick huts they built themselves, with the bricks made from clay they mix by hand and transport by donkey cart. I saw old men squatting down in their big flowing robes, looking like they could have been squatting in that spot for fifty years. The people there are trying to scratch out a living from an unforgiving landscape the same way they did a thousand years ago.

Iraq, on the other hand, was more prosperous. Baghdad was a center of learning in the ancient world, and even further back, the "Fertile Crescent" where it sits was the birthplace of civilization. But the territory has been claimed and fought over down the centuries, by Persians and Ottomans, and later the British, the homegrown dictator Saddam Hussein, and then ISIS.

The dust in Iraq felt like it was six inches deep. It was like walking through talcum powder. But luckily, on one trip, I got to stay in one of Saddam's palaces, which came complete with a pool. Sure, the place had been bombed a few times, but it beat sleeping in a tent or one of those shipping-container shelters where we sometimes ended up.

In the skies over western Iraq, near Fallujah, I thought my life was going to end. We were in a V-22 Osprey, an aircraft that can fly like a twin-rotor helicopter or a two-prop airplane. It also comes equipped with a heat sensor meant to track missiles coming toward it. If it detects one on the way, it automatically takes defensive action.

All of a sudden, the Osprey took a nosedive and started shooting flares out the back to confuse the missile it apparently thought was heading for us. After a few seconds of absolute terror, the pilot leveled us out again and the alarms turned off. As it turned out, we were flying over a farm while the farmer below was doing a controlled burn in one of his fields. The heat from his burning field triggered the heat sensor. Automation doesn't get it right every time.

No matter what kind of aircraft we were flying in, I always made sure to look for the most comfortable seating option.

"Comfort" is a relative term here—pretty much every seat on a military plane is going to be hard. But here's a tip: most of the bigger ones, like C-130s, have a couch built into the passenger area. At least there you can lie down, and if you bring your own blanket and pillow—like I learned to do early on—it's not so bad.

Over time, I developed a few simple rules for every CODEL I helped run. Whether we were going to Afghanistan or Finland, the rules were the same. Rule one: no jackasses; nobody wants to travel with members they don't like. Rule two: we're going to enjoy ourselves; I vowed never to run a Bataan Death March trip like Gingrich did on my first-ever CODEL. Rule three: everybody has to be on time at all times; if you're late, we're leaving without you, whether it's for the next meeting or the flight home. And in lots of these places you did *not* want to be left behind. And the fourth, slightly less official rule: nobody touches my couch but me.

The rules relaxed a bit for stateside travel. Although when I kicked off the Boehner Bus Trip in a buddy's motor coach, we did realize that there was one rule we had to follow: no girls allowed on the bus. That just wasn't going to work. A bunch of guys lived on this bus for weeks . . . it was no place for ladies.

The bus came fully loaded. If you weren't driving you could relax, shoot the shit, watch TV, drink—whatever you wanted. We'd travel through the Midwest and western states mostly, having friends join us for a few days here and a few days there. The golf clubs and fishing rods were always packed along, and we found time to stop and do both despite doing hundreds of events on every trip. And I only made time to stop for my friends. If our route took us right through a knucklehead's district, we just kept going. Tim Huelskamp, one of the head knuckleheads, represented a gigantic district in Kansas bigger than several states. But the Boehner bus never once stopped there.

The bus held up remarkably well, except for the year it broke down in Jackson Hole. That's not a bad place to be stuck in, but we had a schedule to keep. The only mechanic we could find weighed about four hundred pounds and had a giant Grizzly Adams beard. While he was working away underneath the bus, one of our guys accidentally flipped the switch to empty the water tanks. The mechanic got out before he got wet, but demanded that we "turn the fucking water off." He scared the shit out of all of us, but at least he fixed the bus!

Another fundraising trip took me to California, where I met one of the rare Hollywood Republicans, the actor-director Clint Eastwood. A supporter had set up a half-hour drinks meeting with Clint one evening at a restaurant in Carmel, which was fun enough. He was about 80 at this point, and we didn't want to keep him out too late. So we were surprised when Clint, in that distinctive raspy voice of his, invited himself to stick around. "I'll just have dinner with you guys." We sure as hell weren't going to say no to Dirty Harry himself.

They showed Clint, me, and two of my campaign staffers to a little table way in the back of the restaurant. It was near a separate entrance so we could go outside and smoke. My staffers and I got up to smoke pretty frequently. Clint, despite his voice (or maybe because of it), didn't. But it didn't seem right to leave an 80-year-old Oscar winner just sitting there by himself, so we invited him to step out with us to keep the conversation going. It was on these smoke breaks that the conversation got really interesting.

At one point, one of my guys asked Clint: "Why did you get into acting?" His answer was immediate, in that low, iconic growl: "Chicks, man."

"What do you mean?"

"Well, this buddy of mine was in this acting class, and he

kept telling me about all these hot chicks in there," he went on. "I don't give a shit about acting. I just wanted to meet chicks."

That gave us all a good laugh. But a little later, someone else asked him: "How come you decided to teach yourself to play the piano?"

The growl rumbled up again: "Chicks." Again he explained: "I used to go to all these Hollywood parties, and there'd be some gay guy playing the piano and all these chicks hanging around him. I thought, Hell, I want the chicks hanging around me, so I learned to play the piano."

He brought the house down with that. A great career started off for a very simple reason. Unfortunately I had some colleagues in politics who entered politics for the same reason. Usually it didn't work out so well.

I'm lucky to have met all kinds of people all over the world. But for some reason, I've still never been to the Grand Canyon, or Monument Valley in northern Arizona. Just haven't gotten around to it—yet. The Boehner Bus is officially retired—the last fundraising trip was in August 2018—but I still have time to make it out to those spots on my own.

As much as I've learned about America from traveling around it, I've learned just as much from traveling elsewhere. I've seen amazing sights, tasted some of the strangest things you could imagine, and met the best and worst of humanity. There are plenty of things that make humans and our communities similar no matter where you go, but then coming back to America always reminds me of what's exceptional here.

I'm not in a rush to make it to the Grand Canyon. I like the idea of always leaving some spot left to explore, some bend in the road always up ahead. Because, like I said, if you don't keep heading toward the end of the road, how are you going to find out what's there?

# EPILOGUE

## Into the Sunset

I didn't always drink red wine. Somehow over the years a glass of a nice red became part of my "image," and I admit I played along with it. But I sure as hell didn't grow up with red wine, or much of any wine at all (except at communion). A glass of red sitting on the bar at Andy's Café would have been a very rare sight.

In my younger days I was a beer drinker—the crisp German-style lagers that we grew up with in our part of Ohio. That was alright for a while, but once you start to get a little older, beer just fills you up too much with all that carbonation. Too much bloat. So then, as a "young professional," I switched to old fashioneds. I wasn't a fan of hard liquor on its own, but the sugar and the bitters helped take the bite out of the bourbon, and you could sip on a good old fashioned for a long time. But if you've got a long night ahead of you, you usually find that drinking liquor for several hours is pretty much unsustainable. Plus, nothing that sweet can be good for you in the long run.

And so I settled on wine. Drinking wine is a marathon, not a sprint, and makes sense for the more mature drinker. Once I got to Congress and started going to those receptions they throw almost every night in DC, I found I could make a glass or two of wine last the whole night. It was enough to take the edge off after a long day, and then I could still get to bed by ten and wake up ship-shape the next morning.

Over the years I've come to know a thing or two about good wine. I don't know that I'd call myself an expert, but I do know what I like. Merlot is a favorite, but I appreciate plenty of other types—or "varietals," as the real experts say. A cabernet sauvignon can do the trick nicely. Chianti is generally under-rated. One of my go-to bottles at Trattoria Alberto, my favorite restaurant on Capitol Hill, is the Ruffino Riserva Ducale Chi-anti, a Tuscan Sangiovese. It goes great with "veal alla Boeh-ner," a delicacy based on a German dish I had growing up that the folks at Alberto's were kind enough to make for me, and eventually put on their menu. It's a lightly breaded thin piece of veal with two fried eggs and anchovies on top—delicious. Apparently it went off the official menu after I left town, but if you ask nicely I'm sure they'll make it for you. Trust me, it's worth it.

Another good thing about the Ruffino Chianti is that it's a great value. In wine, more expensive doesn't always mean better. It's all about what you like. But everybody has a line. In 2012, when I spoke at the House Radio and TV Corre-spondents dinner—a freewheeling, more fun version of the glammed-up White House dinner for journalists that cover Congress—the organizer who was introducing me announced that they wanted to get me a nice bottle of wine as a "thank you" for speaking. But then they remembered the House eth-ics rules prohibited gifts to members with a value greater than ten dollars. That didn't stop them. They pulled out a bottle of MD 20/20—the concoction you find in convenience store coolers that's nicknamed "Mad Dog" for what it turns you into—and handed it to me right there on stage. It was even the "Red Grape Wine" flavor. That brought the house down. It really was an inspired, and totally legal, gift idea. I was laughing so hard I could hardly keep it together. But I think I "regifted" that bottle to my staff.

I didn't mind being known as a wine guy. Over the years, whenever someone would ask me if I wanted to run for president, I'd give them some version of the same answer: "I like to play golf, I like to smoke cigarettes, I like to drink red wine, and I like to cut my own grass. If you think I'd give all that up to be president of the United States, you're crazy." It got a laugh, but I meant it.

At least nowadays nobody is asking me to run for president anymore. I don't even think I could get elected in today's Republican Party anyway, just like I don't think Ronald Reagan could either. Living through the 2020 election was a pretty strange experience, even for somebody who'd been in politics for quite a while. It showed that, in a lot of ways, America only got more divided during the Trump years, but it showed some unexpected glimpses of possible cooperation too.

It was a little surprising to see Biden win the White House while Republicans held their own in Congress and even picked up a lot of seats in the House. Then again, just about every time I was on the ballot during a presidential election year, about 10 percent of the voters in my district would cast their vote for president and then, apparently, just walk out of the voting booth, ignoring the rest of the ballot. It seemed like that happened a fair amount in 2020, which meant that voters' decisions came down to one factor: Donald Trump. They had four years to watch and listen to him, and came to the conclusion that even if they agreed with him on policy, his personality just rubbed them the wrong way. And Joe Biden, for all of his faults, is basically a nice guy, who didn't suffer from his own personality defects the way Hillary Clinton did.

At the same time, Republicans actually did better with Black and Hispanic voters than they did in 2016, suggesting a more diverse coalition of voters in the party's future. That was something I was gratified, and slightly surprised, to see. If the GOP knows what's good for them, they'll work extra hard to reach out to those communities and make the most of those recent gains.

But I'll admit I wasn't prepared for what came after the election—Trump refusing to accept the results and stoking the flames of conspiracy that turned into violence in the seat of our democracy, the building over which I once presided. Watching it was scary, and sad. It should have been a wake-up call for a return to Republican sanity. And with close divisions in Congress, sane Republicans gained a chance to work with Joe Biden to actually get things done. Biden, Mitch McConnell, and Chuck Schumer are old negotiating pros, after all. Take it from me, I've been around the table with those guys many times.

Whatever they end up doing, or not doing, none of it will compare to one of the lowest points of American democracy that we lived through in January 2021. The mob attack on the Capitol building shocked the nation and killed one Capitol Police officer. Another took his own life days later. Four of the rioters died as well.

Trump incited that bloody insurrection for nothing more than selfish reasons, perpetuated by the bullshit he'd been shoveling since he lost a fair election the previous November. He claimed voter fraud without any evidence, and repeated those claims, taking advantage of the trust placed in him by his supporters and ultimately betraying that trust. It was especially sad to see some members of the House and Senate helping him along—although some of the people involved did not surprise me in the least. The legislative terrorism that I'd witnessed as Speaker had now encouraged actual terrorism.

And it pissed me off. I called on Trump to resign, but I knew that wouldn't be enough. My Republican Party—the party of smaller, fairer, more accountable government and not conspiracy theories—had to take back control from the faction that had grown to include everyone from garden-variety whack jobs to insurrectionists. If the conservative movement in the United States was going to survive, there couldn't be room for them. Time will tell how successful that mission will be, but I hope to be able to do my part, even in retirement.

In the meantime, I still like to play golf, I still like to smoke cigarettes, I still like to drink red wine.

But the summer of 2019 was the last summer I cut my own grass. Age has funny ways of catching up with you. That August, after I cut the grass for the last time, I retired my trusty old lawnmower. I found a spot in the front of the garage with a bunch of boxes piled up. I moved the boxes to make some space, pushed the mower in, put all the boxes back on top of it and buried it, never to be used again.

Okay, so I'm not cutting my own grass anymore. But I'm still me—I was the same jackass when I left the Capitol as I was when I first walked in, and I still am today. And one of the things I'm most proud of is that I left on probably the highest of all the high notes you could think of, a memory that gave me comfort when carnage overtook the Capitol some years later.

I tried for 20 years to get a pope to come visit the U.S. Congress. No luck with John Paul II, no luck with Benedict XVI. But by the time Francis was elevated, I had friends in the Vatican who could help the process along. In fact, I understand His Holiness was especially favorably disposed to the invitation I sent him after he learned about the work I (and my late pal Teddy Kennedy) had done for kids at Catholic schools in Washington.

When Pope Francis agreed to address a Joint Session of Congress, I was beside myself. And imagine how wonderful it was to learn later that my daughter Lindsay, who was pregnant with my first grandchild, was set to give birth shortly before the pope's arrival. I swung into action immediately, leaning on everybody I'd ever met in the Vatican or anywhere else to see if I could get the Holy Father himself to baptize my grandson.

Well, the Vatican has a two-thousand-year head start on bureaucracy over the United States, but eventually the word came back that it wasn't in the cards. He would be happy to bless my grandson, but apparently they don't like to let the pope do baptisms outside of a church.

When the big day came, nothing could dampen my excitement. When Pope Francis first arrived at the Capitol, I officially greeted him for all the cameras from around the world, then sent them away and escorted him into my office. Then I sat down with just the Holy Father, seven cardinals, and my chief of staff, Mike Sommers. "Sommers," I leaned over and whispered, "what the hell are we doing here?" For two kids from Catholic school, this was about as big a deal as it gets. I just hope the Holy Father didn't hear my exact language.

We had a lovely meeting. The pope spoke English well enough that we could carry on our conversation without a translator. As it was breaking up, my family, who had been in an adjoining room, came in to meet His Holiness. As Francis stood up, he turned to his assistant and said, "Could you get me a glass of water?"

My heart leapt. There were Lindsay and Dom with Alistair . . . maybe he was going to get baptized after all. The assistant brought Francis the glass, the Pope took it, raised it—

was he going to bless it?—and then took a drink. That was it. It's still one of the most impressive head fakes I've ever seen.

He gave a wonderful speech that day. He even said a few lines in his native Spanish, which our Spanish-speaking members loved. Before he left, we found ourselves alone near the door where he was to exit. Before I knew it he drew me into an embrace and said, "Mr. Speaker, pray for me."

"Holy Father," I said, "who am I to pray for you?" But I did. And I still do.

I'd never seen Congress more happy than it was that day. Republicans and Democrats, senators and representatives—everybody was uplifted by Pope Francis's visit. And it was the presence of the Holy Spirit he brought there that day that gave me the idea to announce my retirement not in the fall as I'd planned but the very next day.

◆

And I've got to say, I love being retired. For one thing, I get to spend a lot more time with my family. I've got nine siblings to stay in touch with, remember. There would be eleven but, sadly, my brother Rick passed away in 2015 and my sister Lynda in 2018. I miss them both. None of us are here forever, and we've got to make every day count. But the family's growing too. Our daughters and their husbands each have a little boy—Lindsay and Dom have Alistair, Tricia and James have Zak. My grandsons are little guys with big personalities, and they run me ragged trying to keep up with them. I've had a bunch of fancy titles over the years, but it's a lot of fun to just be "Papa" now.

It's nice too to be able to catch up with old friends. Some of the saddest people I knew in Washington were the politicians who got so deep into their work, who only cared about wheeling and dealing, that they never had time to make real friends.

Or if they had them before, they shed them once they got to DC and only went after people they could get something from. Politics is full of people like that. I never resented them, but I did feel bad for them. I'm very lucky to have friends from all stages of life—guys like Jerry Van I've known since we were kids, and my best buddies from Congress like Burr, Chambliss, and Latham— and that we can get together or pick up the phone and still give each other shit like no time has passed at all.

Deb and I also spend a lot of time at our condo in Florida now. Southwest Florida is a beautiful piece of God's earth. We share it with some of the nicest people you could ever hope to meet—neighbors and the folks at shops and restaurants who've become like family over the years. Most of them came from somewhere else. A lot, like Deb and me, came from the Midwest and just followed I-75 south until they ran out of road. An exception was Stan Gober, who came from Alabama and ran Stan's Idle Hour restaurant in Goodland until his death in 2012. Stan was a local legend and a great American, and the restaurant is still run by his family, still serving the best grouper on the Gulf.

There are other neighbors too, like the gopher tortoise and the burrowing owl. These little guys are all over the place. You have to be especially careful driving around our neighborhood because the tortoises are a threatened species, and sometimes, as tortoises do, they like to cross the road. You avoid them if you can, but there are times you have to pull over and get out to give them a hand getting to the other side.

I couldn't cut my own grass in Florida even if I wanted to because, well, we don't have a yard. But we do have a deck, and a view down to the beach and the Gulf of Mexico. We try to watch the sunset out there as often as we can. It's truly amazing. We watch the sun as it moves across the sky from December 21 to June 21. Every night in between it's a whole new show. Sometimes it reflects off the clouds or off the water. It's hard to think of a better way to experience the beauty of God's creation. It's enough to bring a tear to your eye.

And, yes, I still like to play golf. I've got a lot more time for it now. Mark Twain supposedly said that golf was "a good walk spoiled." I don't agree with that. Twain probably wasn't very good and was just pissed off about it. But I *do* believe that "a leader without followers is just a guy taking a walk." When I was Speaker of the House I had to be a leader—sometimes that meant being tough with followers, and sometimes it meant going along with things I didn't agree with because that's what my followers expected me to do.

But whenever I stepped onto a golf course, I didn't have to be a leader anymore. I could just be a guy taking a walk. It didn't matter what crazy controversy had engulfed Washington. It didn't matter who was walking alongside me—even if it was the president of the United States. For a few hours, no matter what else was going on, I could just focus on putting that little white ball where I wanted it to go. Now I'm a little older and I walk a little slower, but the free, calming feeling is the same.

To this day, every time I step off a golf course, I come away a little bit smarter than when I stepped onto it. Each course has its own tricks, and even the most familiar spots challenge you to play better than you did the last time you were there. And you can learn something from everybody you've ever played golf with too—whether it's a lesson in hard work, patience, humility, or humor. Sometimes it takes an 86-year-old former president jumping up and down swearing like a sailor at the top of his lungs to remind you that we all need to let off steam sometimes. And if somebody needs a mulligan after an especially embarrassing shot, remember that it doesn't cost you anything to be nice.

And no matter how bad you're playing, you just keep your head down and keep moving. After all, it's just golf. You hit the ball, find the ball, and hit it again. You just keep going. Sometimes you hit a few bad shots, but the ball has to move forward, and so do you. If you stick to that, you'll come off the course secure in the knowledge that you did your best. Sure, maybe you wish some shots had gone better, but you made the best of it and kept going. The most important thing to remember—in golf, in politics, in life—is that if you do the right things, for the right reasons, the right things will happen for you.

And the right things will happen for this country too. I have just as much faith in America now as I've ever had. Despite all the problems thrown at us—diseases, economic troubles, enemies foreign and domestic—we're still plugging away.

There's a line that's attributed to Winston Churchill that goes, "Americans will always do the right thing—after exhausting all the alternatives." Whether Churchill actually came up with it or somebody else, I've always liked the sentiment. It's true that Americans are the most versatile people God ever put on earth. We're a smart people, a nimble people. We stumble, but we can adapt. And it's our commitment to freedom that makes that possible. Freedom means you can be a genius and invent a new product that makes you millions of dollars and helps millions of people. It means you're free to work your way to becoming the first in your family to go to college. It means you're free to reach as high as you want, no matter where you came from—even if you're a little kid sweeping out a bar in southwest Ohio. Take it from me—you never know where you'll end up. *That*'s freedom.

I'll raise a glass to that any day.

# "BOEHNERISMS":
## Selections from the Boehner Book of Wisdom

- "There's a fine line between stupidity and courage"
- "Never get into a pissing match with a skunk"
- "No need to murder your opponent when they're committing suicide"
- "The mark of a good leader is to prepare those who will succeed you"
- "Get the right people on the bus, and then find them the right seat"
- "A dog that shits quick, doesn't shit long"
- "If you do the right things, for the right reasons, the right things will happen"
- "A leader without followers is a just a man out taking a walk"
- "It doesn't cost anything to be nice"
- "You never get in trouble for something you don't say"
- "If and's and but's were candy and nuts, every day would be Christmas"
- "It's just golf . . . hit the ball, find the ball, hit it again"
- "To you, it's just lines on a page, but I have to do this shit!"
- "I'm a happy warrior today"
- "Why would I voluntarily jump in a cage and let people throw stones at me?"

- "You only pick on the ones you love"
- "It's better to be heckled than ignored"
- "If my aunt had balls, she'd be my uncle"
- "Nothing rolls like a ball"
- "I have 3 goals today: One, play golf. Two, keep my money in my pocket. Three, get my hands into someone else's pocket."
- "Pigs get fat, and hogs get slaughtered"
- "Luckier than a dog with two dicks"

# ACKNOWLEDGMENTS

---

Most of the good things in life start with family, so I'd like to thank them here first. Debbie, Lindsay, and Tricia have given me so much love and support over the years, and I'm very grateful. My sons-in-law, Dom and James, and grandsons, Alistair and Zak, have been terrific additions. And then there's the extended family—all my brothers and sisters whom I love, and all the other Boehners scattered around southwestern Ohio, many of whom have heard a lot of these stories over the years. Now I figured it was time for others to suffer through them as well.

Our part of Ohio is a special piece of the world to me, not only because it's where I grew up, but because it's full of great people who trusted me to represent them in Congress for 25 years. My constituents in Butler, Preble, Darke, Mercer, and Miami counties—and at times Clark, Shelby, and Van Wert counties, too—are some of the best Americans you'd ever hope to meet.

The U.S. Congress, as I've said, also has some of the best Americans you'd ever hope to meet, and some of the worst. I want to thank my colleagues and especially everyone who supported me when I ran for Speaker of the House, an honor I'll always be proud of. My friends on both sides of the aisle made the experience fun, especially Tom Latham, Richard Burr, and Saxby Chambliss. And then, of course, there were the assholes who made the experience more . . . interesting. Some of you are mentioned in this book. The rest of you, well, consider yourself lucky.

I've said many times that I wouldn't have been anything without the great staff I've had over the years. The same goes for pretty much any elected or appointed official, and don't let any of them tell you otherwise. Our team in Washington had some excellent leaders: Barry Jackson, Mike Sommers, and the late, much-missed Paula Nowakowski. Mick Krieger kept things running in Ohio's 8th District, and helped dig up and provide many of the photos in this book. My policy directors in the Speaker's office, David Stewart and Brett Loper, did a lot of the heavy lifting on projects of major importance to the American people. Loper helped with the fact-checking in this manuscript too. Three longtime staffers—David "Schnitt" Schnittger, Amy Lozupone, and John "BJ" Criscuolo—still help keep me in line to this day, and were instrumental in co-ordinating lots of the moving parts of this project.

The fact that this project kicked off in the first place is the fault of the guys at Javelin—Matt Latimer, Keith Urbahn, and Dylan Colligan. They helped bring this thing into being and encouraged me to let the expletives fly. If someone is offended by that, I'll send you their address. I got to know them through Tim Alberta, one of the sharpest journalists writing today, who had a knack for getting me to tell him more than I probably intended to. The editorial team at St. Martin's Press—Thomas Dunne, Stephen Power, Tim Bartlett, and Alice Pfeifer—were all helpful and understanding and believed in the project all the way. I'm grateful to each of them for making this possible.

Finally, I'd like to thank all my friends and supporters all across the country who were so good to me and my team over the years. From Boehner Bus visits to golf outings to barbecues, I enjoyed getting to know all of you during my time in office, and I'm proud that so many of our friendships from the Team Boehner days have kept up to today. Never in my life, when I was one of a dozen kids in a tiny house, or working every rotten job there was, did I ever imagine someone would coin the term "Boehnerland" and put me in the middle of it. But having been here for a few decades, surrounded by so many great people, I would say "Boehnerland" is a damn fine place to be.

# INDEX

# Index

# Index

# Index

# Index

# Index